SOUTH CAMPUS

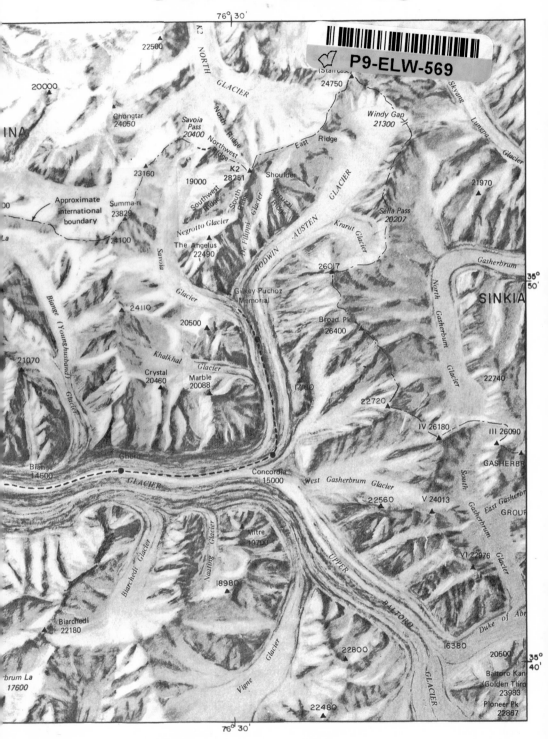

76° 30'

K2 NORTH GLACIER

22500

20000

Chongtar 24050

Savoia Pass 20400

North Ridge

Northwest Ridge

East Ridge

[Staircase]

24750

Windy Gap 21300

Skyang Lungma Glacier

23160

19000

K2 28251

Shoulder

Approximate international boundary

Summa-ri 23829

Southwest Ridge

South Ridge

Abruzzi Ridge

De Filippi Glacier

GODWIN - AUSTEN GLACIER

21970

Sella Pass 20207

35° 50'

24100

La

Savoia

Negrotto Glacier

The Angelus 22490

Krarut Glacier

Gasherbrum

SINKIA

Biange (Younghusband)

24110

Glacier

Gilkey-Puchoz Memorial

26017

North Gasherbrum Glacier

20500

Broad Pk 26400

21070

Khalkhal

Crystal 20460

Marble 20088

Glacier

17160

22720

22740

Biange 14500

Ghoro

GLACIER

Concordia 15000

West Gasherbrum Glacier

IV 26180

III 26090

GASHERBR

Biarchedi Glacier

Nauling Glacier

Mitre 19700

18980

22560

V 24013

South Gasherbrum Glacier

East Gasherb

V 22976

GROU

GASHERBR

UPPER

Biarchedi 22180

Vigne Glacier

22800

BALTORO

16380

Duke of Abr

20500

35° 40'

brum La 17600

22480

GLACIER

Baltoro Kan (Golden Thro 23983

Pioneer Pk 22867

76° 30'

LYONS T.H.S. LIBRARY
WESTERN SPRINGS, ILLINOIS

K2

K2

Life and Death
on the World's
Most Dangerous
Mountain

ED VIESTURS

with David Roberts

Broadway Books

NEW YORK

BROADWAY

Copyright © 2009 by Ed Viesturs and David Roberts

All rights reserved.
Published in the United States by Broadway Books, an imprint of the
Crown Publishing Group, a division of Random House, Inc., New York.
www.crownpublishing.com

BROADWAY BOOKS and the Broadway Books colophon are trademarks
of Random House, Inc.

Library of Congress Cataloging-in-Publication Data
Viesturs, Ed.
  K2 : life and death on the world's most dangerous mountain / Ed
Viesturs with David Roberts.
      p.   cm.
  Includes bibliographical references and index.
  ISBN 978-0-7679-3250-9
  1. Mountaineering—Pakistan—K2 (Mountain)
2. Mountains—Pakistan—K2 (Mountain)—Difficulty of ascent.
3. Mountaineers—Pakistan—K2 (Mountain)   4. Mountaineering
accidents—Pakistan—K2 (Mountain)   5. K2 (Pakistan : Mountain)—
Description and travel.   I. Roberts, David.   II. Title.
  GV199.44.P18V54 2009
  796.522095491—dc20   2009016390

ISBN 978-0-7679-3250-9

Printed in the United States of America

10   9   8   7   6   5   4   3   2   1

First Edition

As always, to my loving wife Paula and our kids—
still and forever the best reasons for coming home.

And also to those who have been inspired and challenged
by the holy grail of mountaineering that is K2.

Contents

28,251

Gilkey-Puchoz
Memorial

K2 from the South

The Shoulder

VIII

VII 3

VI

Abruzzi Ridge

V

2

IV

III

1

II

I

Godwin Austen Glacier

1953 Base Camp

TRADITIONAL EXPEDITION CAMPS I–IX
MODERN EXPEDITION CAMPS 1-4

1

THE MOTIVATOR

In the wee hours of the morning of August 1, 2008, some thirty climbers from ten different expeditions set out from their high camps on the Abruzzi Ridge of K2. At 28,251 feet the world's second-tallest mountain, K2, thrusts skyward out of the Karakoram Range of northern Pakistan. After weeks of sitting out bad weather, the mountaineers were poised to go for the summit on a clear and windless day. During the endless storms, morale at base camp had reached rock bottom, and some climbers had thrown in the towel and gone home. But now everybody still on the mountain was jazzed. As they emerged from their cramped tents to clip on crampons and hoist packs, the climbers were riding a manic high. Sometime that day, they thought, they would claim one of the most elusive and glorious prizes in mountaineering. For most of these men and women, K2 was the goal of a lifetime.

Although the various teams were operating independently, they had tried to cobble together a common logistical plan that would help everyone get to the top. The crucial feature of that plan was the fixing of thin nylon ropes—to be used on the way up, in effect, as handrails, and on the way down as lines that could be easily rappelled. Those fixed ropes were intended to ensure the climbers' passage through the Bottleneck, a steep and dangerous couloir of snow and ice that rises from an altitude of 26,400 feet.

The Bottleneck and the sketchy leftward traverse at the top of it form the "crux" of the Abruzzi Ridge. Although climbing the Bottleneck is only moderately difficult, what makes that high gauntlet so nerve-racking is a gigantic serac—a cliff of solid ice—that looms above it. Weighing many tons, poised at a vertical and, in places, an overhanging angle, the serac looks as though it is barely attached to the mountain. Yet in the sixty-nine years since mountaineers first came to grips with this formidable obstacle, the serac had proved remarkably stable. It seemed, indeed, to be a permanent feature of K2's summit pyramid.

Thirty climbers crawling up the same route on the same day would have been business as usual on Mount Everest. On K2—a far more serious mountain, and one that has seen far fewer attempts—such a crowd was unprecedented. Still, as they approached the Bottleneck, thanks to the perfect weather for which they had waited so long, the climbers were awash in optimism. The summit was within their grasp.

And then things started to go subtly wrong. Small mistakes were made. Miscommunications, fueled by the many different languages the climbers spoke, flared into angry words. The slower climbers began to block the way for those who were capable of moving faster. Yet the single event that turned an awkward day into a catastrophe was nobody's fault.

Within the next thirty-six hours, eleven of those mountaineers would die high on the Abruzzi Ridge. The disaster that unfolded on August 1 would end up as the worst single-event tragedy in the mountain's history, and the second worst in the long chronicle of mountaineering in the Himalaya and the Karakoram.

And nobody saw it coming.

———————

Almost sixteen years earlier, on August 16, 1992, with my partners Scott Fischer and Charley Mace, I had left our high camp in the predawn darkness and started trudging up toward the Bottleneck. On that day, I, too, had been full of bursting hope, tempered by the wary alertness that is the obligatory state of mind for any alpinist who wants to stay alive in the great ranges. I had previously climbed Everest and Kangchenjunga, the first- and third-highest peaks in the world, but I knew that K2 was in another league of difficulty and danger.

Like 2008's climbers, Scott, Charley, and I had had to bide our time for interminable weeks before we finally got a crack at the summit. Not only storms but all kinds of logistical snafus and interpersonal conflicts had delayed our final assault again and again. It was not until fifty-seven days after arriving at base camp that we finally set out for the top. On the other hand, on that August day in 1992, the three of us had had the Bottleneck to ourselves. And fixing ropes up the couloir was not part of our plan.

In *No Shortcuts to the Top,* the memoir I wrote about climbing the world's fourteen highest peaks, I devoted a full chapter to my K2 expedition. Even after K2, it took me several years before I began to consider that it might be possible for me to reach the summit of all fourteen 8,000-meter peaks. For one thing, I didn't think there was any way that I could ever afford to go on so many expeditions. For another, climbing all fourteen 8,000ers seemed far too ambitious a goal. The first person to accomplish that feat had been the great Tyrolean mountaineer Reinhold Messner, who knocked off his fourteenth in 1986. And Messner was like a god to me.

Yet with K2, I became the first American to climb the world's three highest mountains. The outdoor magazines ran a few short profiles about me. One of them was titled "Ed Who?" Even after those pieces appeared, I was still relatively unknown to the general public, but with the boost in confidence they gave me, I finally got up the nerve to start approaching potential sponsors.

K2 was a huge turning point in my life. Yes, it brought me my first modest taste of what you might call "mountaineering celebrity." But far more important than any faint whiff of fame were the lessons K2 taught me.

In the aftermath of 2008's disaster, all kinds of armchair "experts" delivered their scathing critiques. Nonclimbers clogging the online chat rooms, in response to sensational newspaper articles, took a macabre delight in the tragedy. This was Everest 1996 all over again, they seemed to think—the melodrama of clueless dilettantes who had no business on the mountain buying their way into a catastrophe at the cost of their own lives, as well as the lives of professional guides entrusted with caring for them. (Hundreds of readers of Jon Krakauer's bestseller *Into Thin Air* reduced his complicated narrative to that simplistic morality play.) After the August 2008 tragedy, Messner himself sounded off in this vein, decrying the "K2 package deals" that he assumed had lured novices to the mountain and concluding, "Something like this is just pure stupidity."

Messner was not the only famous mountaineer to criticize the victims of the 2008 disaster. The temptation to second-guess those luckless climbers' decisions was all but irresistible. Newspapers, magazines, and radio and TV shows called me for my commentary. I was already beginning to think that what had happened on K2 on August 1 was far more complicated than the first tabloid and Internet versions of the story. It would take several weeks for more detailed accounts to trickle down from the slopes of the mountain and find their way to responsible media outlets. And I was not about to cast facile aspersions on climbers who had died on the mountain, or had barely survived it.

In 1992, K2 had not only proved to be a turning point in my life—it had been the scene of what I still regard as the greatest mistake I ever made as a mountaineer. The most important lesson I learned from that beautiful and dangerous peak was a blunt one: *Don't ever do that again, if you want to stay alive. Listen to your instincts, and follow them.*

Recently, I reread my diary from the K2 trip. I was struck by how different it seemed from the account I had written in *No Shortcuts*. Events and relationships that seemed really important when they were happening barely made it into the chapter I wrote thirteen years after the expedition. Conversely, some of the most dramatic turning points of my weeks on K2 got covered in my diary in only a few deadpan sentences. I wasn't writing the diary, of course, for anybody else to read. At the time, I thought I was simply making a day-by-day record of the most ambitious mountaineering attempt of my life up to that point.

Now I wonder. Any "story" can be told in dozens of different ways. For that very reason, I believe, every time you go back and reexamine an important chapter in your life, you learn something new about it. And the reactions of audiences when I give slide shows, as well as the e-mails I received from folks who read *No Shortcuts to the Top,* gave me many new insights into my own experience.

I have always believed that climbing mountains teaches you lessons. And more than that, I firmly believe that those lessons can be applied to the rest of your life. It's not an easy process, however. Mountaineering literature is full of trite clichés about "conquering an enemy" or "transcending your limits." For at least two centuries, philosophers of the outdoors have insisted that nature is "a school of character."

Would that it were all so simple! The most important lesson I learned from K2 was that by simply putting off making a decision, I made the worst decision of my life: to climb on into a gathering storm. I was lucky to survive our summit push on K2. Scott and Charley didn't agree with me about this. That day, they never seemed to suffer from the nagging doubts—the knot in my gut, as I've always thought of it—I carried with me hour after hour. Yet my partners' comparatively blithe attitude about our climbing on that August 16 doesn't even begin to tempt me to revise my judgment. It's ultimately a personal thing.

K2 is often called the hardest mountain in the world. It's also often called the deadliest. This may not be strictly true: in terms of the ratio of climbers who get to the top compared to those who die on the mountain, Annapurna is more deadly than K2. (I succeeded on Annapurna, in fact, only on my third try, in 2005, and only after I'd begun to wonder whether it was too dangerous a peak to justify another attempt. It became my nemesis—the last of all the fourteen 8,000ers I was able to climb.)

Even before I went to K2, however, I had started calling it "the holy grail of mountaineering." It seemed to me to pose the ultimate challenge in high-altitude climbing. To prepare for that challenge, I read everything I could about K2's history.

I've often puzzled over the fact that the public seems so fixated on Mount Everest. At one point in 1998, there were about ten books published in English by climbers who had been involved in the Everest disaster two years earlier—not just Krakauer's *Into Thin Air* but memoirs by such survivors as Beck Weathers, Anatoli Boukreev, Lene Gammelgaard, and Matt Dickinson.

In the chaotic summer of 1986, thirteen climbers died on K2, including several who were among the finest alpinists in the world. That's five more than died in the 1996 "killer storm" on Everest. Yet only one book chronicling the K2 disaster was published in the United Kingdom or the United States—Jim Curran's *K2: Triumph and Tragedy*.

As I did my homework before our 1992 expedition, I couldn't help comparing Everest's history to K2's. The highest mountain in the world has its dramatic stories: Mallory and Irvine disappearing into the clouds in 1924, Hillary and Tenzing's smooth first ascent in 1953, Messner's astonishing solo climb without bottled oxygen in 1980, and the like. But taken as a whole, the saga of Everest seems to me a sprawling, even tedious narrative, especially in recent years, now that guided commercial expeditions throng the mountain each spring and fall and as many as five hundred men and women per season claim their fifteen minutes each on the summit.

The history of K2, in contrast, pivots around a few intense and troubled campaigns, separated from each other by years of inactivity or total failure. As I first read about those campaigns, it struck me that each one had a lot to tell us about the most basic questions mountaineering raises—the questions of risk, ambition, loyalty to one's teammates, self-sacrifice, and the price of glory. As of 2009, moreover, K2 still has not developed anything like the guided-client scene on Everest. The world's second-highest mountain is simply too difficult for beginners.

In focusing on the six most dramatic seasons in the mountain's history—August 2008, 1938, 1939, 1953, 1954, and 1986—my aim is not just to tell the stories of those campaigns, not just to write chapters of a K2 history, but to muse and probe my way through those episodes as I attempt to glean their lessons. This book might in fact be called "Lessons Learned from K2." Plenty of mistakes were made during those campaigns, leading to shocking tragedies. But it's not my intention to sit back and second-guess my predecessors. Instead I want to imagine my way into their company, where I can ponder the what-might-have-been of their dilemmas.

Each of those six campaigns evolved into complicated human predicaments. Faced with adversity, the members of the 1938 and 1953 expeditions drew together, forging brotherhoods so deep that they lasted for decades thereafter. That kind of brotherhood is not only truly admirable but, I think, almost unique to mountaineering. The camaraderie born of shared adventures was one of the chief things that drew me to climbing in the first place.

Faced with other kinds of adversity, however, the 1939 and 1954 teams split into bitter factions, sparking personal animosities so intense that some of the men never spoke to each other again for the rest of their lives. During the 1986 and 2008 seasons, when many separate teams thronged K2 (unlike the single expeditions of '38, '39, '53, and '54), any semblance of order degenerated into a kind of every-man-for-himself anarchy.

In chapter 2, I retell my own story of K2, bringing in details and events I either neglected or forgot to mention in *No Shortcuts*. During the four years since I wrote that other book, I've reflected many times on what went right and what went wrong on K2 in 1992, and—not surprisingly—my take on that turning point in my life has shifted. By reorganizing my own story in a more straightforward, chronological narrative, I hope to uncover stones I've never looked under before.

There's all too much tragedy in K2's history. But I hope this book serves as a hymn of praise to the great mountain. As well as being dubbed the hardest or the deadliest mountain in the world, K2 is often called the most beautiful. It still seems to me a holy grail—and I am neither the first nor the last of its many worshippers to travel to the ends of the earth for the chance to grasp it in my hands.

A sharp pyramid of black rock, sheer snow gullies and ridges, and ominous hanging glaciers, K2 has a symmetry and grace that make it the most striking of the fourteen 8,000ers. Rising from the Baltoro Glacier in the heart of the Karakoram, K2 is flanked by five other of the world's seventeen highest peaks. That range, in fact, holds the densest constellation of skyscraping mountains anywhere in the world—even denser than the Himalaya around Everest. Yet K2 soars in proud isolation over Broad Peak, Gasherbrum I, Gasherbrum II, and its other formidable neighbors.

When you approach Mount Everest from the south, as do all teams that attempt the classic first-ascent route through the Khumbu Icefall and up to the South Col, the great mountain only gradually comes into view. Most of the way to base camp, Everest is effectively hidden behind the bulk of its satellite peak, 25,790-foot Nuptse. During the multiday trek into base camp, you get only sporadic peekaboo glimpses of its summit. As a result, for climbers the first sight of Everest seldom comes as a stunning, unforgettable moment.

It's just the opposite with K2. As they march up the Baltoro Glacier, most climbers get their first view of the mountain from Concordia, where several glacial streams converge. All at once, after a week's trek from the last village, Askole, K2 springs into sight. Even though it's still a dozen miles away, the sheer, towering presence of the mountain overwhelms you.

Sir Francis Younghusband, the great Victorian explorer, was one of the first Westerners to see K2 from a distance, in 1887. The prospect moved him to an uncharacteristic effusion in his book about the expedition; he later recalled "saying emphatically to myself and to the universe at large: Oh yes! Oh yes! This really is splendid! How splendid! How splendid!"

Reinhold Messner, who climbed K2 in 1979, unabashedly called it "the most beautiful of all the high peaks." He added: "An artist has made this mountain."

In 1992, Scott and I got our first view of K2 not from Concordia but days earlier, when we hiked up a wooded hill out of our Paiju camp. All of a sudden, there the mountain was, sticking up into the sky, a perfect white pyramid. "Holy shit, that's big!" said Scott, and I answered, "Wow, we're almost there!" That evening, I wrote in my diary, "After breakfast, Scott and I scrambled up the ridges above camp and got some great views of K2. That is one huge mo-fo!"

By the beginning of the summer of 2008, some sixty climbers had assembled at base camp on the south side of K2. Several had tried the mountain before, but for most of the men and women on the Baltoro, it was their first go at K2. After their own first sightings of the magnificent mountain, some of their Internet dispatches had gushed with the same sense of wonder and astonishment that Scott and I had felt in 1992 and that Younghusband had expressed way back in 1887. Nearly all of the climbers were planning to try the Abruzzi Ridge or its variant spur, the Cesen route.

Too many days spent sitting out storms at base camp, however, had taken their toll on the various teams' morale. By the end of July, more than a few of the climbers had chucked it in and left for home. Others hovered on a teeter-totter of indecision. A sixty-one-year-old Frenchman, Hugues d'Aubarède, decided on July 20 to give up his attempt. No sooner had he started packing his gear than several forecasts arrived predicting a coming spell of excellent weather. According to journalist Matthew Power, the Dutch leader of another team told d'Aubarède, "Just skip your work for another two or three weeks and then you can summit K2." Changing his mind, d'Aubarède called his wife in France to tell her he was going to give the mountain one more shot. It would be a fatal decision.

The window of clear, windless weather arrived at the very end of July. In the group of thirty who set out early on August 1 to go for the top, there were no superstars. Many of those climbers, however, had previous experience on the world's highest mountains. A Norwegian couple, for instance, had climbed Everest together in 2005; they had also reached the north and the south poles the same year. The Dutch leader, who had made it to the top of Everest without bottled oxygen, was on his third expedition to K2. Besides Norway, Holland, and France, the mountaineers came from an assortment of countries, including Korea, Serbia, Singapore, Italy, Germany, Spain, Sweden, Australia, the United Kingdom, and the United States. There were also several Pakistanis and a number of Sherpa from Nepal.

Nearly all those climbers set out on August 1 from Camp IV, situated on a broad snow ridge known as the Shoulder, at about 26,000 feet. The Shoulder is the last place on the Abruzzi Ridge where you can reasonably pitch a tent. In 1992, Scott, Charley, and I placed our own Camp IV as far along the Shoulder as we could, just below where the snow slope steepens toward the start of the Bottleneck couloir. Last summer's climbers, however, pitched their tents on the lower, southern end of the Shoulder. The difference may not seem like such a big deal, but we had good reasons for camping where we did. At altitude, in soft snow, it can easily take a full hour to trudge from one end of the Shoulder to the other. That's an hour we saved over last summer's climbers. That's an extra hour added to their grueling summit day on the way up, and at least twenty minutes on the way down.

If there was one guy last summer who really had his act together, it was the Basque mountaineer Alberto Zerain, who started his own summit push from well below the Shoulder, leaving Camp III at 23,600 feet. Operating as a soloist without teammates, Zerain got moving by 10:00 P.M. on July 31, and he climbed the 2,400 feet up to the Shoulder in the astonishing time of only two hours. When he reached the other climbers' Camp IV, he found them still struggling to get ready. According to Freddie Wilkinson, who covered the tragedy for the magazine *Rock and Ice,* "Zerain called out to the others still in their tents, trying to cajole them into hurrying up to leave with him. He received few responses. . . . After an hour of waiting, Zerain finally continued alone."

I must admit that when I first saw photos from last summer, I was shocked. There those guys were, still crossing the Shoulder, and it's already broad daylight! As I said, I'm generally not comfortable criticizing other climbers' decisions. But that late start on summit day meant that the climbers had reduced what was already a small margin of safety by that much more.

It's easy to succumb to high-altitude lassitude. You lose your motivation. It takes longer not only to do something but even to think about doing something.

It's no fun getting off in the middle of the night from a high camp on an 8,000er. You're in this closet-sized tent with your buddy. It's dark, it's cold, there's ice everywhere. You have to brew up a drink—something warm, like a cup of tea. And that seemingly simple task alone can consume an hour of precious time. If your partner has to take a crap, you have to move aside and let him go out and do that. Then you have to put on your boots, your overboots, the rest of your clothes, and your harness. I always sleep with my boots in my sleeping bag, though not on my feet. Lots of climbers don't. So in the morning they have to put on cold boots, which will instantly suck precious warmth from their feet, whose blood circulation is sorely taxed to begin with. That contributes to a bad start.

On my expeditions, I've always been the clock-watcher. I always have a plan. I want to be in control of the time. In a way, that's just part of my nature—I tend to be punctual. The night before, I'll remind my partners, "We need to be out the door by one or one-thirty A.M." Other climbers seem to have the attitude of "Oh, I'll leave when I'm ready." Next thing you know, they've lost two or three hours.

So I have to think that a crucial mistake made by nearly all the climbers on August 1 was getting off late from Camp IV. That delay was compounded by what happened when the first climbers reached the bottom of the Bottleneck.

As you head up that steep couloir, you're excruciatingly aware of the huge ice cliff hanging over you. It's a monstrous-looking thing, some 400 feet high, and the whole time you're under it, you can't help wondering, *What's holding that damned serac in place?*

In 1992, I nicknamed the ice cliff "the Motivator." It certainly motivated Scott, Charley, and me. It threatens you the whole time. You don't want to stop, you can't take a break, and as you kick steps up the couloir, you're literally holding your breath while you climb as fast as humanly possible. Your muscles almost scream from oxygen deprivation.

The first mountaineer who ever came to grips with the Motivator was the great Fritz Wiessner, in 1939. He was so leery of it that he chose to climb a different route, on the rock bands well to the left of the Bottleneck, even though that forced him onto much more difficult terrain.

Before our 1992 expedition, I'd studied every photo I could find of that serac. Oddly enough, the Motivator looked much the same year after year. It seemed to be pretty stable. It had a fairly smooth face—there weren't big broken chunks that looked ready to plunge with the first gust of wind. And in more than fifty years, no one had ever reported seeing ice calve away from that face.

Since we had the Bottleneck to ourselves in '92, we climbed it as fast as we could. That was a luxury 2008's climbers didn't have. As soon as the guys in the lead reached the bottom of the couloir, the whole procession stalled. The climbers lined up, one after another, but no one could move faster than the slowest man. The climb quickly turned into a traffic jam. On top of that, matters were made much worse by the climbers' common assumption that they needed fixed ropes to get up and down the Bottleneck safely.

Afterward, some of the survivors lashed out at other climbers on the mountain, accusing them of making mistakes that led directly to the tragedy. No one was more critical than Wilco van Rooijen, the forty-year-old leader of the Dutch Norit K2 expedition. "Everything was going well to Camp IV," he told the press from his hospital bed, "and on the summit attempt everything went wrong." To a reporter from Reuters, van Rooijen elaborated: "The biggest mistake we made was that we tried to make agreements. . . . Everybody had his own responsibility and then some people did not do what they promised. With such stupid things lives are endangered."

Since there were so many different teams on the mountain, their leaders had crafted the "agreements" to which van Rooijen referred. The plan was for nine climbers to string almost 2,000 feet of rope up the Bottleneck and across the leftward traverse that leads to easier ground. On August 1, however, the available supply of rope was at least 300 feet short—causing the leaders to doubt whether there was enough to equip the whole dangerous passage. In addition, as van Rooijen complained to *Men's Journal* correspondent Matthew Power, several of the nine lead climbers "just didn't show up."

Then, to make matters worse, the rope fixers started stringing their lines too low, on the relatively easy ground before the Bottleneck really commences. By the time they got to the most hazardous part of the climb, they were out of rope. "We were astonished," van Rooijen later told the Associated Press. "We had to move [the fixed ropes]. That took, of course, many, many hours. Some turned back because they didn't trust it any more." Speaking to Power, the Dutchman was even more scathing: "We lost many, many hours because of this stupid thing, which we already talked about many, many times at Base Camp."

I'm sorry, but I just don't buy it. Van Rooijen claims he couldn't climb because the ropes had not been fixed in the right places. Well, whose fault was that? Does your success depend on what other people do? Van Rooijen blames the others for the delay. Why didn't he get out and do something?

Meanwhile, the solo Basque climber, Alberto Zerain, was hours ahead of all the others. He had cruised up the Bottleneck and across the traverse without even thinking about fixed ropes. Zerain would reach the

summit at 3:00 P.M.—the only climber that day, in my opinion, to top
out at a reasonable hour.

Some 1,600 feet lower on the mountain, the traffic jam had ground to
a halt. According to Power, "A decision was made to cut a lower section
of the rope and use it to protect climbers as they made their way across
the traverse [leading leftward from the top of the Bottleneck]. A knife was
passed down to cut the rope near its bottom anchor, and the rope was
pulled back up to the head of the line."

At around 11:00 A.M., the first fatality occurred. Somewhere in the
middle of the traffic jam, a Serbian climber, Dren Mandic, unclipped
himself from the fixed rope. Afterward, all kinds of explanations about
what Mandic was attempting to do appeared in print and on the Internet. Among other things, he was accused of trying to leapfrog past other
climbers. The most accurate account was probably that offered in the
public announcement by the Serbian team, mourning the loss of their
comrade. In broken English, the team leader reported, "Wishing to replace himself with climber behind him DREN undo his assurance. Fix-
rope relocated suddenly. DREN loosed his counterbalance and fell down
to 8020 m [26,300 feet] where his body was stopped."

As he fell, Mandic slammed into the next climber on the fixed rope,
Cecilie Skog. (Skog and her husband, Rolf Bae, were the experienced
Norwegian couple trying to climb K2 together.) Skog was knocked off
her feet but managed to stay attached to the fixed rope. According to
Wilco van Rooijen, as reported by Matthew Power,

> Still falling, Mandic grabbed wildly at the rope, jerking two other
> climbers off their feet. He then lost his grip and tumbled down
> the steep couloir, pinwheeling hundreds of feet back down
> toward the Shoulder. "Just one moment, and he was gone," says
> Wilco.

Uncertain whether their teammate was still alive, two Serbians and a
Pakistani porter descended to his body. By the time they got there,

Mandic was dead. According to Power, however, over the radio from base camp, the Serbian team leader ordered that trio to try to haul the body back to Camp IV. As they began the effort, the porter, Jehan Baig—described by Power as "inexperienced"—suddenly slipped and fell. Eyewitnesses claimed that Baig never tried to self-arrest with his ice ax. Instead, he cartwheeled down the slope and plunged out of sight over a cornice.

If Power is correct in his assertion that the body recovery was ordered by the team leader, that directive strikes me as questionable at best. It's hard enough to help a sick or wounded climber descend under his own power from 26,000 feet on an 8,000er; it's virtually impossible to haul a dead body from such a perilous perch back to camp. It's not clear what the ultimate point of that mission would have been, since the body could never have been taken all the way down the mountain. That order, if in fact it was given, cost Jehan Baig his life. It's curious that in his public announcement, the Serbian team leader made no mention of Baig's death. Instead, he wrote, "We muffled our friend's body in the Serbian flag, secured it with pickaxe and put it on 7,900 m [25,900 feet] to the right from direction C4-Bottleneck. Our friend rest near the heaven. Let God bless him."

It's also unclear how many of the climbers stuck in the traffic jam were even aware that Mandic had fallen to his death. Almost certainly, none of them knew about the second fatal accident down below. In any event, now that the rope salvaged from the bottom of the Bottleneck had been fixed in place on the culminating traverse (the hardest part of the whole route), most of the climbers in the traffic jam kept plodding, ever so slowly, upward.

One of the few in the crowd who had decided to turn around and give up his summit attempt, the American Chris Klinke took an amazing photo of the upper mountain from Camp IV just after noon on August 1. (The shot, which captures in a single image the fiasco that was unfolding on K2 that day, was run splashed across a two-page spread in *Men's Journal*.) The picture is so sharp that you can clearly see twenty-two tiny, insectlike human figures on the route. At the bottom of the photo, well below the Bottleneck, two of them are engaged in the effort to recover Mandic's body, only minutes before Baig would fall to his death. Most of the climbers have finally escaped the Bottleneck and the traverse, but the traffic jam is alive and well: nineteen of the climbers are so tightly bunched that it looks as though each one is on the verge of stepping on the heels of the climber in front of him. Far, far above even the leader of the traffic jam, a solitary climber—Alberto Zerain—rests in the lee of a small serac before starting on to the summit.

In my view, many of those climbers still heading upward ought to have thought a little more seriously about turning back. Turnaround times aren't an ironclad rule on K2, but I believe in them for myself. On our own summit day, Scott and I got moving from Camp IV at 1:30 A.M. Charley, who started a little later, caught up with us, having followed the tracks we'd kicked in the deep snow. I had resolved that if we didn't summit by 2:00 P.M., I'd turn around. As it was, we topped out at noon.

In August 2008, I suspect, summit fever took over in the traffic jam. All those climbers were piled together. They were slow together, and they were late together, and that probably rationalized their decision to continue toward the summit together, so late that the sun would be setting as they topped out. Only a few of them thought better of it and turned around. On a mountain like K2, nobody gives you credit for making the smart decision to give up the summit and go down.

In 1990, an acquaintance of mine, Greg Child, an outstanding Aussie mountaineer transplanted to the United States, climbed K2 by its north ridge, a considerably harder route than the Abruzzi. Recently I reread Greg's account of the climb, published as "A Margin of Luck" in his collection of essays *Mixed Emotions*. Greg has a sardonic, even self-mocking style, so some of the things he writes in that piece may be tongue-in-cheek. Even so, it's clear that he had a desperate time on summit day.

At 27,500 feet, only 750 feet below the top, Greg and his partners Greg Mortimer and Steve Swenson discussed what to do. It was already past 4:00 P.M.

Swenson looks down: "Should we go for it?" A long pause follows. Nothing could be more uncertain.

"Yes!" Mortimer finally shouts, prodding us into action and out of this inertia of doubt.

"This is crazy," I think to myself. "A storm is moving in and we're going for the summit, without oxygen, without bivouac gear." But, I rationalize, this is our last shot at the mountain. If we go down now, we'll never climb K2. A little more luck is all we need.

That exchange is incredibly similar to the one I had in 1992 with Scott and Charley as heavy snow began to fall. We, too, were above 27,000 feet. I remember asking, "Hey, what do you guys think?" "Whaddya mean?" Scott answered, and Charlie chimed in, "We're going up!"

In 1990, Greg Child reached the summit only at 8:05 P.M. He didn't start down until 9:00. That descent in the dark—"staggering, falling in the snow"—turned into what climbers mordantly call "an all-out epic." Greg started to have hallucinations. Finding an empty oxygen cylinder in a circle of rocks, he fantasized:

> I'm seeing an image in my mind of me hunkered among the rocks, warming my hands over a campfire. "That's right," I think, "I'll build a fire down there. When Mortimer arrives we'll get nice and warm." I've got it all worked out.

Only 300 feet short of the tent, Greg became "completely apathetic" and collapsed. He literally crawled the last stretch to safety.

Man, I thought, as I reread Greg's essay, *that was scary, to go that long and that late.* I wouldn't have done that. Greg's a really strong climber. A weaker mountaineer wouldn't have survived.

Messner himself is famous for having wild hallucinations on the 8,000ers, especially when he was climbing alone. But I've always felt that if I started to hallucinate, I was doing something wrong.

The fourth member of Greg's team in 1990, Phil Ershler, did turn back. And Ershler, as a senior guide at Rainier Mountaineering, Inc. (RMI), had been one of my most important mentors. On our own summit day in 1992, as I carried that knot in my gut and couldn't make up my mind whether to go up or down, I kept thinking, *Well, Ershler turned around.*

As he headed down from the summit in August 2008, Alberto Zerain passed no fewer than eighteen climbers still going for the top. According to *Men's Journal:*

> Though he doesn't speak English, [Zerain] claims he tried to tell the others that it was getting too late to continue. "As I descended," he explains, "everyone stopped to ask me how far it was to the summit. Did I tell the people to turn around? No, you can't. There are a lot of people, and they are all going up together. It's the majority against you."

(There's a succinct definition of summit fever!)

Some of the climbers that day may well have pondered turning around. But one of the more experienced, the Italian Marco Confortola, tried to rally them onward. "I started shouting," he later told reporters. "I told them that the first person to reach the summit of K2 [in 1954] did it at 6:00 P.M., so let's move!"

At least one climber in the throng, the Norwegian Rolf Bae, stopped below the top. Only 300 vertical feet short of the prized goal, Bae waited for his wife, Cecilie Skog, and another teammate to tag the summit and return.

Besides Zerain, seventeen others reached the top. Their arrival times ranged from 5:20 P.M. to after 7:00 P.M. For some, this meant that they had been going for twenty hours since leaving camp that morning. They were already pretty worn out.

By the time those summiteers got back to the diagonal snow ramp that leads down to the tricky traverse and the Bottleneck, it was pitch-dark. And most of them were exhausted.

It's at this point that it's hard to figure out just what happened on K2 late on August 1. The various accounts that filtered back from the survivors are so mutually contradictory, you can't stitch them together into a coherent narrative. It seems that the strongest climbers hoped to down-climb in the night all the way to Camp IV. But others, upon realizing how late they would arrive on the summit, apparently planned to bivouac well above the crux traverse and the Bottleneck.

By "planned to bivouac," I don't mean to suggest that this was part of their preconceived agenda. As far as I can tell, none of them carried a bivouac sack, or a half sleeping bag, or even a stove, and by now nearly all of them were without food and water. It may be that they had become so wasted that there seemed no alternative to bivouacking. But one thing is clear: whether that night or the next morning, they were counting on the fixed ropes to get down through the Bottleneck to Camp IV.

The weather was still perfect. But to survive a night in the open above 27,000 feet without shelter, food, or water, you have to hang your life out on a limb. Yet it's amazing how many climbers on K2 seem to take for granted the option of bivouacking on the way down as the price to pay for bagging the summit. On our own 1992 expedtion, the ostensible leader of our team, Vladimir Balyberdin, bivouacked above 27,000 feet. Vlad was a tough dude, he had a mild night, and he got away with it. The next night, Chantal Mauduit thought she had no choice but to bivouac at 27,500 feet, but Aleksei Nikiforov, coming down from the top three hours later, roused her out of her apathy and cajoled her into descending with him—probably saving her life.

In 1978, my friend Jim Wickwire was one of the four climbers who became the first Americans to climb K2. Jim and his partner, Lou Reichardt, got to the top at 5:15 P.M. Lou realized the importance of heading down at once, and took off after only a few minutes. But Jim lingered, almost in a trance, taking photographs, changing the film in his camera, and savoring that indescribable achievement, until he had spent close to an hour on the summit. It's uncannily similar to what happened on Annapurna on the first ascent in 1950: Louis Lachenal was obsessed with getting back to camp, while Maurice Herzog, the team leader, stayed and stayed, caught up in a euphoric vision that would ultimately cost him his toes and fingers.

On K2, Lou made it down to high camp that night, but Jim had to bivouac just below 28,000 feet. He barely survived; by the time he reached base camp, he was suffering from both pneumonia and pleurisy, his vocal cords were paralyzed, and he had incurred some frostbite. He was absolutely wrecked. Porters had to carry him in a litter back to Concordia, and he was eventually helicoptered off the Baltoro.

There's an old joke: "bivouac" is a French word for "mistake." I'm proud of the fact that on all thirty of my expeditions to 8,000-meter peaks, I never once had to bivouac. On several occasions, I turned around short of the summit rather than submit to a night out without shelter. In 1990, if Greg Child, Greg Mortimer, and Steve Swenson had bivouacked instead of calling upon their utmost reserves to get back to camp, they might well have died on the north ridge.

After Zerain and several of the Sherpa, the strongest climbers that day were probably the Norwegian trio: Cecilie Skog; her husband, Rolf Bae; and their teammate Lars Nessa. At dusk, ahead of all the others, they climbed down the ramp and clipped in to the last fixed rope on the near end of the traverse to the Bottleneck.

It was at this precise moment, sometime between 8:00 P.M. and 9:00 P.M., that the geologic fluke that would transform the gathering fiasco into a true catastrophe occurred. As Freddie Wilkinson reconstructed the event in *Rock and Ice*:

> Bae [was] in the lead. Skog traversed next and heard the sickening roar of a large avalanche in the darkness. A second later, Skog was wrenched off balance as the rope she was clipped to broke somewhere below. Bae's headlamp disappeared.

Skog called out in the black night for her husband, but got no response.

A huge section of the Motivator, that ferocious but apparently stable ice cliff hanging over the route, had collapsed at the worst possible moment.

Despite the unfathomable shock of having her husband crushed by tons of ice as he traversed just ahead of her, then hearing his body plunge and vanish with the falling debris, Skog kept her wits about her. She carried a thin 165-foot rope in her pack. Now she and Nessa tied that cord to the broken end of a dangling fixed rope and rappelled into the Bottleneck. They downclimbed the couloir in the dark and made their way back to Camp IV in the early morning hours.

When the first bulletins from K2 hit the newspapers and the Internet, the initial scenario made it sound as though the collapsing ice cliff had wiped out most of the climbers who had died on the mountain. But Bae was apparently the sole direct victim of the crashing ice blocks. Far more consequential was the fact that the debris took with it a sizable section of fixed ropes—estimates by the climbers themselves ranged from 600 to 1,500 feet. And this unforeseen event effectively stranded all the climbers above the Norwegians in a cul-de-sac that was, paradoxically, of their own making.

By the time Rolf Bae was killed, several of the other climbers had already decided to bivouac. The Dutch leader, Wilco van Rooijen, later reported that he never saw the serac collapse, and didn't know until much later that it had. At something like 27,200 feet, van Rooijen carved out a seat in the snow slope and settled into it as he anticipated a grim night with neither sleeping bag nor food nor water. Beside him, two other members of the Dutch Norit team prepared their own bivouac seats. They were the Italian, thirty-seven-year-old Marco Confortola, and a thirty-seven-year-old Irishman, Gerard McDonnell. A fun-loving folk musician and oil worker, McDonnell was especially well liked by his teammates. A few days earlier, he had left a farewell note on his online blog upon leaving base camp, a phrase in Gaelic that translates as "That's all for now, friends. The time is coming." On reaching the top late on August 1, McDonnell phoned his girlfriend in Alaska. He had become the first Irishman to climb K2.

From a hospital in Islamabad, Confortola recounted his bivouac to a reporter from the British newspaper the *Independent*. "Since Gerard was having a difficult time," the Italian said, "I made his hole bigger to help him lie down for a little bit. Gerard was very cold. I was also cold and began to shiver on purpose to create heat. I was wasting energy, but I needed to get warm." The bivouac ledge was perilously exposed. "I made sure not to fall asleep," Confortola added, "because I could have fallen [off the mountain]."

The three men managed to get through the night, then started down in the morning. Somewhere they came across three Korean climbers, tangled up in a single rope with which they were tied together. "There was a Korean guy hanging upside down," van Rooijen recalled. "There was a second Korean guy who held him with a rope but he was also in shock and then a third guy was there also, and they were trying to survive but I had also to survive."

Van Rooijen said that the Koreans declined his offer of help. But Confortola insisted that he and McDonnell spent three hours trying to disentangle the Koreans from their snarled rope and get them started down, to no avail.

At this point, even Confortola's several accounts of what happened didn't quite jibe. To the *Independent* reporter, he claimed that "for some strange reason," McDonnell started "to walk away." To others, he reported (in Matthew Power's paraphrase), "Suddenly . . . Gerard turned around and began to climb back up the slope, back toward the Koreans, offering no explanation." McDonnell's friends later concluded that he went back up in a final attempt to give aid to the Koreans.

I'm not surprised at these discrepancies. By the time Confortola finally reached base camp, he was so wiped out that his memory could well have been playing tricks on him. And all climbers accept the sad fact that nonclimbing journalists can never seem to get our stories right.

We have all had the experience of thinking that we explained very lucidly to some reporter just what happened on some mountain, only to have a completely garbled version appear in print.

In any event, at this point, while he was still in the Bottleneck couloir, Confortola fell asleep from sheer exhaustion. He awoke to a loud booming noise. He later told the website K2Climb.net, "I saw my friend Gerard's boots falling among the blocks of ice and snow. That was the worst moment."

Apparently, a second, smaller serac collapse—a kind of aftershock of the massive initial breakdown of the night before—had engulfed McDonnell and carried him to his death. Later, the grieving Italian remembered his friend: "I used to call him Jesus. The beard, everything, he looked like Christ. He was always smiling. He was a flower."

By now, chaos reigned among the climbers still trying to negotiate the descent. Van Rooijen bitterly recaptured the scene: "People were running down but didn't know where to go, so a lot of people were lost on the mountain on the wrong side, wrong route. They were thinking of using my gas [bottled oxygen], my rope. So actually everybody was fighting for himself and I still do not understand why everybody were [sic] leaving each other."

Had the climbers been members of a single unified team—like the Americans on K2 in 1953, for example—they might have rallied to one another's aid. But given how many different teams were on the mountain in 2008, with only whatever rudimentary English each one commanded as a common language, it is not surprising that anarchy prevailed.

By this point, van Rooijen and Confortola had separated. Their solo descents took on the nightmarish quality of last-ditch retreats. And both men became effectively lost. Van Rooijen later told *National Geographic Adventure,*

> The next morning after I spent the night, it was difficult to come
> down. I had radio contact with my climbing partners in Camp IV,
> but . . . [I] didn't find Camp IV. I was on the wrong side of the

mountain. People at base camp saw me go over the wrong side of the ridge. . . . I had to sit out a whiteout because I couldn't see anything and I knew I couldn't go down any further. So I waited.

And to his brother over a satellite phone from Pakistan, Confortola recalled, "During the descent . . . due to the altitude and the exhaustion, I even fell asleep in the snow, and when I woke up I could not figure out where I was."

Even without a sleepless night in a bivouac, it's easy enough to get lost descending a mountain like K2. Coming down from the summit in '92, Scott started to veer off in the wrong direction, too far east. If I hadn't corrected him, he might have led us completely off the Abruzzi Ridge, into uncharted terrain on the east face.

On the way up, a lot of climbers gaze ahead; they never look down at the way they came. But at some point in the descent, they start wondering, "Now, where was it that I came up this thing?" I've always made it a fundamental principle to keep looking down on the way up, to memorize the landmarks that will guide my descent. It's partly instinct, and it's partly my training as an RMI guide. On Rainier, on Denali, that was hammered home as a crucial thing to do.

The chaos on the morning of August 2 was so total that we don't even know what happened to some of the climbers who died. One of them was the sixty-one-year-old Frenchman, Hugues d'Aubarède, the guy who almost pulled up stakes and went home, before van Rooijen talked him into giving the mountain a last shot. On the summit, d'Aubarède radioed his final message home: "It's minus twenty [degrees Celsius], I'm at 8,811 [meters]. I'm too cold, I'm too happy. Thank you."

Somewhere on the descent, d'Aubarède simply vanished. In all likelihood, he fell off the mountain as he tried to downclimb. Like those of many K2 victims over the decades, his body may never be found.

By the time the disaster had run its course, eleven climbers had died in a single thirty-six-hour period on K2. Besides the Serb Dren Mandic, the Pakistani porter Jehan Baig, the three Koreans, Rolf Bae, Gerard McDonnell, and Hugues d'Aubaréde, the victims included another Pakistani porter who was climbing with the Frenchman, and two veteran Sherpa.

To be sure, a lot of mistakes were made on K2 in August 2008. Too late a start by too many climbers from Camp IV; too many people on the route at the same time, climbing too slowly, which created the traffic jam; the further delay when the team leaders insisted that the fixed ropes in the Bottleneck had to be repositioned; summit fever, which kept so many from turning back short of the summit; too late an hour when all but Zerain topped out; the panic that set in after the serac collapse in the night.

The initial media coverage, however, made it sound as though the collapse of the Motivator was the direct and sole cause of the tragedy, almost like an act of God. But except for Rolf Bae, people didn't die because of the serac collapse. They died because of what that serac collapse created, after all the other ominous conditions surrounding the ascent had come into play.

It's very much like what happened on Everest in 1996. The "killer storm" of May 10–11 wasn't the single direct cause of the tragedy. It was simply the straw that broke the camel's back. That camel had already been overloaded by climbers starting too late, going too slowly, refusing to turn around, and using up their reserves of energy and bottled oxygen.

Even so, I was shocked by the viciousness of the public response to 2008's tragedy. All kinds of nonclimbers riveted by the news from K2 seemed to derive a kind of spiteful glee from the terrible events. After the *New York Times* ran its front-page story about the disaster, scores of folks weighed in online. Something like 90 percent of their comments were derogatory I-told-you-sos. The *Times* article said nothing about "heroes," yet carpers made such comments as "It's long past time to stop calling these egomaniacs heroes and call them what they are. Selfish, egomaniacs, and stupid." Another reader wrote in, "Heroes my ass. No one should feel an inch of sympathy for these egg heads." Yet another proclaimed, "They engaged in marginally suicidal behavior and wound up dead. To me, they were stupid and reckless beyond all limits."

It was as if mountaineering itself were considered by the public—or at least by a significant sector of the public—to be nothing more than a selfish, idiotic form of Russian roulette. It was also assumed that the climbers on K2 were fat-cat millionaires. Wrote another *Times* respondent, "Because someone is rich enough to travel to the end of the Earth to play chicken with suicide does not make him a hero."

Call this the Krakauer effect, though you can't blame it on Jon Krakauer. Since I was involved in the '96 Everest catastrophe, when our IMAX team temporarily gave up our own summit plans to try to rescue climbers in trouble, I had a front-row seat as the tragedy unfolded. At the time, I was critical of some of the decisions made by both clients and guides that May, and I still feel they made fatal mistakes. But I can't imagine sitting in some armchair back home and rejoicing that these "clueless dilettantes" got what they were asking for. Sadly, a major vein ·in the public response to *Into Thin Air* ran along just those lines.

But there's no viable analogy between Everest in 1996 and K2 in 2008. Not a single one of the eleven climbers who died that August on the world's second-highest mountain was a true client in the sense that Scott Fischer's Mountain Madness or Rob Hall's Adventure Consultants customers were. None of them were paying big bucks to have a commercial guiding company get them up the mountain. They were almost uniformly experienced climbers in their own right. The Pakistani porters may have helped the Europeans carry loads and establish camps, but they were not acting as true guides. And the Sherpa on K2 were not hired hands but climbers going for the top themselves, on an equal footing with their Western counterparts.

Yet in one respect, 2008's mountaineers allowed themselves to slip closer to the status of clients than nearly anyone had on previous K2 campaigns. This had to do with their dependence on fixed ropes. In the aftermath of the tragedy, too much focus has been put on the collapse of the serac, too little on the whole business of the fixed ropes.

In general in the mountains, it's harder to climb down a pitch than to climb up it. And if you've relied on fixed ropes to get yourself up the Bottleneck and across the traverse—just "jugging" along, with your ascender clipped to the line—it can be terrifying to face having to descend those same passages without fixed ropes. Especially in the dark, after you're really strung out from taking so long to get to the summit.

In 1992, Scott, Charley, and I had no fixed ropes to help us get up and down the Bottleneck. We climbed the couloir; then, on the descent, despite the dangerous accumulation of new snow, we simply faced in, kicked in our crampons, planted our ice tools, and climbed down that steep, 600-foot slope. Even Jim Wickwire in 1978, though near death after his bivouac, summoned the nerve and the technique to climb down the traverse and the Bottleneck unaided by fixed ropes or partners.

No one even thought of fixing ropes all the way through the Bottleneck until about two years ago. How quickly, though, the comfort of fixed ropes gets taken for granted. It even starts to seem to some climbers like a privilege that ought to come with the K2 package, as reflected in Wilco van Rooijen's petulant complaint that some of the designated fixers didn't "show up" and that other climbers placed the ropes in "the wrong places."

If you're counting on fixed ropes to get you over all the hard places, you're much less likely to carry your own rope, much less any pitons or ice screws. Cecilie Skog and Lars Nessa may have survived because Skog carried her own thin rope, with which the two of them improvised a rappel over the most difficult passage. It doesn't seem as though any of the other "stranded" climbers even thought about rappelling—probably because they didn't carry their own ropes and hardware. It's easy to imagine this scenario, since carrying extra gear for those "just in case" situations is not a priority anymore, while trimming weight and traveling light is. The three Koreans were found tangled up in their climbing rope. Why didn't they untie and try to rappel with it? Perhaps they were simply too exhausted, too befuddled by hypoxia, their fingers too stiff with cold to manage the operation. We'll never know.

After the tragedy, a member of the Dutch Norit team, Cas van de Gevel, who reached the summit and downclimbed successfully, was quoted in *Outside* magazine as saying, "On the mountain there were no heroes."

Instead, there was full-blown chaos, the every-man-for-himself panic that van Rooijen later so vividly described. The chief reason for that, I believe, is that there was nothing like a unified band of mountaineers on K2. Instead, there were ten different teams with climbers from fifteen different countries. Most of them didn't know each other beforehand, and at base camp they didn't form lasting friendships beyond the boundaries of their own teams.

But there was also something relatively new going on that summer, something that has already played itself out with a vengeance on Everest in recent years. It's a kind of dehumanization, and if it's inevitably the wave of the future, as I think it may be, well, that says something sad about mountaineering. It involves a scenario in which one climber comes across another climber who's in a truly desperate situation. And it's as if the climber who's not in trouble says to himself, *I don't know you. You're not my problem.* And so he leaves the victim to die—or at least to get himself out of his own predicament.

I just don't understand that way of thinking. Six times on 8,000ers, I've given up my own plans to try to help save the lives of others. Sometimes they were partners and good friends, such as Dave Carter on Everest, J.-C. Lafaille on Broad Peak, and Jimmy Chin on Cho Oyu. But others—like Beck Weathers on Everest and Gary Ball and Chantal Mauduit on K2—were strangers to me before we met at base camp. I can't really say what other people should have done in comparable predicaments; I just know what seemed instinctively to me to be the right thing to do. I couldn't live with myself if I'd just walked past someone in bad trouble and left him to save himself.

Van de Gevel was wrong, however. Last summer, there *were* heroes on K2. As seems increasingly to be the case on the world's tallest mountains, they happened to be Sherpa.

From Camp IV, on the afternoon of August 2, several climbers could see the three Koreans at about 27,000 feet, above the traverse and the Bottleneck. They were still moving feebly, though making no downward progress. With them was a Sherpa, Jumic Bhote, who had also summited, and who may have been effectively guiding the Koreans. In Camp IV were Tsering Bhote and Pasang Bhote, Jumic's brother and cousin, respectively.

These two Sherpa performed an incredible feat. They climbed the Bottleneck and the traverse—without fixed ropes, of course. In the lead, Pasang reached the three Koreans, who were almost unconscious, and Jumic. Pasang managed to revive two of the Koreans and his cousin and get them started down the mountain again.

Just as the four climbers reached the top of the Bottleneck, according to Freddie Wilkinson, who reconstructed what happened for *Rock and Ice,* another huge chunk of the Motivator cut loose. It scoured the Bottleneck, sweeping the two Koreans and the two Sherpa with it. As Tsering Bhote watched in horror, all four men plunged to their deaths. Deeply shaken, Tsering managed to descend safely to Camp IV.

Meanwhile, the media were focused on the survival stories of Marco Confortola and Wilco van Rooijen, reporters hanging on every word the Italian and the Dutchman uttered from their hospital beds in Islamabad. Thus this last and most deadly episode of the tragedy, which concealed the genuine heroism of Pasang Bhote and Tsering Bhote, nearly passed beneath the radar.

Sherpa heroism did not end there. Along with Alberto Zerain, the two most competent and experienced climbers on K2 that summer were thirty-four-year-old Chhiring Dorje and thirty-four-year-old Pemba Gyalje. Chhiring had climbed Everest ten times, Pemba six. In the early morning hours of August 1, Pemba had been one of the lead climbers fixing rope up the Bottleneck. Far stronger than the Europeans, he could have left them behind and gone for the top on his own. But on the summit, he waited until the last European topped out, just to make sure everyone was all right, and only then descended with the stragglers.

Pemba did this not because he was a "hired gun," which he was not, but just, I suspect, because he was a Sherpa. The best Sherpa have far more endurance at the end of a long summit day. Westerners tend to think, *Boy, that was hard. I'm exhausted.* Sherpa think, *Well, yes, it's hard, but that's what it is.*

They've worked hard every day since they were kids. They're used to carrying heavy loads from village to village. Their whole lives are about hardship and struggle.

When climbers such as McDonnell, van Rooijen, and Confortola chose to bivouac, both Chhiring and Pemba decided to climb down toward Camp IV in the dark. Near the top of the Bottleneck, Chhiring ran into another Sherpa, Pasang Lama, who had also reached the summit, but who by now had dropped his ax. If anyone was truly stranded on the mountain, it was Pasang.

"Pasang Lama was worried, but I said don't worry," Chhiring later e-mailed Freddie Wilkinson. "We have only two options—one is staying here, which is very dangerous under the serac. The other option is to descend down with one ice ax, which may lead us to Camp IV . . . if we don't slip."

So Chhiring cut off a short hank of broken fixed rope, tied Pasang to him in a tight tether, then, facing in, used his ax and his crampons to descend the Bottleneck, with his fellow Sherpa almost dangling from his harness like a haul bag. The two eventually reached Camp IV without mishap.

That's a pretty astounding deed. But I can just imagine how you might pull it off: kick each foot in solid, plant the ax, then tell the other guy to kick with his own feet and even punch holds with his hands. Don't move until he's secure. Still, if Pasang had come off, he probably would have taken Chhiring with him. Talk about selfless!

It's a Sherpa thing. They're loyal. It's their ethos, instilled in them on Everest. They just feel it's the right thing to do.

But if Chhiring and Pasang could make it down with one ice ax between them, one guy short-roped like a dead weight to the other, why couldn't those Europeans have downclimbed the Bottleneck unencumbered?

Pemba Gyalje reached Camp IV by 1:00 A.M. on August 2. In the morning, on learning that a bunch of climbers were still unaccounted for, he simply headed back up the mountain. To do that, after an exhausting summit day of your own—and both Chhiring and Pemba had summited without supplemental oxygen, the first Sherpa to do so on K2—takes incredible fortitude. And, once again, incredible selflessness.

Pemba reached Marco Confortola halfway up the Bottleneck. The Italian was unconscious and probably suffering from severe altitude sickness. With bottled oxygen, Pemba got Confortola going again. But almost as soon as the two men had started down, the third serac collapse—the one that carried the two Koreans and Pasang Bhote and Jumic Bhote to their deaths—nearly took out Confortola and Pemba. The Italian was struck in the back of the head by a chunk of falling ice. He started to fall, but Pemba grabbed him from behind and held him. The Sherpa then shepherded the Italian the rest of the way down to Camp IV. There is no doubt that Confortola would have died had Pemba not rescued him.

This time, as he collapsed in his tent, Pemba was truly worn out. But the next morning, when he learned that Wilco van Rooijen was still missing, he went out again.

Van Rooijen had gotten wildly off route as he made his impulsive and desperate descent. He had wandered to the west not only of the Abruzzi Ridge but of its western variant, the Cesen route, by which the Dutch team had ascended. He may have glancingly intersected the prominent snow ridge called "the Shoulder," but he missed Camp IV altogether. After a second night out, van Rooijen was truly lost—and near death.

Bizarrely enough, the ring of the Dutchman's sat phone in the darkness gave his team the first inkling of his whereabouts. On August 3, Pemba and Cas van de Gevel found van Rooijen. They led him slowly back to Camp III, which the three men reached only well after dark.

In his interviews with reporters, van Rooijen made scant mention of Pemba's rescue. Recounting his epic to *National Geographic Adventure,* the Dutchman credited instead his own skills: "My mountaineering experience let me be quiet and patient enough to wait for better weather. . . . I took a risk climbing some difficult technical parts to traverse to easier slopes and to easier glaciers. I finally survived."

This is a sad trend in recent mountaineering on the 8,000ers. When something screws up, the Sherpa are the first ones to be blamed. But when a Sherpa performs heroically, as Pemba did in saving the only two climbers who bivouacked above the Motivator and then got off the mountain alive, they barely get credited, and often they are not even named.

I was very gratified, then, when Pemba Gyalje was hailed by *National Geographic Adventure* in December 2008 as its Adventurer of the Year, an award I had won in 2005. The National Geographic Society, or NGS, flew Pemba to Washington, D.C., for the ceremony, and I heard that he really enjoyed it, as he stood beaming and holding aloft his trophy, while the audience in the posh society headquarters gave him a wild standing ovation.

Topping off the encomiums, the American Alpine Club bestowed its most prestigious honor, the David A. Sowles Memorial Award (for heroism in saving the lives of other climbers), on Pemba at its annual meeting in Golden, Colorado, in February 2009.

People often ask me if a disaster like last summer's is bound to happen again on K2. And my answer, sadly, is yes. Too many of the climbers who survive such a fiasco tell themselves, *Well, I got away with it.* And too many others, planning their own future expeditions, think, *Oh, it's not going to happen to me.*

The most those of us who have climbed the world's highest mountains can hope to do is educate others. I also tried to educate myself every step of the way on all of my climbs, realizing I could never learn enough. But sometimes I wonder if even trying to educate others is a lost cause. Little that we say or do seems to sink in. The appeal of risk seems to outweigh the rewards of discipline on hazardous peaks. To cite an oft-quoted statistic, after the 1996 season, when so many inexperienced clients came to grief on Everest, in 1997 the numbers of applicants willing to pay as much as $75,000 apiece to get guided up the highest mountain significantly increased.

After *No Shortcuts to the Top* was published in 2006, I got hundreds of letters and e-mails from readers. Very few of them were negative or critical, and many folks wrote to say that they were captivated or even inspired by my story. But the e-mail that probably moved me the most—the one that almost stunned me, it came so out of the blue—didn't arrive until December 2008. That e-mail alone helped reaffirm for me that it was worth writing and talking about the risks and rewards of our glorious but dangerous pastime—that some good may yet come out of sharing with others what the mountains have taught me.

The e-mail was from Chris Klinke, the American on K2 in 2008 who, dismayed by the traffic jam on August 1, turned back. Klinke and I had never met, but he wrote:

> *Hi Ed,*
>
> *I wanted to thank you for something that you are not even aware of at this point. But as I was making my decision to turn around just below the Bottleneck I kept remembering a discussion that I had with my teammates at BC. . . .*
>
> *The thing that helped me make the decision was the discussion we had about your feeling of regret about your summit on K2 because you violated your own personal rules of listening to your gut. . . .*
>
> *In remembering that conversation with my teammates and your description of that feeling in your book I made the decision to turn around. Despite the fact that there were 24 people heading to the summit, despite the fact that the*

weather was amazingly perfect, I felt my gut telling me something entirely different.

Listening to that feeling was a good decision for myself, and I appreciate the fact that I had the ability to get guidance from those on the mountain and those who came before me.

I hope to meet you in the future and I thank you for blazing the trail on so many mountains.

Be Well,
Chris Klinke

2

DECISION

In 2007, after another controversial spring season on Mount Everest—record numbers reached the summit, but seven climbers died—I was asked by the *New York Times* to write an op-ed piece. The editor's only half-articulated premise was *What can we do about this mess?* As we talked and e-mailed back and forth, I began to realize that what she really wanted from me was a rigid set of rules and restrictions that somehow could immediately be put into action. When I told her that I thought you couldn't make rules about mountaineering, she quickly lost interest in my writing a piece.

All kinds of commentators shared the *Times* editor's sentiments in the wake of 2008's K2 disaster. There was also a widespread determination to pinpoint the supposed "villains" of the story. If we could only identify the cause of the tragedy, these armchair judges implied, we could fix it so it wouldn't happen again.

I'm afraid I just don't see things that way. About arriving on the summit as late as 7:00 P.M., for instance, I have no trouble saying that I'd never do that. But that doesn't mean that I can tell other climbers what to do. In mountaineering, right and wrong aren't black-and-white. For every "rule" you might try to apply to our pastime, you can come up with a classic example of some daring alpinist who flagrantly violated it, and in the process became a legend. In 1953 on Nanga Parbat, according to the wisdom of the day, the Austrian climber Hermann Buhl should never have gone for the summit alone. He should have turned around rather than reach the top as late as 7:00 P.M. Above all, he should not have let himself get so strung out that he would have to bivouac on a ledge so tiny he couldn't even sit down on it. But Buhl did all of the above, and although he lost toes to frostbite, by making the only first ascent of an 8,000er ever to be accomplished solo, he immortalized his deed as one of the boldest climbs ever performed in the Himalaya.

Suppose you did try to establish rules about climbing on Everest or K2. What committee would enforce them? What gatekeeper is going to stand at base camp and say, "Okay, *you* can head on up the mountain. Nope, *you* better turn around and go home." Suppose the American Alpine Club tried to tell Nepal or Pakistan that they ought to limit the number of permits they give to expeditions every year or screen the applicants for competence. Forget it—those impoverished countries make serious amounts of money from expedition permits. Who are we to tell them how to run their business? In 2008, when the Chinese government cleared all other climbers off the north (Tibetan) side of Everest so that they could carry the Olympic torch over the summit, and even persuaded Nepal to make radical restrictions on the south side of the mountain, a lot of Western climbers got pretty pissed off. But the real victims were the Sherpa. By now, a significant portion of the whole Sherpa economy depends on the spring and fall seasons on Everest. A Sherpa who goes high to carry loads, fix ropes, and establish camps for American or German or Korean climbers can earn from a single expedition most of the yearly income that supports himself and his family. You didn't read much about it in

the newspapers, amid all the coverage of protests in Paris and San Francisco and Lhasa, but thanks to Chinese arrogance, in 2008 a lot of
Sherpa people were hit hard by the financial backlash.

As for disasters: we can't stop the kind of catastrophe that played out
on K2 in August 2008 from happening again. We shouldn't even try.

Paradoxically, the glory of mountaineering has everything to do with
this state of affairs. Climbing is about freedom. There's no prize money;
there are no gold medals. The mountains are all about going there to do
what you want to do. That's why I'll never tell anyone else how to climb.
All I can say is, *This is how I prefer to do it.*

These feelings, which are central to my philosophy of mountaineering,
rose to the surface not only in the aftermath of 2008's disaster on K2, but
as that tragedy made me think all over again about my own expedition to
the world's second-highest mountain in 1992. Among all my thirty expeditions to the 8,000ers, I feel now, the K2 campaign was the one most
marked by ecstatic highs alternating with abysmal lows. And it was also
morally the most complicated.

That expedition was a roller-coaster ride of a learning experience for
me, but I was young, ambitious, and hungry for any type of opportunity.
That's why I was willing to accept and suffer all the difficulties that were
thrown into my path.

Scott Fischer and I would have preferred to go to K2 with a solid team
made up of good friends. When I first heard that he was organizing an
expedition, and I got up the nerve, in effect, to invite myself along, Scott
had so many teammates lined up that all he could promise was to put me
on the waiting list. But as the trip drew near, one by one the others
dropped out, until the "team" consisted only of Scott and me. By then we
were so broke that both of us doubted whether we could afford an expedition to K2.

That's why we ended up buying slots on somebody else's expedition.

We joined a Russian team led by Vladimir Balyberdin, or simply "Vlad," as everybody called him. On paper, the deal looked like a reasonable quid pro quo: the Russians were eager to sell places on their permit in order to afford the expedition themselves, since what they lacked above all was hard currency. Vlad proved to be a strong climber (like me, he'd already gotten up Everest and Kangchenjunga), but he was a leader in name only. Almost from the start, there were tensions between the Russians and the rest of us who had bought places on the team. The word "team," in fact, would be an oxymoron that summer.

It was only in 1975 that the Pakistani government caught on to the lucrative trick of selling multiple permits to K2 in a single season. That summer, instead of leasing the mountain only to Americans (as it had in 1953) or Italians (1954), the Ministry of Tourism granted simultaneous permits to teams from the United States, the United Kingdom, France, Italy, the Netherlands, Poland, Switzerland, Austria, and Japan. "Throughout the summer," writes K2 historian Jim Curran, "there was a more or less continuous procession of porters carrying supplies and equipment up the Baltoro Glacier. The result was chaos.

"Porter stages, load sizes, fees, rest days, etc., all became open to negotiation," Curran elaborates, "and almost every expedition was dogged with strikes, go-slows, and thefts. Some expeditions even failed to reach Base Camp and a vast amount of ill-will was generated."

By 1992, the authorities had worked out most of the logistical kinks. Porter strikes were not a problem on our approach to base camp. After the chaos of 1975, the Pakistani Ministry of Tourism had established fixed wages for the porters. Foreign climbers had to pay the standardized rates, and the porters had to accept them or go home. On the other hand, when I had to hire my own porters in Askole for the eight-day trek to base camp, I was so poor I could afford only three porters to carry my four loads, so I ended up humping my own sixty-pound pack all the way in.

Our so-called team was disorganized from the start. To save money themselves, the Russians had decided to drive overland all the way to Rawalpindi. They got there long after we Americans did. After cooling our heels for a frustrating week as we waited for the Russians, my teammate

Thor Kieser and I decided to snag a last-minute trekking permit and hike in by ourselves. Scott had already left Askole with his own trekking permit, escorting two paying clients to base camp in an effort to fill his nearly empty pockets. Along the way, Thor and I caught up with Scott and his trekkers. By the time we arrived at base camp on June 21, only a five-person Swiss team was on the mountain.

In retrospect, it's obvious to me that from the very start, our expedition was plagued by stress and frustration. But I was so gung ho at the time that I ignored the distractions. After all our preparations, it was beyond my wildest dreams to be camped beneath the holy grail of mountaineering, and for weeks I floated along on a manic high of enthusiasm and hard work.

Not long ago, I let a friend read my K2 diary. He made an interesting observation. "Ed," he said, "do you realize that the writing in your diary is far more blunt and critical than anything you write for publication, or anything you say when you give a slide show?"

No, I hadn't realized. But when I recently reread my dairy, I saw that my friend was right. As I've said, the diary was for myself—I never expected that someday someone else would read it. So I'm sure I used those daily entries to vent my frustration. I tend to be nonconfrontational, so I guess that writing in my diary was a way for me to let off steam. I also believe that in certain tense situations, it's often best to let it ride, rather than venting immediately, because hard feelings tend to smooth out with time and reflection.The question, though, is, which version is the truer account of what happened on K2—my diary or what I've written for publication?

There's an old and honored tradition in exploration literature that you don't air your dirty laundry in print. Whatever bickering, name-calling, grudge nursing, and dark funks really took place on the expedition, they're nobody else's business. You can read the whole of Sir John Hunt's *The Ascent of Everest* and never suspect that a single cross word was exchanged by the climbers who supported Hillary and Tenzing's monumental push to the summit. Maurice Herzog's *Annapurna*—the bestselling mountaineering book of all time, and the book that more than any other inspired me as a teenager and made me want to become a climber—characterizes the 1950 French team as an ideal brotherhood, with each member making heroic sacrifices to support the others and, in the end, even to save their lives.

When I learned, about a decade ago, that that wasn't the whole story, that there had been plenty of conflict and resentment on the first ascent of Annapurna, I felt only slightly dismayed. By then I'd been on enough expeditions to see for myself how interpersonal conflicts and team dynamics play out. The new revelations about Annapurna didn't change the feelings I'd had decades earlier, when I'd first read Herzog's book. It still seemed a heroic tale of struggle, camaraderie, sacrifice, and eventual success.

With the counterculture revolution of the late 1960s and the 1970s came a new trend in expedition literature. In the new narratives, the dirty laundry was not only brought out of the closet, it was put on prominent display. No two books more vividly embodied this tell-it-like-it-was aesthetic than Galen Rowell's *In the Throne Room of the Mountain Gods* and Rick Ridgeway's *The Last Step,* which chronicled, respectively, the 1975 and 1978 American K2 expeditions. Rowell and Ridgeway not only highlighted every interpersonal showdown among their teammates, they remembered (or recreated) blistering dialogues to dramatize them. A sample from Ridgeway:

> "I just talked to Lou," Cherie said acidly. "I'm tired of hearing all this stuff about Terry being upset. Everyone whispering behind our backs. You're all bastards. Bastards, bastards, bastards."
>
> "Look, we could care less what goes on as long as it doesn't affect the team and the climb," John said.
>
> "What do you mean what goes on? I'm sick of all this gossiping," Cherie started to cry.

After those two books were published, some of the team members—the ones portrayed in the most unfavorable light, of course—felt betrayed. But a younger generation of readers responded with gleeful enthusiasm: *So this is what really goes on during expeditions.* The elders of our tribe, the traditionalists, were aghast. I read Rowell and Ridgeway's books when they came out, and I could relate to what they wrote. But I'd never publish the kinds of intimate details from my expeditions that they sprinkled on virtually every page of their books.

The debate persists today, although the tell-all school has gained a comfortable edge. I've never been exactly sure where on this spectrum my own views lie, though they're certainly far to the right (if right is con-servative) of Rowell and Ridgeway. Since I've never written a book-length account of any of my expeditions, I've never had to commit my beliefs on this matter to print. In *No Shortcuts to the Top,* there were certainly plenty of real antagonisms that I downplayed or even avoided mention-ing altogether. At the same time, I've sometimes been accused of being too much of a "nice guy," even of subscribing to that old motherly ad-monition "If you don't have something nice to say about somebody, don't say anything at all."

I'd be the first to admit that the kinds of rows and resentments re-counted by Rowell and Ridgeway are exactly what goes down on expedi-tions. The question remains, whose business is it beyond the members of the team?

What my friend pointed out was that in the privacy of my diary, I'm closer to Ridgeway than I might otherwise think. K2 in 1992 was unde-niably an expedition fraught with conflict. It may be that the version of the story that I told in *Shortcuts* soft-pedals that conflict.

From the hike in onward, for instance, one of my teammates really bugged me. Let's call him "Joe" to protect his identity. Here's some of what I wrote:

> Joe already split to go to base camp. I'm kinda glad because he's starting to drive me nuts. He's always gotta pipe into a conversation and add something. He's already "conquered" K2 in his mind. He has no patience and he can't keep his mouth shut.

. . .

> Joe went up alone today [to Camp I] and is spending the
> night. That is a bit stupid in my opinion. He's in a hurry for
> no reason. Climbing K2 is a marathon and he's sprinting!
> He's a bit of a lost soul and I think he's looking for recogni-
> tion and attention.
>
> .   .   .
>
> Joe talks & talks & talks. Sometimes it's nice to have peace
> & quiet but he doesn't know when. Scott & I keep on read-
> ing & Joe keeps on talking. He also keeps borrowing stuff.
> Doesn't have a spoon, toilet paper, shave cream, etc. Not
> very well prepared.

Inevitably, on expeditions, cabin fever sets in. You're in such close proximity to your partners day and night, 24-7, and under such tension about whether you can get up the mountain or not, that every last thing some guy does or says can drive you crazy. It gets especially bad when you're trapped together inside a small tent during a long storm. It can get so that the very sound of him chewing his breakfast or blowing his nose threatens to push you off the deep end.

This can happen even between best friends, let alone among virtual strangers you're thrown together with on an expedition. Fortunately, in 1992 I was with Scott most of the time, and we got along great. That was a particularly good thing, since neither of us ever bonded with the Russians.

Another source of tension that summer was the perception on the part of a few that we were competing with the international team led by Rob Hall and Gary Ball. Both of our teams would be hard-pressed to find adequate campsites on the Abruzzi Ridge. It was usually first come, first served when it came to grabbing those precious sites.

It was at base camp that I first met that famous New Zealand duo— Hall & Ball, as everybody called them. They had a vast amount of experience in the Himalaya, and they'd pulled off a tour de force by climbing the Seven Summits—the highest peak on every continent—in only seven months. And this was already their third attempt on K2.

When I first shook hands with Hall & Ball, I thought, *Oh my God, these guys are superstars. They'll leave me in the dust.* But Scott told me, "Take it easy, Ed. They're just normal guys." Then, on the mountain, I discovered that I was as strong as or stronger than these superclimbers. There were days when I broke trail and fixed rope for them and Hall & Ball trudged into camp hours after I did. That was a real revelation.

During those first weeks, Scott and I paired up with Hall & Ball to fix ropes up the lower part of the Abruzzi Ridge. (Only a few of the other members of our team contributed to this effort; the rest seemed unwilling or unable.) In general, Hall & Ball cooperated well with Scott and me as we shared the grunt work of establishing the route. I got more and more frustrated by some of the half-assed efforts of other guys on the mountain. Some of them would carry only the lightest loads; they'd claim the conditions weren't good enough for a heavy carry. And sometimes they'd get only halfway to the higher camp so they'd just dump their loads in the snow and head down. I picked up a bunch of those loads, but I drew the line at carrying other guys' oxygen bottles for them. If they couldn't get their own oxygen to the higher camps, how the hell did they expect to use that oxygen to go for the summit? Eventually, we worked it out so that the folks hoping to use oxygen higher up labeled their bottles with their names. That made them solely responsible for moving the bottles up the mountain.

It would have helped a lot if Vlad had turned out to be a real leader. But from the get-go, Vlad was strictly doing his own thing. He was just not a team player. So without any real plan or structure in place, everybody else started doing his or her own thing as well.

The frustration of taking on more than my share of the work, of having other climbers shirk their responsibilities, and of having no leader who would assign tasks built inside me into a towering resentment. But I kept it all inside; I never blew up and chewed anybody else out. (That's typical for me, I'm afraid—I tend to avoid overt conflict.)

I didn't mention this in *Shortcuts*, but the reason I tried Everest solo the next year was because of my disappointment with the poor teamwork on K2. I'll always pull my own weight, and I'm happy to pull even more than my weight, as long as others genuinely try to contribute. But after I got back from Pakistan, I said to myself, *Look at how much time and energy you wasted on other people. Why not go on an expedition where all that time and energy benefits yourself?*

On rereading my diary, I discovered that even before I got to Pakistan, I'd anticipated the underlying problem that would divide our team from within. On June 6, as I sat in JFK airport waiting for my flight to Asia, I wrote:

> Hopefully Scott & I will jell and climb as a strong team on K2. There will be a fair amount of attrition from the other team members but that doesn't surprise or worry me. It's typical on a long, arduous trip such as this. Scott is built like a brick shithouse and we've put a lot of sweat & tears into this, so there is no lack of desire. We haven't climbed together, but I feel we know each other well enough by now to form a solid, strong team.

By 1992, I already knew that the thoroughness and intensity of preparation you put into an expedition translate directly into commitment on the mountain. Before K2, Scott and I had spent ten months planning, training, and scrounging together the dough to afford our expedition. By the time we got to base camp, we were truly committed, and we were willing to stay as long as we needed to in order to get up the mountain.

The same wasn't true of all of our American teammates. They were all gung ho at the start, but after a month, some of them lost motivation and started complaining about how hard everything was. Scott and I wanted to say to them, "Of course it's hard. What did you sign up for?" (In their defense, a few members of our team did have inflexible deadlines by which they had to return to their jobs.)

Climbing an 8,000er is a sufferfest. You need a lot of patience. As it turned out, after forty days on K2, Scott and I weren't even thinking about going home. I didn't have a girlfriend then, or a steady job, or any other particular reason to go home. I thought, *Hell, I'll stay here for four months if I have to.*

That doesn't mean I didn't have my apprehensions about the climb beforehand. Downing a couple of beers at JFK, I wrote:

> So many things can happen for better or worse. I just hope we all return safe and can count to 20 using our fingers & toes. With the right weather, good conditions and health, we can climb K2. But it's gonna be a bitch.

Throughout my eighteen years of attempting 8,000-meter peaks, I've always been a stickler for getting into great physical shape before each expedition. I've felt that my training during the months prior to a climb would not only increase my chances of success but would make me climb more safely. If I could climb faster and stay strong day after day, I could minimize some of the inevitable risks of exposure on those great peaks. With a bank of endurance stored up, even if something went wrong at the end of a long day, I hoped I would have the strength to keep moving. If I failed on an expedition because of lack of preparation or training, I would have only myself to blame.

Not every Himalayan mountaineer feels the same way. The legendary British climber Don Whillans was famous for letting himself go between expeditions, drinking heavily and eating so much he actually got fat. On the hike in to his next objective, his own porters sometimes teased Whillans about how out of shape and overweight he was. Amazingly, on the mountain he always rounded into form. He reached the summit on one of the greatest expeditions in Himalayan history—the south face of Annapurna in 1970—and he was one of the strongest climbers on the pathbreaking attempts on the southwest face of Everest in the early 1970s. On the other hand, Whillans died of a heart attack at the age of only fifty-two. His lifestyle almost certainly contributed to his early death.

Right from the start on K2, my training paid off. Even in my diary, I'm not comfortable bragging about being fitter than other guys on a climb, but some of my entries make it pretty clear that that's what was going on. On July 2, I wrote:

> We had planned to finish fixing all the way to C II today. Everyone was slow today, so I grabbed 3 ropes and started out by 6:45 A.M. Had to re-break trail to our high point of last eve. Got there by 8:30. Everyone was still way back so I started stringing rope on my own. . . . Fun, 3rd class stuff.
>
> Rob [Hall] finally caught up but was going slow so I kept leading out.

Scott typically didn't train as hard as I did, but he had tremendous natural stamina. The genes he was born with enabled him to look like Captain America without really having to work too hard at it. He also had the distractions of a family and a business, which limited his workout time. As early as June 26, I wrote, "It was fun to climb with Scott today. He's super strong, competent and easy-going. I hope we summit together."

From the start, as it turned out, Scott and I were slightly stronger than Hall & Ball. And they were planning to use supplemental oxygen up high; Scott and I were not. Still, we felt a huge respect for these likable veterans, and I was thrilled to work hand in hand with them. Their previous knowledge of the route was invaluable. On July 1, Scott and I reached Camp I before Hall & Ball and set up our tent. From my diary: "We left a bomber site for the Kiwis just to be nice & diplomatic. Otherwise it looks like we're racing each other up the mountain just for good tent sites." Usually, when you get to a camp—especially on a route like the Abruzzi, where there are so few good platforms—you grab the best site you can find and claim it with your tent. Instead, Scott and I deliberately left the best platform for Rob and Gary, just so they wouldn't think we were being hypercompetitive about getting up the mountain first.

At about 21,500 feet on the Abruzzi, you encounter the first real technical obstacle on the route. It's an 80-foot-tall fissure that splits a nearly vertical rock cliff; in the back of the fissure there's usually a narrow gully of hard ice. The pitch is called "House's Chimney," after Bill House, the

American who first climbed it in 1938. It took House two and a half hours of desperate struggle to get up the chimney, which forms the crux of the route all the way up to the Shoulder, at 26,000 feet.

According to Jim Curran:

> In 1980 Peter Boardman, arguably Britain's best Himalayan climber at the time, climbed House's Chimney and was impressed and surprised at its technical difficulty. He thought that when it was first climbed it must have been the hardest pitch in the Himalaya. Certainly it was far harder than anything climbed on Everest in the 1920s and 1930s.

As it turned out, on July 2 Scott and I were the first climbers from our team to reach the base of House's Chimney. One of us would get to lead it, going first on the rope and placing "protection" to shorten a possible fall. Then, once the leader had climbed the pitch, he'd string fixed ropes for all the other climbers to use. Although the Swiss team had gone up the chimney before us, as they were attempting a fast and light ascent, they'd relied on the decaying strands of rope from previous years that still hung down the crack. Scott and I didn't trust those old, frayed ropes, and we weren't about to put all our weight on them.

We'd been anticipating this moment since long before we'd left Seattle. Now Scott and I drew straws to see who would get the "sharp end." I won and led the pitch. My diary sounds almost nonchalant about the climbing: "It was a narrow, vertical snow & ice-choked crack. Fun climbing up and stemming." I remember, however, being quite impressed with the lead Bill House had pulled off fifty-four years earlier.

We'd been on K2 for only two weeks, but already, scattered around the Baltoro, other expeditions were throwing in the towel and going home. From my diary:

> Many failures so far in the Karakoram area. The Swiss tried to climb K2 in just 4 wks. From a very low C II they tried alpine style to go for it. They encountered deep snow on the

Black Pyramid. Too early in the season? IE still too much
snow yet?

Germans & Koreans just gave up yesterday on Broad
Peak also. [Steve] Swenson & company gave up on GIV
[Gasherbrum IV] due to deep snow also. Now they're on
GII we believe.

It's only early in the season yet. We've still got lots of
time.

By July 8, we were on the verge of establishing Camp III at 24,000
feet. I'd had one bad day at Camp II; I'd felt lightheaded after breakfast,
then unusually tired going up the hill. "Not quite acclimatized I can tell,"
I wrote in my diary. By the next day, however, I felt as good as new, and
I was raring to go. Because of the weather, though, we descended to base
camp, at 16,800 feet, to rest for several days. "Climb high, sleep low"
has become a formula for success on the 8,000ers, overturning the earlier notion that the longer you stayed high, the better you acclimatized.
The truth of the matter is that above 20,000 feet or so, the body slowly
deteriorates, no matter what kind of shape you're in. Those rest days
down low are vital to regenerating for the summit push.

I still felt vexed by the unequal efforts some of our teammates were
putting out. On July 11, I complained to my diary, "No real 'power-carriers'
on this trip. 10# [pound] loads are about max. I'm used to climbing with
guys from RMI that carry 50# no sweat & don't even bat an eye. Scott carries big like me, but that's the exception." Despite this disappointment, I
was feeling increasingly positive about our chances, and I sketched out
possible scenarios for the upcoming days. The most optimistic had us establishing Camp IV on the Shoulder at 26,000 feet only four days hence.
From that camp, we hoped eventually to reach the summit in a single day.
"If it all works out," I scribbled, "come down rest 4–5 days, wait for good
weather & go for it!"

Fat chance. K2 wasn't going to give up that easily. On July 12, we suffered our first real setback. At the time, it felt like a huge one.

Scott and I had set off from base camp that morning at 5:00 A.M., hoping to climb all the way to Camp II in one day. Just before you reach the base of the Abruzzi Ridge, you have to wend your way through a funky little icefall. It's technically trivial but potentially dangerous. We always roped up going through the icefall, even though most of the others, including the Russians, didn't bother.

That morning, Scott was leading as he wound his way through the maze of cracks and ice towers. He stepped on a chunk of ice that was wedged across the mouth of a small crevasse. The chunk shifted under his weight, and he fell. There was no danger that he'd fall very far into the crevasse, as I held him on a tight rope. Instinctively, Scott stuck out his arms to catch the fall. And as he hit the glacial surface, he screamed in pain. "Shit!" he yelled. "I've dislocated my shoulder again!"

It turned out that Scott had dislocated the same shoulder in a fall about twelve years before. "We got him slung up and left his pack," I recorded that evening in my diary. "[Scott] walked to the end of the moraine in extreme pain & had to stop a few times. I left him there and ran to get Yuri, our doctor."

Once they realized Scott had had an accident, a number of other climbers helped out with the "rescue." Yuri Stefanski, the Russian doctor, relocated Scott's shoulder and gave him painkillers and muscle relaxants. But he told Scott, "You must go home. The expedition is over for you."

Scott refused to accept that verdict, claiming he'd be back in action in a week. I'm not sure either of us believed his boast. "Scott is way bummed," I wrote in my diary, back in base camp. And I was just as bummed myself. In a silly little accident, no more dramatic than tripping over a street curb, my partner had been put out of commission indefinitely.

Until that moment, I don't think I'd realized how much I was counting on our two-man teamwork. I'd always envisioned Scott and I working our way up the mountain together, then embracing on the summit. Now, as I brooded in the night, I faced the real possibility that if I got to the top of K2, it might be with some other partner. I had begun to connect with a couple of the stronger climbers on my team, Neal Beidleman and Charley Mace, as well as Hall & Ball. Perhaps they would be the ones I could go to the summit with. Yet at this point in the expedition there wasn't another guy on our team I thought of as a truly close friend, and there sure wasn't anybody I trusted the way I trusted Scott.

In the absence of any real leadership from Vlad, the rest of us decided we needed to designate someone as climbing leader. During one of our mealtime meetings, with Vlad absent, off doing his own thing, we took a vote, and to my surprise, I got elected. Right away, I tried to put some semblance of order into the logistics—figuring out who would carry what supplies to which camp, and so on. There was no telling the Russians what to do, however. The only loyalty they had was to one another, and as far as I could tell, there wasn't even much of that.

Another thing that disturbed me was that the Russians seemed willing to climb in really dangerous conditions. In turn, they sometimes acted as if the rest of us were wusses. One day when Vlad got back to camp, he turned to me and asked, "Why do you not go today?"

"Because I thought there was tremendous avalanche danger," I answered. I didn't say out loud what I really thought: *Dude, we're not suicidal like you!*

I wondered at the time whether this propensity for really hanging it out there was part of a peculiarly Russian style in the Himalaya. On Everest in 1990, I'd climbed with Soviets on Jim Whittaker's International Peace Climb. There, the Russians had also seemed willing to climb in worse conditions than the rest of us. They tend to be highly competitive within their own ranks, as they gain status and honor in their home country with every success they achieve. On later expeditions, though I wasn't partnering with Russians, I noticed that they often acted in a similar way. Right or wrong, they have their own way of winning a prized spot on an expedition, and once on the team they all silently push one another very hard.

During the ten days after Scott dislocated his shoulder, the weather was consistently bad. My optimism took a solid hit. Even though I was the nominal climbing leader, I couldn't bully some of the others into pulling their own weight. Instead, I just got frustrated and grouchy—and my diary reflects that mood.

> July 14: Our goal is to establish CIII, finish fixing to CIII &
> pick up all the shit between CII & CIII. That's a major
> problem on these trips. Most people only make half carries
> & dump shit all over the place!
>
> July 15: Always anxious only because got lots to do & I
> have to get people organized. I wanted to work with Rob to
> finish fixing into CIII cause he knows where it should go so
> I waited for him. By 7:30 he still wasn't ready so I took off
> alone.
>
> Same day: Got down to CII at 4 P.M. after a lot of raps
> [rappels]. . . . Got to CII and Alex, Gnady and Dan
> arrived. A full-on cluster fuck! They all wanted to sleep @
> CIII tomorrow as did we. They don't even give us room to
> breathe! I was pissed off!

We simply didn't have enough tents for all of us to sleep at Camp III. Our
climbing logistics still needed some fine-tuning.

In my frustration, in the privacy of my diary, I recorded my own nick-
names for some of the other climbers. The Swedish team were "sheep."
A pair of brothers whose last name rhymed with my epithet became "the
weenies." But my bitching in the diary was more than sour grapes. I really
thought that our so-called team effort was held together by less than a
shoestring.

> July 17: I can't keep the group organized as climbing leader
> cause they (most anyway) aren't strong enough or experi-
> enced enough to be out front so they just scoot around
> dropping loads all over the mountains! They are gonna falter
> big time up high."

Even sometimes when a teammate genuinely tried to help lead or
push supplies, it backfired. On July 19, as we were carrying loads from
Camp I to Camp II, an American teammate told me to go first, since I
was faster. But then, inexplicably, as I wrote in my diary,

Just as I get going he jumps on the [fixed] ropes right in
front of me. What am I supposed to do? Climb up his ass?
So I wait & wait & just go slowly right behind him & take
my time. He stopped constantly to bend over & breathe,
looking back down at me—staring. Drove me nuts! . . .
Finally he stopped @ CII & I blew by to CIII.

There was one woman on our team, but it was clear to me from early
on that she wasn't strong or experienced enough to get high on the mountain. That summer, the only really talented and ambitious woman on K2
was Chantal Mauduit. Although she was French, she had been a member of the Swiss team. When they gave up and went home, Chantal
stayed on—which, strictly speaking, in terms of her permit, was illegal.
According to the rules in Pakistan, once the expedition leader leaves the
mountain, the rest of the team must do so as well.

By 1992, only three women had climbed K2—all three during the dis-
astrous summer of 1986. And by now, all three were dead. Liliane Barrard and Julie Tullis had died on the descent that year, after making the
summit. The Pole Wanda Rutkiewicz, the finest high-altitude woman
climber of her day (and perhaps of all time), had survived K2 only to die
just a month before the beginning of our 1992 expedition on Kangchenjunga, when she was caught in a storm near the summit.

Though it may seem macabre, the fact that no living woman had succeeded on K2 lent a huge cachet to Chantal's effort. She was already famous in France for other exploits, but it would mean a huge boost in
celebrity and sponsorship if she could get up K2.

Chantal was a very beautiful woman, with long brown hair and spar-
kling eyes. She had a habit of flirting with virtually everybody. I found it
disconcerting—when she gave me a certain look, did it mean something
special or was it simply the way she interacted with all the male climbers
on the mountain? In any event, everybody seemed to like Chantal.

One of my American teammates, Thor Kieser, had had a previous relationship with Chantal, but she had broken it off. I got the feeling that

Thor was still in love with her. And she still liked him well enough to agree, after the Swiss had gone home, to pair up with him for her own summit effort.

With Scott out of action, I started to climb a lot with Neal Beidleman. He was an aerospace engineer from Aspen, very successful in his profession. He was also a solid climber, one of the few guys on the mountain who really pulled his own weight. We got along well right from the start. What I especially liked about Neal was his strength, the depth of his climbing experience, and his easygoing personality. Unfortunately, he had work commitments back in the States and planned to leave base camp on August 5 to get back to his job, so it looked as though he'd have at most one shot at the summit.

Through the last week of July, the weather remained mostly bad. This didn't stop the more overeager climbers from trying to force their way up the mountain. They included three of the Russians, Vlad, Gennadi Kopeika, and Aleksei Nikiforov (I called the last two Gnady and Alex), as well as Thor and Chantal. Because it had snowed so much, the climbing conditions were pretty sketchy.

On July 20, Neal and I finally got a tent pitched at Camp III, at 24,000 feet, and spent the night in it. In the morning it was snowing and windy, with a smothering whiteout. It was obvious to me that it was still too soon for a serious summit effort, but the more antsy climbers didn't see it that way. I wrote in my diary that night, "Vlad took off with personal gear & Thor decided he was also gonna sleep @ CIV & try for the top. Yuk, yuk, yuk!"

The only sensible thing was to go down. But still trying to be team players, Neal and I carried a tent, a rope, willow wands, and a snow shovel above Camp III toward where the route steepens to gain the Shoulder, in support of Vlad.

> I caught up to Vlad & told him it was no use to continue
> with zero vis[ibility] and snowing. He insisted on continuing
> so we gave him the tent and bailed. Thor & Chantal were

also more than happy to turn. (Vlad eventually camped right about where we left him! He learns the hard way.)

Neal and I went back down to Camp III and spent the rest of the day debating what to do. As the weather progressively worsened, we made our decision and started descending with headlamps. By 9:30 that night, Neal and I got all the way down to base camp.

For weeks now, I'd been almost constantly irritated by the lack of teamwork within our "team." At base, I had a long, hard think about it, at the end of which I had what I called in my diary a "revelation." "I've done more than my share of teamwork—fixing, hauling, etc.," I wrote. "From now on I make my own moves/decisions." I went on to jot down a possible scenario. If the weather settled and the snow conditions improved, on my own summit attempt I'd take a one-man bivy tent and a stove. I hoped Neal or even Scott could go with me, but I was ready to try for the top solo. Energized by this decision, I wrote in my diary, "It's a good plan and the rest of the team can cluster fuck all they want! Hoka hay!"

Meanwhile, at base camp Scott had been recuperating faster than anyone thought possible. We had helped him rig a special kind of shoulder brace that allowed him to use his injured arm for jumaring up fixed ropes but prevented him from raising that hand above chest level. On July 25—only thirteen days after he had dislocated the shoulder—he gave it a test run on a solo carry up to Camp I. He still felt a fair amount of pain, but, tough guy to the end, he figured he could climb all right with it. I was overjoyed to have my buddy back in action.

Finally the weather was turning good. I still wasn't in any hurry to dash up the mountain, because I knew that after all the storms, the snow conditions would be atrocious. But by July 27, a kind of anxious frenzy had taken hold of the climbers who were ambitious to get to the top. I was still entertaining thoughts about going solo on my own summit push, and the last thing I wanted to do was get railroaded into an attempt because others were chomping at the bit.

Ambivalence is one of the hardest states of mind to handle on an expedition. That night, in a fit of vexation, I wrote in my diary:

> The weather *is* good. I'll get ready to go & decide
> tonight. . . . So I'll be ready to go whenever. Everyone
> keeps hounding me—when am I going up? Fuck, leave me
> alone! I don't want to go with a huge pack of idiots. Too
> many people & they all want to go at once. We have so
> much time, but all of a sudden it's got to be a mad dash.

The Abruzzi Ridge may indeed be the easiest route on K2, but it's no cakewalk. All through that summer on the mountain, I was acutely aware of a startling historical fact. The last successful ascent of the Abruzzi had come in 1986—and of the many climbers on the route that year, six had died on the descent. In the intervening years, 1987 through 1991, fourteen different expeditions had attacked the Abruzzi Ridge. Not a single climber from any of those fourteen parties had reached the summit.

By 1992, only five Americans had climbed K2: Jim Wickwire and his three teammates by the northeast ridge in 1978, and Steve Swenson on the north ridge in 1990. No Americans had yet climbed the Abruzzi. Although that was not a major factor in my motivation, I couldn't help but realize that I might be part of the first American team to get up the classic line by which K2 had first been climbed in 1954.

On July 29, Thor, Chantal, Neal, and I fought our way back up to CIII. We found it completely buried in snow—there wasn't even the top of a tent pole sticking out of the drifts. We spent hours digging out the camp. One tent had been completely destroyed; the other was salvageable, but when we repitched it, it was so cramped that it offered room, as I put it in my diary, only "for one and a half people." I helped Thor and Chantal set up their own tent, then crawled into my coffinlike bivy tent. Neal settled into the tent we had just repitched. Later in the day, Vlad and Gnady arrived from below, climbed through, and eventually camped slightly above us. Alex was also headed up, about a day behind.

It was a miserable night; I didn't sleep very well, as I had to keep getting up to shovel new snow and spindrift off my shelter. In the morning, the wind was still howling. "Tough decision as to what to do," I wrote later. "It's Neal's last shot but it's terrible up here. Decided to bail down. Thor & Chantal stayed. *Really* bad going down."

From the lower camps, our communication with our "teammates" was limited to a prearranged 7:00 P.M. radio call. These calls were cryptic and frustrating at best, as the Russians translated little of their information for us. Sometimes the Russian chatter droned interminably on and we simply gave up listening, since we seemed to be excluded anyway. On July 31, those of us back in base camp waited nervously. Finally we got some news. "Vlad [and Gnady] made it to bottom of summit pyramid," I recorded in my diary. "Alex is at CIII and Thor is ? Very nice day, but Vlad said snow was chest deep."

August 1 was another good day on the mountain. I was still biding my time before making my own surge up the mountain. For Neal, any hopes of the summit had been dashed, but by now Scott was back in good shape and ready to charge. That day, we knew, Vlad and Gnady were going for the top. Forty-one days after I'd arrived at base camp, somebody from our team was finally making a serious assault.

Yet 7:00 P.M. came and went with no radio call from the summit pair. Granted, I had never formed any close friendships with the Russians, and Vlad had really ticked me off with his every-man-for-himself philosophy. That day, however, I couldn't help but worry about what was going on high on K2, as I silently pleaded with the mountain gods to be kind to those two determined climbers. We all tried to send positive energy their way.

Finally we found out what had happened. Vlad and Gnady had left Camp IV, pitched on the Shoulder at 26,000 feet, at 3:00 A.M. Hindered by deep snow, they had climbed agonizingly slowly, but they'd refused to turn around. They'd reached the summit together at 9:00 P.M., after eighteen hours of climbing.

When I found this out, I was astounded and disturbed. In my book, eighteen hours was far too long to keep going for the summit, and 9:00 P.M. was far too late to get there. But these were really tough guys. Did I think I could climb any faster? On my own summit attempt, what could I do differently? "Should we leave CIV @ 8 P.M.?" I mused in my diary. "Gonna be a bitch!"

That night, Gnady made it down to Camp IV, but Vlad bivouacked, exhausted, below the summit. Remarkably, he not only survived the night but suffered no frostbite. The two Russians descended all the way to base camp on August 3.

Meanwhile, on August 2, Thor, Chantal, and Alex had climbed to the Shoulder and set up their own camp at 26,000 feet. Their plan was to go for the summit in the morning.

The same day they made their attempt, August 3, Scott and I finally launched our own summit bid. At last, all our hard work on the mountain was paying dividends. To save time and take advantage of the good weather, we climbed 7,500 vertical feet, from base all the way to Camp III, in a single sustained push. It took me only eleven hours to make that monumental ascent, Scott a few hours longer. In terms of sheer efficiency of movement, that day remains one of the best I have ever had in the mountains.

As we climbed, of course, we had no idea what was going on with our three teammates above. At Camp III, we listened to the 7:00 P.M. radio call, but there was no word of their progress. In those days it was not unusual not to make any calls during a summit push, because you were so caught up in the effort of climbing or hadn't even bothered to carry the bulky radio with you. Our only option was to keep the radio on and wait for word from the summit trio.

As you climb the Abruzzi Ridge, for thousands of feet the summit pyramid is out of sight, eclipsed by the cliffs and slopes above you. It's only when you reach the Shoulder, at 26,000 feet, that the majestic upper sweep of the mountain suddenly bursts into view.

Caught up as we were in our own great day of climbing, Scott and I didn't give much thought to Thor, Chantal, and Alex. They were experienced climbers who ought to be able to take care of themselves. Inside our sleeping bags at Camp III, Scott and I were wired and exuberant. The next day we would push on to Camp IV. If the weather held, we would go for the top on August 5.

We were too excited to get to sleep at first. Instead, we just tossed and turned in our bags. And then, at 10:00 P.M., we heard the crackle of our radio. I sat up, turned on my headlamp, grabbed the walkie-talkie, and answered the call.

It was Thor, transmitting from Camp IV. "Hey, guys," he said. I could hear the tension in his voice. "Chantal and Alex aren't back. I don't know where they are."

Oh, shit! I said to myself. In the headlamp beam, I looked at Scott. He had the same look of disgust and concern on his face. *There goes our summit try,* I thought.

Thor and Alex, it turned out, had left Camp IV at 5:30 that morning. Chantal hadn't gotten off until 7:00. But then, even though she was climbing without bottled oxygen, she caught up with the two guys in the Bottleneck and surged past them. It was an extraordinary performance at such an altitude.

After a long, hard day of climbing, realizing he would reach the summit too late in the day, rather than risking a bivouac, Thor prudently gave up his attempt just a few hundred feet below the top and headed down. As he would learn only the next day, Chantal had pushed on and reached the summit at 5:00 P.M. Alex didn't top out until 7:00. On the descent, he came across Chantal. Afraid to go down by herself in the dark, she had started to bivouac. Almost berating her, he roused her out of her apathy and convinced her to go down with him.

At first light on August 4, Scott and I prepared to head up from Camp III. Our summit attempt had been transformed into a rescue mission or, even worse, into a search for missing climbers. But then, at 7:00 A.M., Thor came on the radio again. Alex and Chantal had just arrived, staggering into camp after a descent that had stretched through the whole night. Chantal was completely exhausted, snowblind, and suffering from what she thought was frostbite. Alex had saved her life, but now, as if he felt he had done all that was required of him, the Russian dumped Chantal in Thor's lap and headed on down the mountain. He barely said good-bye.

Chantal was still virtually helpless. So, Scott and I realized, it would now be our job to go to her aid. Thor could never get her down to base camp by himself. At least, I thought as I gathered gear for our mission, it was a rescue and not a search.

That morning, however, everything seemed to conspire against us. By the time Scott and I got going, the visibility had dropped to almost zero, and the snow conditions were really bad. For a couple of hours, barely able to see where we were going, we plowed upward through deep snow, before deciding to call it quits and head back.

Late that evening, Alex came into sight above Camp III. He was pretty wasted. We climbed up a little way to help him down, got him into a tent, and brewed up lots of drinks, because he was severely dehydrated. It surprised me that at this point, Alex didn't even seem curious about what was going on with Chantal.

That same day, Thor had started down from Camp IV, leading Chantal, who could barely see her feet in front of her. Because of the marginal conditions, they got only a short distance before having to stop on the lower edge of the Shoulder. Fortunately, Thor had brought a tent, but the emergency shelter he set up on that precarious slope was more like a bivouac than a true camp. I could only imagine the monumental task he had taking care of Chantal in such trying circumstances.

The next day, August 5, Scott and I got up at 4:30 A.M., then waited for a break in the weather to head back up, since the situation above us seemed to be getting more dire by the hour. Alex was too wiped out to help at all; later that day he would head down from Camp III on his own. Finally the weather improved just enough. Scott and I were off at 7:30. There were clouds scudding by, alternating with sunbursts. The snow everywhere was deep and soft.

By midday, we had reached the last headwall beneath the Shoulder.

Suddenly we caught sight of Thor and Chantal, two small dots above us flickering in and out of clouds and mist. The wind was blowing steadily in a minor gale, and little spindrift avalanches had started sliding down the headwall.

Throughout the expedition so far, I had always erred on the side of caution. I'd refused to climb in conditions the Russians seemed to think were worth the risk. I'd headed down when cockier climbers headed up. Now, all at once, I felt that the slope Scott and I were trying to climb was ready to avalanche. Scott hadn't yet come to the same realization—I attribute that to the fact that I'd done a lot more guiding than he had and had learned to be hypervigilant about avalanche conditions. "Wait a minute, Scott," I said. "This is not a good slope."

It's an eternal and inevitable fact in mountaineering, as in most dangerous pursuits, that you can get sucked into exceeding the boundaries of your own best judgment of acceptable risk when you go to the rescue of someone else in trouble. The classic example occurred on K2 in 1953, when, trying to save the life of a crippled teammate, seven members of the American expedition came extremely close to dying in one horrible, interlinked fall. That accident had taken place almost exactly where Scott and I now stood.

Later I would think about the sad fate of Jean-Marc Boivin. One of the finest French climbers of his day, he was also, during the 1980s, the boldest extreme skier in the world. Boivin performed scores of first ski descents in the Alps, on couloirs and faces where the slightest slip meant certain death. He also perfected the arts of BASE jumping and parapenting (hang gliding with a frameless parachute that unfurls from a pack on your back). In 1988 he electrified the climbing world by jumping off the summit of Everest and parapenting to a lower camp in only twelve minutes.

In 1990, at the age of thirty-nine, Boivin was starring in a made-for-TV adventure for *Ushuaïa,* a chic French documentary show about extreme sports. He and a female costar were set to BASE jump off a cliff near Angel Falls, Venezuela—a piece of cake for Boivin. But when the woman, jumping first, hit the cliff glancingly on the way down, Boivin impetuously jumped to go to her aid, without making his usual meticulous preparations. He hit a tree near the bottom of the jump, then lay on the ground, injured. A helicopter flew by to rescue him, but Boivin signaled the pilot to go after his costar first. She survived, miraculously, with only minor injuries. By the time the chopper had returned to gather up Boivin, he had died of internal hemorrhaging. He left behind a wife and small children.

If we had been climbing only for our own reasons, to get to the Shoulder and establish Camp IV, Scott and I would not have pushed the headwall in the conditions that now engulfed us. It was the very real possibility that Chantal—and perhaps Thor, as well—might die without our help that drove us to such an extreme and dangerous effort.

Scott and I were roped together with a fifty-foot line I had scrounged at Camp III. By now, I had a foreboding sense of imminent disaster. "Man," I said to Scott, "let's not get ourselves killed doing this." The slope we were climbing seemed triggered to avalanche at any moment. Scott, who was above me, sat down on the slope, facing out. Almost in a panic, I started digging frantically with my ice ax, trying to excavate a hole I could hunker down in if the avalanche came. My thought was that this pocket in the snow would protect me from the brunt of the blow if the slope cut loose.

And then, sure enough, it came. Scott never saw it. I had time just to look up and see a wave of snow swallow him before he disappeared from sight. I quickly tucked my head and upper body into my hole, thrust the pick of my ax into the slope, and put all my weight on top of it. The slide took so long to carry Scott down the slope and then past me that I began to think, *Wow, I got away with it!*

Then—*boom!* The rope came tight in a wrenching jolt, and I was plucked out of my little hole like a knife out of butter. I started careening down the slope fifty feet above Scott. There was just enough time for me to anticipate the 8,000-foot fall to the glacier—and to oblivion.

The instincts born of my years of RMI training clicked in. *Arrest! Arrest!* my brain screamed. Even as I cartwheeled down the slope, I flipped onto my stomach and got my head uphill, with the ax held in both hands under my chest. I dug and dug with the pick, only to feel it slice through soft snow. Scott, I later learned, had been unable to get in position even to attempt a self-arrest.

We had probably fallen a couple of hundred feet when all of a sudden my ax bit into some ice and we came to a stop. My self-arrest had finally done the job. I rolled over and yelled out, "Scott, are you okay?"

I couldn't have been more relieved by his answer. "Yeah, but my nuts are killing me!" he screamed. If Scott was together enough to complain about his harness jamming his balls, he had to be all right.

All the same, we had come within inches of taking the big plunge. That was by far the closest brush with death I had experienced in my sixteen years of mountaineering.

Scott and I pulled ourselves together. I got Thor on the radio and warned him not to come down the slope that had just avalanched. "Go over to your left," I pleaded, "toward this ice-cliffy area, and maybe rappel." Then we climbed up, still hoping to guide Thor and Chantal down. Finally, at 25,500 feet, we closed the gap. "Man," Thor exclaimed, "am I glad to see you guys!"

We laid Chantal on her back, right there in the snow. I managed to pry her eyelids open and douse her eyes with anesthetic drops. Then we tied in as a rope of four, with Scott going first and myself in the rear as anchor. Late that afternoon, we at last made it down to Camp III. We got Chantal into a sleeping bag. I checked her feet; they weren't frostbitten, just terribly cold. We melted pot after pot of snow to nurse both Thor and Chantal with hot drinks.

Throughout the retreat, Chantal never thanked us once. Instead, over and over again, she pealed, "I made the summit! I'm so happy!" It would not be the last time this strong and beautiful Frenchwoman would use up all her reserves getting to the top of an 8,000er only to collapse and depend on other climbers to get her down the mountain.

Scott and I knew what the rescue had cost us. Our summit attempt was now on indefinite hold. The more pressing duty was to get Chantal, still exhausted, and Thor, in only marginally better shape, safely down the mountain.

By midnight on August 6, all of us had made it back to base camp in one piece. Scott and I were pretty tired ourselves, but beyond that, we were profoundly disappointed. Any summit attempt we might make would now require a whole new launch out of base camp. Morally, however, we had had absolutely no choice but to abort our summit try to help Thor and Chantal get down the mountain. That's why I find it so hard to stomach all the accounts in recent years—especially on Everest—of climbers ignoring others in trouble for fear a rescue effort would sabotage their own summit bids.

The next night, the Russians and Chantal celebrated their victory. Scott and I weren't invited, so we lay in our own tents listening to their drunken cheers and toasts. That was hard enough to take, but not nearly as hard as the bombshell that exploded in the morning.

Vlad gathered his "team" in the cooking tent at breakfast. Then he announced that the expedition was over! Everyone on his permit would now have to go home. And as if that edict weren't severe enough, he decided to insult the rest of us for good measure. We Americans, he announced witheringly, just didn't climb fast enough. We had wasted our time and weren't willing to push it.

I simply stared at Vlad. I was so angry, I couldn't get a single word out. I couldn't remember ever being so pissed off at a fellow climber on a mountain. I couldn't believe that a so-called leader could be so selfish. If we needed any further proof that Vlad, in the end, was a complete jerk, he had just provided it.

By August 7, Scott and I had been on the mountain for nearly seven weeks. There were five of us on the Russian permit who still dearly wanted another crack at climbing K2. And there was another team still at base camp—Hall & Ball, with their Swedish and Mexican teammates. After so much effort, I wasn't about to give up just because Vlad had told us to go home.

Chantal, of course, had ignored the whole permit business after her

Swiss team had packed it in. She had climbed the mountain illegally and had apparently gotten away with it. That wasn't my style, however; I've always pretty much played by the rules. And I knew that other climbers who had tried to circumvent permit restrictions had been banned from Pakistan by the Ministry of Tourism.

Since our leader, Vlad, was leaving, technically our expedition was over and all of us had to leave as well. But, working with Hall & Ball and our liaison officer, we eventually cobbled together an arrangement that allowed us to stay on the mountain. Dan Mazur, one of our five determined to give it another shot, became the nominal leader of what was left of our party.

Meanwhile, the weather refused to cooperate. Day after day, we saw fierce storms raking the upper slopes of the mountain. Scott and I had left all our gear at Camp III. But now we started to worry that Camp IV, on the Shoulder, could have been buried under new snow or destroyed by the winds that we had seen scouring the upper reaches of the mountain. Instead of counting on the tents and gear left by others at Camp IV, we'd have to pack up Camp III and carry it up to the Shoulder.

We rested at base camp for four days. I was preoccupied with logistics. On August 10, I wrote in my diary:

> Scott & I have all of our own stuff @ CIII—tent, bags,
> fuel, stove, food. Last trip up we ate like sparrows—
> granola for breakfast, 2 power bars during the day & soup
> for dinner. We gave up on hot drinks because it took too
> much time to cook on the Bleuet stove. . . .
>
> We could do it in 3 days if conditions were right. If not
> deep snow. Base to CIII, to CIV, to summit. *Please* give us
> some good weather!

It wasn't until August 11 that the weather cleared. We all decided to head up the mountain the next day. After all our waiting, all our setbacks, all the interpersonal conflicts, I was supermotivated. You can see the tension in my very handwriting in my diary, and in my use of exclamation marks:

> We are going to CIII tomorrow. Scott, me, Gary & Rob will
> leave here at 2 A.M. . . . Many will follow. But most of the
> rest haven't even been above CII yet! Plus they will carry
> O's [bottled oxygen]. It's gonna be tough for 'em.
>   GET PSYCHED!!
>   GO! GO! GO! GO!

On August 12, Scott and I and Hall & Ball left base camp at 2:00 A.M., planning to climb all the way to Camp III that day. Several others had left the day before and spent the night at Camp II, in hopes of meeting up with us at CIII when we arrived. In the lead all the way, I reached Camp III at noon. I'd climbed those 7,500 feet in ten hours—an hour faster than my great time on August 3. Charley Mace, who had spent the night at Camp II, arrived at 2:30 P.M. Scott didn't get in until 4:00. Hall & Ball and the rest of their teammates were even slower. From my diary:

> Rob & Gary arrived totally fried-out & hypothermic. Had to
> set up camp for 'em & give hot drinks. Mex's & Swedes
> showed between 7–8 P.M.! Not a lot of strength here that's
> for sure.
>   Beautiful clear evening. High hopes for good weather
> tomorrow.

But as it turned out, the weather the next morning was decidedly iffy, with lenticular cloud caps covering all the major peaks—almost always a sign of a coming storm. None of us was sure what to do, until Scott and I decided to head up to the Shoulder. We didn't get off until 9:30 A.M. The others eventually followed us.

As part of my homework for K2, I had studied all the things that had gone wrong on previous expeditions on the Abruzzi Ridge. In particular,

I'd learned a sobering lesson from the 1986 tragedy. On their descent, a number of climbers that year had been marooned on the Shoulder during a long storm. One reason some of them didn't seize the lulls in the storm to head down was that they were afraid of losing the route. And the reason for that was that they had not adequately wanded the stretch from Camp III to Camp IV.

"Willow wands" are ordinary garden stakes painted green, with little red ribbons attached to one end. On the way up, if you plant a wand in the snow every hundred feet or so, you're marking the route so that you can find it even in a whiteout on the way down. I'd been trained on Rainier and Denali always to wand a route.

Thus I'd been stunned to learn that the climbers marooned on the Shoulder in 1986 simply had not brought enough willow wands to mark the route on the featureless white expanse below Camp IV. On a nice sunny day, it's hard to imagine the need for those markers. But I'd always been taught to plan for the worst and hope for the best. Wanding doesn't seem to be a European thing—it's not quite chic to be seen lugging a pack with dozens of green sticks protruding from the top flap. Even the Russians on our trip had not bothered to wand the route above Camp III.

Now, on the way up from Camp III to Camp IV, I placed wands at regular intervals. I knew that this stretch was the most likely place for us to get lost on the way down. As I climbed, I kept repeating to myself, "Remember '86!" It wasn't easy, since we had lost a bunch of wands when the tents were buried. In the end, as I began to run out, I had to break many of the wands in half and plant them short to eke out our supply. We had even scrounged tent poles from broken tents at Camp III to use as wands. Several days later, those markers would save our asses.

Scott and I reached Camp IV at 2:00 P.M. Once again the others straggled in hours later, some as late as 8:00 P.M. I'd deliberately placed our campsite as high on the Shoulder as was feasible, to shorten the climb on summit day. Now we all settled in to wait. In this incarnation, Camp IV was a small cluster of freshly erected and newly occupied tents. Charley Mace was camped just below us. In various tents were the members of

Hall & Ball's team: Rob and Gary, two Swedish climbers, and the three Mexicans.

Scott and I had also chosen to go superlight. Our tent was not a regular two-man model but a five-pound bivy tent. We had only one sleeping bag to share between the two of us. The idea was to sleep in our down suits, with the bag unzipped and draped over us like a blanket. In the claustrophobic confines of our cramped tent, we thought, this arrangement should keep us warm enough.

Our only rope was the fifty-foot line I had scavenged at Camp III. All of the rope we had originally brought had either been fixed in place or lost in the intervening storms.

That evening, August 13, Scott and I planned to get up at 10:30 P.M. and be out the door by midnight. But I knew better than to count on perfect weather for the next day. As I wrote in my diary—presciently, it turned out—"Weather is so fickle on K2 the only way to get good weather is to go high & wait it out. That's our plan. Hang out here @ CIV until it looks good enough to go."

The days that followed severely tried our patience. Scott and I got up to check the weather at 10:30 P.M., then again at midnight, 3:30 A.M., and 5:30 A.M. Each time we stuck our heads out the tent door, we saw that it was blowing hard and snowing—too nasty for a summit attempt. We had decided that if we could not take off by 5:30 A.M., it would be too late to get to the summit and back with a margin of safety. Once we'd made up our minds not to go on August 14, we simply lay in our cramped tent, trying to make the hours pass. "Dozed all day," I wrote in my diary. "Didn't eat shit. Try again tonight."

During our time at Camp IV, we tried to yell over the wind to let the others know our plans. All of Hall & Ball's team, including the Swedes and the Mexicans, were now intermittently using their bottled oxygen even while they slept. That made for a cruel trade-off: the longer they hung out at Camp IV, the less oxygen they'd have left to go to the summit with. We weren't surprised, then, in the middle of the day on August 14, when two of the Mexicans, Ricardo Torres-Nava and Adrián Benítez, decided to bail. They were experienced climbers—both had topped out on Everest—so we figured they wouldn't have any trouble getting down to Camp III.

What happened on their descent we learned about only secondhand, over the radio from Dan Mazur and Jonathan Pratt, two of our team-mates who were still at Camp III. The news shocked us badly, but I'm disturbed, upon rereading my diary, to see that I recorded it at the time with more outrage than compassion:

> Apparently they tried to do a ski pole rappel (stupid!) @ the traverse & Adrian pulled it out & fell 3000' to near CII—he's dead! Idiots! Dan & Jonathan tried to get to him but it was too dangerous.

Below the Shoulder, at about 25,500 feet, there was a small ice step. Rather than downclimb it, Ricardo and Adrián set up a rappel. Despite having gotten up Everest, the two Mexicans apparently weren't very tech-nically skilled. As the anchor for their rappel, they simply thrust a ski pole into the slope. Even in the most desperate situation, that would have been an incredibly foolish thing to try. In fact, I'd never before heard of anybody trying to rappel off a ski pole. Ricardo got away with it, but when Adrián put his weight on the rope, the pole pulled. He never had a chance to stop himself. Even though they were sure he was dead, Jonathan and Dan spent the better part of two days trying to get to Adrián's body; eventu-ally they decided that it was so hazardous, they would be inviting an-other accident.

I'd guess now that the tone of my diary entry reflected the weeks of tension and frustration that had built up inside me by mid-August. The accident showed how close to the edge some of the climbers were on this unforgiving mountain. Adrián was a friendly and likable guy, and we were all saddened by his death. But the accident was entirely avoidable. He could have easily faced in and downclimbed the steep step where he fell; he didn't need to rappel.

That's where my anger came from. I'd been on the mountain too long with other climbers who weren't even my teammates, let alone my friends, and whose judgment and technique I didn't trust. What's more, the irritation in my diary must have been a defense: I didn't want this needless tragedy to undermine in any way my own determination to climb K2. Had it been Scott or Charley who had died, more than likely I would have given up my attempt.

August 15 came and went with no improvement in the weather. That day, having run out of bottled oxygen, the Swedes bailed, and the third Mexican, Héctor Ponce de León, descended to console his surviving teammate. So now there were only five of us left at Camp IV: Hall & Ball, Charley, Scott, and me. We had to pass the hours resting and daydreaming. My mind was filled with anxious thoughts: How strong would I be during the final ascent after surviving here for two or three days? Would the weather finally break? Could we get up to the summit and back before nightfall, as no one this season had yet done?

My diary entry that day is a testament to uneasiness:

> Tried again last night & no go. Still funky weather. Barely eating. We either go up tonight or bail down tomorrow. . . .
>
> Weather is OK. Not great. Cloudy, no wind, poor visibility. We seem to be at the top edge of clouds. Very anxious. Tonight we must go up or go down tomorrow & start all over—ugh! I want to get this over with! We snooze all day like coon-hounds. Dreaming of food—salad, beer, pizza.

That line about going down and starting all over again, I now realize, was pure rationalization. All five of us knew this was going to be our last chance that summer to climb K2.

On August 16, Scott and I were up at midnight. It was still cloudy, but calm, so we decided to go for it. Breakfast was a cup of coffee apiece. Altitude deprives you of hunger, and forcing yourself to eat can stir up waves of nausea. It's one of the paradoxes of high-altitude climbing that even though you are burning thousands of calories each day, you simply cannot get enough back into your system to balance things out.

We had slept in our down suits, so it was just a matter of putting on boots, overboots, harnesses, mittens, hats, goggles, and headlamps. Ice that had coated the inside walls of our confining tent showered us as we tried not to elbow each other. Finally we were out the door. We strapped on our crampons and were moving by 1:30 A.M. Charley didn't get off for another hour, and Rob and Gary were even further behind.

I wasn't carrying a pack, just two liter bottles filled with a powdered energy drink; in my chest pockets I'd stuck a couple of Power Bars. I also carried a spare pair of mittens, a camera, and extra headlamp batteries. Scott and I were roped together with our fifty-foot line, in anticipation of the crevasses that we knew lay above.

The slope gradually steepened as we headed up into the mouth of the Bottleneck. We kicked steps in the firm snow, inclined at a 45-degree angle. Following in our tracks, Charley caught up to us in the Bottleneck. During the whole expedition so far, Scott and I had scarcely climbed with Charley, but in that instant he became our partner. We managed to tie in all three of us on that fifty-foot rope, which was almost absurd, yet roping up together gave us a certain feeling of security.

Near the top of the Bottleneck, the snow conditions worsened, alternating deep, soft powder with a scary breakable crust. We swapped leads often.

We'd been climbing for two hours before we finally saw Rob and Gary's headlamps as they left Camp IV. Despite that late start, and despite using supplemental oxygen, they were moving very slowly. Was something wrong?

At the top of the Bottleneck, we began the leftward traverse, the crux of the whole route. Vlad had fixed a 150-foot rope here on August 1, and it was still in place—the single fixed rope on the mountain above Camp IV. It was anchored, with a pair of ice screws, only at either end, so if you came off in the middle of the traverse, you'd take a horrendous yo-yo plunge before the stretchy nylon rope would catch you—assuming that neither of the anchors pulled. All the same, we clipped in to the rope and used it like a handrail, counting on what climbers jokingly call "psychological" protection.

The traverse was sketchy. The points of our crampons barely gained purchase on the downward-sloping slabs of rock that lay just beneath the sugary snow. Falling was not an option, but staying attached to the face took all the concentration we could muster.

By shortly after sunrise, we were past the traverse and had started up the long diagonal ramp that leads to the summit snowfield. We were still more than a thousand feet below the top, with some five or six hours of climbing ahead of us, but we knew that the ground only got easier above. Things were looking really positive.

All morning, however, a sea of clouds below us had been slowly but steadily rising. At 7:00 A.M., the sea engulfed us. It was still completely calm, and eerily warm—so warm that I took off my hat. But then it started to snow; the big, soft, fluffy flakes quickly grew so thick that I started inhaling them as I panted in the thin air. We were still roped to-gether, because even on the summit snowfield there are crevasses you could fall into. We continued to swap leads as we plowed through the breakable crust.

As we trudged slowly upward in silence, I started calculating. Five hours to the summit, three back down to here—what are conditions going to be like eight hours from now if it keeps snowing? It was then that the knot started to form in my gut. As I later wrote in my diary, I was won-dering, "What to do? The prudent thing is to turn back, but we keep going. Stupid? Probably. This is the worst part of climbing big peaks. Spend tons of $ & time to get to this point & you're faced with this decision."

Scott and Charley obviously weren't going through the same kind of agonizing appraisal. When I finally stopped them and asked, "Hey, what do you guys think?," Scott answered, "Whaddya mean?" and Charlie sec-onded him: "We're going up!"

So I kept heading upward, putting off my decision from one half hour to the next. I thought, *Why are they comfortable with this and I'm not? Am I a sissy? Do I worry too much? Am I too conservative?* All that ambivalence, all that self-questioning just ate away at me, and the knot in my gut grew heavier.

As we got closer to the summit and the falling snow showed no signs of letting up, I knew I was making the greatest mistake of my climbing life. And yet I kept going.

During the seventeen years since K2, I've thought long and hard about why I didn't turn around on August 16, 1992. There was certainly a voice in my head taunting me: *What are other people going to say if I go down while Scott and Charley make the summit?* Yet today I can honestly state that my partners' eagerness to push ahead was not what swayed me. It was, instead, my perverse inability to make a decision. In my head at the time, a broken record was playing: *I wish I didn't have to make this decision right now. This is the worst decision in the world.*

What happened to me in 2002 on Annapurna gave me much-needed clarity about what had gone on a decade earlier on K2. On May 14 of that year, J.-C. Lafaille and Alberto Iñurrategi completed an exposed and dangerous snow-and-ice traverse under a tower called the Roc Noir, then began climbing the steep face to regain the crest of the east ridge. Coming along a little behind the lead pair, Veikka Gustafsson and I reached the traverse at 7:30 A.M. I started to lead across, but I realized at once that the slope was loaded with snow ready to slide. All it might take to trigger a fatal avalanche was somebody kicking steps in the unstable surface.

J.-C., the most talented climber I had ever paired up with, had led the traverse, but I balked. He kept yelling down to us how dangerous the conditions were—a fact that was already obvious to me. Torn by conflicting impulses, I remembered being in a similar predicament in 1992. This time a voice in my head warned me, *Ed, don't do now what you did on K2.* I turned back, and without hesitation Veikka turned back with me. J.-C. and Alberto pushed on to the summit, but they had a true epic getting down. It was only after they had reversed the traverse under the

Roc Noir that they, as J.-C. would later write, "once more entered the land of the living."

That was the only time on my thirty expeditions to 8,000ers that I ever turned back while a partner went on. But I've never second-guessed my decision. The sense that I'd made the right choice helped me congratulate J.-C. and Alberto on their triumph with unalloyed joy and admiration. I believed they had just pulled off one of the most daring ascents in recent mountaineering history. By 2002, I was comfortable with the notion that someone like J.-C. might tread a thinner line of acceptable risk than I would.

On August 16, 1992, Scott, Charley, and I broke free of the clouds just short of the summit. We saw it shining in the sun ahead of us. At noon, we stood on top, hugging each other and gasping in the thin air. My elation was genuine, but it was tempered by a mounting anxiety as I stared at the boiling black clouds below us. After only thirty minutes on top, we headed down.

Almost immediately we plunged back into that sea of clouds, which was now darker and more ominous than ever. Soon we were stumbling downward in a thick whiteout. It was then that Scott, in the lead, started to head off in the wrong direction, toward the top of the unknown east face. On the way up, I'd memorized even the subtlest landmarks, and now I was able to shout, "No, no, no! Wrong way, Scott! Farther to the right!"

By the time we got to the ramp that led down to the Bottleneck, the snow conditions were appalling. Most of the drifts were thigh-deep, and as I broke trail, I kept knocking loose huge slabs that thundered out of sight into the void below. By now, I was convinced that we were going to die. I kept telling myself that I'd probably just made the last and most stupid mistake of my life. That realization brought with it a weird sense of calm: *Well, you might as well give it your best effort. You've got nothing to lose now.*

At last we reached the near end of the crux traverse. There was no hope of reversing the pitch in the footsteps we had kicked on the way up—they were lost under layers of deep new snow. Instead, one by one we rappelled the fixed rope until we reached its sagging midpoint, then jumared back up to the farther anchor. From there, at the top of the Bottleneck, we faced in and started to kick steps downward. We were un-roped, since we knew that if one guy fell here, the rope would also pull the other two off.

Miraculously, none of the snow slabs broke loose beneath our feet. We downclimbed slowly, until at last the angle gentled out where the summit pyramid meets the Shoulder. By now, the whiteout was so thick, we couldn't see Camp IV. So we spread out, three abreast, and clomped on down, like searchers looking for clues in a crime scene in the forest. When we got to the top of the Shoulder, we started calling out, hoping Rob and Gary could guide us into camp. At last they heard us and shouted back.

We reached the tents at 5:00 P.M. We'd been climbing for almost sixteen hours.

I sat down in the snow outside our bivy tent. At that moment, I felt no happiness whatsoever at having climbed K2. Instead, I felt only anger at myself. That very evening, I wrote in my diary, "We'd pushed our luck beyond the max. I hope I never do that again! No summit is worth dying for. You can always come back."

K2 was not done messing with us. As we'd reached Camp IV, I'd asked Rob, "What happened to you guys?"

A stricken look had crossed his face. "Gary's pretty sick," he'd said softly.

That morning, Rob and Gary had barely gotten started when Gary collapsed with severe breathing problems. It was all Rob could do to get his partner back to camp. Throughout the day, as he lay in the tent, Gary's condition steadily worsened. Eventually we would conclude that he had a bad case of pulmonary edema.

Exhausted though we were, Scott, Charley, and I would now have to get a nearly helpless climber down the mountain. It would have been tempting to take a rest day on August 17, but I knew better. I wrote in my diary, "We gotta get outta here. Don't want to get trapped here & die like all those people in '86. . . . This mountain is gonna kick our ass all the way down."

In terms of avalanche danger, the conditions were still terrible. Knowing there might not be any tents still standing at the camps below, I packed our bivy tent, and we carried our sleeping bags with us. Tired as we were from our summit climb the day before, plowing through waist-deep snow exhausted us even further. Adrenaline was our fuel, and saving Gary's life was our motivation. Once we'd left the Shoulder, we improvised a descending technique born of desperation. I would try to kick a solid stance in the snow, then belay Charley down on our fifty-foot rope. Then the other three would use the rope like a static hand line, with me as the anchor. Finally, when everybody was down, I'd face in and descend without a belay. All the while, Gary seemed only half-conscious.

Needless to say, this was incredibly slow and tedious. After a while, however, we found the uppermost willow wand. Now, when I belayed Charley, he would sweep back and forth at the end of the rope until he found the next wand. It was here that those humble green garden stakes saved our lives. By 1:00 P.M., we had reached Camp III. We wanted to push on down to Camp II, and since there were fixed ropes all the way from III to II, Scott, Charley, and I decided to go ahead, break trail, and prepare camp for Rob and Gary.

Rappelling the fixed lines was a lot easier and safer than downclimbing the steep slopes above Camp III. The three of us got to Camp II at 5:00 P.M.; Gary and Rob arrived three hours later. Weakened by his illness, Gary had abandoned his pack, containing all his gear, somewhere above, so Scott and I gave him one of our sleeping bags (we had left a second bag at Camp II). Once again the two of us cuddled underneath a single sleeping bag in a half-collapsed tent. It was a miserable night, but knowing we were slowly descending into richer air gave us strength and hope.

Each day after we'd summited, the weather got worse and worse. This mountain just did not want to let us go. It was almost as if we now had to pay some sort of toll for having stood on her summit. Had we not had to help Gary get down the mountain, we could have moved fast, but now we were confronted with a moral responsibility that none of us could ignore. We would all go down together.

By the next morning, Gary was in really bad shape. Only marginally aware of what was going on, he pleaded with us to leave him there to die. Scott yelled at him, "We're not leaving you! Get your shit together!"

It took six hours on August 18 to get Gary down to Camp I, even though we now had him breathing supplemental oxygen. He was so weak that we had to unclip and reclip his figure-eight device from each fixed rope. The snow and wind pummeled us relentlessly. At Camp I, Gary completely collapsed. I quickly erected the bivy tent Scott and I had spent our nights in at Camp IV, then sat inside it as I cradled Gary in my lap and monitored his symptoms. His breathing was rapid and shallow, and he was coughing up blood and green phlegm, some of which splattered onto the tent walls. "He looks 90 years old and ready to die," I wrote in my diary.

Blessedly, Jonathan Pratt and Dan Mazur had climbed up to Camp I to help out. They administered fresh oxygen to Gary, but it didn't do much good. He could no longer stand, let alone climb down under his own steam. Eventually the Swedes arrived to lend a hand. Spurred on by the fear of losing Gary, we pushed through the night, wearing headlamps as we lowered and slid our completely helpless partner down the slopes below Camp I. We reached advance base camp, at the foot of the Abruzzi Ridge, only at midnight. From there the Swedes and Mexicans took over, while Scott, Charley, and I stumbled on down to base camp, arriving at 3:00 A.M. We had been on the move for twenty hours straight.

The next day, a helicopter picked up Rob and Gary and flew them to Islamabad. Gary slowly recovered, first in a Pakistani hospital, then back home in New Zealand. He had survived K2 by the skin of his teeth.

I don't think I've ever been more physically or emotionally exhausted in my life than after that climb and descent. But finally I could relax and begin to savor the joy of accomplishment. "What an epic!" I wrote in my diary on August 19. "But we're done! Alive! Summited! No frostbite! Saved 2 people!" Beneath those triumphant boasts, however, I was still haunted by our summit day. *You made a big mistake up there,* I thought. *You happened to get away with it.*

During those reflective moments at base camp, I made a solemn vow to myself—one that, I'm happy to say, I stuck to throughout the following thirteen years of going after 8,000ers. The vow: *Your instincts are telling you something. Trust them and listen to them.*

Before K2, although we had never climbed together, Scott and I thought we might have found the perfect partnership. We were already planning an expedition for the summer of 1993 that might have been even more ambitious than K2: a two-man, alpine-style assault on the huge Diamir Face of Nanga Parbat.

Despite all the setbacks and animosities, Scott and I got along great on K2. In all the pages of my diary, though I tended to let fly at other climbers on the mountain who weren't doing their jobs, there's scarcely a harsh word about Scott.

Yet Scott and I never climbed together again. And that was my decision. We simply had different styles. Scott was a freewheeling, let-it-happen kind of guy. I was more calculating. Ours, I realized, was not an equal partnership in terms of planning, decision making, and bearing the burden of stress. And although we had gotten along well, I could see that Scott and I had different levels of risk we were willing to take.

So when Nanga Parbat came up again, I made some kind of excuse. And I politely declined other invitations from Scott in the following years. We stayed great friends, but we never again shared a rope.

I don't really regret that choice. But it makes what happened in 1996 all the more poignant. That spring, Scott and I were on the south side of

Everest, on different teams: I was part of David Breashears's IMAX project, while Scott was leading his Mountain Madness clients up the standard route on the world's highest mountain.

It was great to see my old buddy again. At base camp, we spent some happy hours just shooting the breeze and reliving K2. Some evenings he would wander over to my tent with a couple of bottles of beer, and we would sit outside chatting. Scott seemed to need someone who wasn't on his team to talk to about their interpersonal dynamics. This was the first time he was guiding a group of clients on Everest. For the future of his Mountain Madness business, it was a huge event. A successful climb in 1996 would boost sign-ups for the following years.

By early May, Scott had decided to join forces with Rob Hall's Adventure Consultants team for their summit attempt. This would mean a relatively large group working its way along the serpentine southeast ridge toward the summit. Scott and Rob announced May 10 as their summit day. Not wanting to be part of this large assault team, our IMAX crew chose to bide our time: we wanted the mountain to ourselves when we tried to shoot our big-screen movie. Scott and I crossed paths on the Lhotse Face as he headed up to the South Col. I gave him a big hug and said, "Have a great trip. Be safe."

That whole spring, something wasn't right with Scott. He was sick much of the time, and uncharacteristically weak. He probably should have let his other guides take the clients to the top, but Scott was so used to being big and strong that it never occurred to him not to summit himself. And he had famously nicknamed the South Col route the "Yellow Brick Road," since he thought he had its ascent down pat.

On May 10, Scott was dragging when he got to the summit, the last member of his team to top out. On the descent, he collapsed at 27,300 feet. We think now that he was probably suffering from cerebral edema. Despite the strenuous efforts of others to save him, Scott died there, curled up on his icy ledge.

Twelve days later, when our IMAX team went to the summit, I knew that I would have to pass Scott's body above the South Col. And I knew that it would be an emotionally wrenching task. So I saved my last "visit" for the way down.

In midafternoon, I sat down next to Scott's body. His upper torso and head had been covered by a pack, but he lay on his back with a flexed knee sticking up into the air. Scott's wife had wanted me to try to retrieve the wedding ring that he carried on a cord around his neck, but I couldn't bring myself to do it.

Instead, I sat there in silence for long minutes. I looked at his surroundings, then back at the body of my friend. "Hey, Scott," I said, "how you doing?" The only answer was the droning of the wind.

"What happened, man?"

In 2003, I climbed Broad Peak with J.-C. Lafaille. As we sat basking on top, we stared at the beautiful pyramid of K2, six miles to the northwest. Just two years earlier, J.-C. had had his own epic on K2. His intention was to make a rapid solo ascent of the Cesen route, the western variant of the Abruzzi Ridge. But the conditions were hideous. As J.-C. later explained, "The snow had a bizarre, almost dusty consistency. Above 22,000 feet, you had the feeling of swimming in polystyrene, or in polenta."

Instead of soloing the route, J.-C. teamed up with the great Tyrolean climber Hans Kammerlander, a longtime partner of Reinhold Messner, who had also been eyeing a solo ascent. The two superalpinists left base camp on July 20. Only two days later, at 2:30 in the afternoon, they embraced on the summit. But the descent became a nightmare. Like me in 1992, J.-C. was all but certain that an avalanche would sweep Kammerlander and himself off the mountain. That same day, a Korean climber fell to his death from the Abruzzi Ridge.

Now, on top of Broad Peak, as we stared at K2, I said to J.-C., "Boy, I'm glad I don't have to climb that again!" A thin-lipped smile seized his face. "*Oui,*" he answered, "*moi aussi.*" Then, remembering my ignorance of French, he added, "Yes. Me too, I am very happy not to do it again!"

3

BREAKTHROUGH

People always wonder how K2 got its name. The answer is, in one sense, completely mundane, but in another, it's an object lesson in just how hard it is to find an appropriate name for a great geographical feature. Rising from the middle of the Karakoram Range, K2 is guarded on all sides by other towering mountains and by major glaciers. It is much harder to see from the lowlands than Mount Everest is.

It was the Great Trigonometrical Survey of India, that indefatigable and classically British mapping project, that "discovered" both Everest and K2. The Everest story is fairly well known. In 1849 three surveyors trained a theodolite on a far distant summit peeking over ridgelines in front of it. They jotted down their data, then soullessly named the summit Peak XV. It was not until three years later that a Bengali "computer"—a clerk whose job it was to work out calculations—came rushing into the office of India's surveyor general to announce that he had "discovered the highest mountain in the world."

Carrying the survey through hundreds of stations all the way from the seacoast, the computer, Radhanath Sikdar, had deduced an altitude of 29,002 feet. This was an amazingly accurate measurement: today, the mountain's official altitude is 29,035 feet above sea level. It took another thirteen years, however, for the surveyor general to discard the name Peak XV and replace it with Mount Everest, commemorating his predecessor, Sir George Everest.

In 1856, another plucky field-worker for the Great Trigonometrical Survey, Lieutenant T. G. Montgomerie, dragged his heavy theodolite to an altitude of 16,000 feet on a mountain overlooking Srinagar, in Kashmir. From that lofty vantage point, Montgomerie gazed at the Karakoram, 130 miles to the north. Taking fixes on the two most prominent summits, he labeled them K1 and K2 (K was short for Karakoram). K1 is known today as Masherbrum, a handsome 25,660-foot mountain first climbed by Americans in 1960. Two years after Montgomerie took his readings, the altitude of K2 was calculated to be 28,287 feet—also an astoundingly accurate measurement, only 36 feet in excess of its official altitude today. Several other peaks labeled in the K series still retain their original names, including the beautiful and formidable 22,744-foot tower K7.

I'm so used to calling the world's highest mountain Everest that it's hard for me to stop and think whether it's a good name or not. Everest has been the official name for so long that it just seems to fit. But long before the British surveyed it, the great peak was known to Tibetan natives as Chomolungma. (That name first appears in print on a 1733 French map of Tibet, drawn after a group of monks returned from a quarter century of work in Lhasa to report their findings.) It's a great name, full of the reverence Tibetans feel for the mountain: it translates to "Goddess Mother of the World." There have been efforts over the years to change the official name, or simply to use Chomolungma unofficially rather than Everest, in the same way that climbers now universally refer to Mount McKinley as Denali, even though McKinley is still the official name. But that revisionism hasn't taken hold on Everest. Only the Chinese regularly call the mountain Chomolungma.

After the survey discovered the great height of K2, there was a sincere effort to find a native name for the mountain. Montgomerie himself wrote, "Every endeavour will be made to find a local name if it has one." Somebody learned that the Balti people living south of the Karakoram called K2 Chogori. The problem is, *Chogori* means simply "Great Mountain." As K2 historian Jim Curran sardonically puts it, "Chogori . . . is likely to have been the sort of bemused answer given to the question 'What's that called?' "

Instead, through the rest of the nineteenth century a number of names honoring British pooh-bahs were tried out. None of them came close to sticking, except Mount Godwin Austen, the name honoring another tireless worker for the Great Trigonometrical Survey, Lieutenant Henry Haversham Godwin-Austen, who was one of the first Westerners to explore the Baltoro Glacier. Thank God that name never won the day! (The branch of the Baltoro that sweeps under the Abruzzi Ridge, however, is officially named the Godwin Austen Glacier.)

The fact is, K2 turns out to be a memorable name. There is no better defense of it than the one mounted by Fosco Maraini, whose 1959 chronicle of the first ascent of Gasherbrum IV, *Karakoram,* is one of the best expedition books ever written. Maraini argued,

> K2 may owe its origin to chance, but it is a name in itself, and one of striking originality. Sibylline, magical, with a slight touch of fantasy. A short name but one that is pure and peremptory, so charged with evocation that it threatens to break through its bleak syllabic bonds. And at the same time a name instinct with mystery and suggestion: a name that scraps race, religion, history and past. No country claims it, no latitudes and longitudes and geography, no dictionary words. No, just the bare bones of a name, all rock and ice and storm and abyss. It makes no attempt to sound human. It is atoms and stars.

Remote from civilization though K2 is, the first attempt to climb it came as early as 1902. That's nineteen years before the first attempt on Everest. The main reason for this discrepancy is that throughout the nineteenth century and the beginning of the twentieth, both Tibet and Nepal were virtually closed to foreigners, whereas K2 lay in what was then British India.

The 1902 expedition was the joint brainchild of Oscar Eckenstein, a superb German climber who had immigrated to Britain, and Aleister Crowley, one of the strangest men ever to become a mountaineer. Crowley would later grow famous as "the Beast 666"—his own nickname for his identification of himself with the devil. He was a magician, a drug cultist, an advocate of complete sexual freedom, a poet, an egomaniac— and a climber. In the early 1970s, his autobiography, *The Confessions of Aleister Crowley,* first published in 1929, became a hippie cult classic.

Crowley unabashedly referred to himself as the best rock climber in Britain. In reality, he wasn't even in the same league as George Leigh Mallory and several other contemporaries. But Crowley and Eckenstein's assault on K2 was conceived as a wildly audacious project. Before they left England, the two men signed a memorandum of agreement in which they pledged "that they should together climb a mountain higher than any previously ascended by man."

The team was rounded out with a twenty-two-year-old Englishman, a former Swiss ex-army doctor, and two Austrians. In his *Confessions,* Crowley is downright withering about these four companions. The Englishman "knew practically nothing of mountains, but he had common sense enough to do what Eckenstein told him"; the Swiss "knew as little of mountains as he did of medicine." But Crowley's contempt rises to a fever pitch when he writes about the Austrians, Pfannl and Wessely. Pfannl was "reputed the best rock climber in Austria," but during the expedition, he "went actually mad," while Wessely "brooded on food to the point of stealing it." In retrospect, Crowley decided, "we should have done better to take none of the foreigners." (Needless to say, Crowley's memoir is a startling exception to the traditional narrative convention of keeping all the expedition's dirty laundry out of sight.)

With the team only in Askole, the last village before the Baltoro Glacier, Pfannl and Wessely (if Crowley can be believed) asked their leaders if they could put three days' provisions in their rucksacks and go off and climb K2! Even today, Askole is a good six- or seven-day march away from base camp. In *Confessions*, Crowley ridicules the näiveté of the Austrians: "It is really astonishing that so many days of travel had taught them nothing about the scale of the mountains."

Yet the Austrians' mistake was one commonly made by Europeans during the early attempts on the great peaks of the Himalaya and the Karakoram. In 1895, A. F. Mummery, the finest British climber of his generation, organized the first expedition to Nanga Parbat. Mummery had put up many bold routes in the Alps and Caucasus, but he didn't seem to recognize that Nanga Parbat was of a different order of magnitude from, say, the Matterhorn. He set off to reconnoiter the lower slopes of the mountain so casually that he took with him only two porters, rather than any British teammates. None of the three men was ever seen again.

The Europeans dimly recognized that the sheer altitude of the world's highest peaks would present problems unknown in the Alps. But they developed some pretty wacky theories about how to deal with thin air. Norman Collie, Mummery's teammate on Nanga Parbat and a mentor to Crowley, was convinced that "the only chance of getting up a big mountain was to rush it." On the K2 expedition, Crowley wholeheartedly endorsed this absurd formula. "The only thing to do," he wrote, "is to lay in a stock of energy, get rid of all your fat at the exact moment when you have a chance to climb a mountain, and jump back out of its reach, so to speak, before it can take its revenge."

On the Baltoro, after many days, the expedition established a camp right at the base of what would come to be called the Abruzzi Ridge. Crowley recognized that spur as a plausible route, but now it was his turn radically to underestimate the scale and difficulty of K2. After study-ing the slopes above him for a full day, he concluded, as he later wrote, "that while the south face, perhaps possible theoretically, meant a com-plicated climb with no half-way house, there should be no difficulty in walking up the snow slopes on the east-south-east to the snowy shoul-der below the final rock pyramid."

Whew! The south face, on which Reinhold Messner would later iden-tify the fiendish but beautiful route he called the "Magic Line," would not be climbed until 1986. And it would be another thirty-six years after Crowley camped at the base of his "east-south-east" route that the first climbers pushed the Abruzzi Ridge as far as the Shoulder, at 26,000 feet. When they did so, it was not by "walking," but only by virtue of some of the hardest climbing yet performed at such an altitude anywhere in the world. (Crowley's very vocabulary betrays his dependency on the Alps as reference point: "no half-way house" sounds like a lament for the ab-sence of a good hut in the Bernese Oberland, not for the lack of a decent tent site in the Karakoram.)

The *Confessions* reads like a 1,020-page I-told-you-so. On every con-ceivable matter, all the experts turn out to be wrong, while Crowley is proved right. But it does seem that on K2, Crowley wanted to attack his east-south-east spur, only to be overruled by Eckenstein, who insisted on turning the team's efforts to the long and complicated northeast ridge. During the next few days, the climbers wore themselves out simply get-ting to the col they named "Windy Gap." The high point reached (by the supposedly worthless Pfannl and Wessely) was estimated at 21,000 feet. But the party made no dent in the northeast ridge, a route that would not be climbed until 1978, when my friend Jim Wickwire and his three American teammates finally solved it.

The first attempt on the Abruzzi Ridge came seven years after the Crowley-Eckenstein expedition. It was led, appropriately enough, by Luigi Amedeo di Savoia-Aosta, the Duke of the Abruzzi. Though a titled nobleman and grandson of the first king of Italy, the duke became one of the greatest explorers of his era. Before turning his attention to K2, he had led brilliantly successful expeditions to Mount Saint Elias (at 18,008 feet the fourth-highest mountain in North America) in 1897 and to the unknown Ruwenzori Mountains of Africa in 1906, where he made the first ascents of all the highest peaks. He had also spearheaded an ambitious dogsled attempt on the north pole in 1900, which reached a farthest north of 86°34', breaking the record of the great Norwegian explorer Fridtjof Nansen by twenty-three miles.

The style of Abruzzi's expeditions mixed opulence with efficiency. On Saint Elias, for instance, the party was made up of six Italian "amateurs" (gentleman climbers like the duke), four professional guides from Aosta, and ten porters hired in Seattle. To avoid the indignity of sleeping in direct contact with the ground, the amateurs brought along brass bedsteads, which the porters hauled fifty-five miles from the Pacific Coast to base camp. Yet high on the mountain, the team went light and fast. On July 31, 1897, all ten climbers reached the summit together. Mount McKinley, the highest peak in North America, would not be climbed for another sixteen years.

For K2, the Duke of the Abruzzi's party included Filippo de Filippi, the expedition doctor, who would write the now classic account of the expedition, and four professional guides and three porters from Courmayeur, the Italian village nestled under Mont Blanc on the south side. Rounding out the team was Vittorio Sella, the finest mountain photographer of his day and one of the greatest ever. Laboriously exposing large-format glass plates and developing them in the field, Sella brought back portraits of previously unknown mountains so glorious they would inspire several generations of climbers. These were published in the lavish folio volumes that the duke produced after each of his expeditions.

Nowhere in the world did Sella find himself enclosed by such a dazzling panorama as when the 1909 team marched slowly east up the Baltoro Glacier. One by one, the peaks filed by on either side—Uli Biaho, the Cathedrals, the Trango Towers, Paiju Peak, Mustagh Tower, Chogolisa, Masherbrum, and Gasherbrum IV. Though they're all lower than 8,000 meters, these technically severe mountains would demand the best efforts of some of the world's top climbers from the late 1950s, through the 1980s, and they continue to lure cutting-edge alpinists today.

Long before I went to K2, I'd seen Sella's photos of those mountains. So as Scott and I hiked up the Baltoro Glacier in 1992, I experienced a feeling of déjà vu. Even so, I had my socks knocked off by the sheer majesty of those peaks. There's no approach to a high mountain anywhere else in the world that compares. By the time I'd finished my quest for the 8,000ers, I'd hiked up the Baltoro four times, since the approach to Broad Peak, Gasherbrum I, and Gasherbrum II is the same as the trek in to K2. Yet even on my last Baltoro march in 2003, I was still struck with wonder as I passed beneath those graceful and legendary mountains.

In 1909, the duke's party turned north at the glacier junction called Concordia. On May 27—much earlier than most later parties would attack the mountain—they pitched a base camp at the foot of the mountain's southeast spur. To the duke, unlike Aleister Crowley, that steep and complicated arête rising almost 9,000 feet to the Shoulder looked like anything but a walk-up. So Abruzzi postponed his attempt, while the team made a quick foray toward the northeast ridge, the route attempted by the Eckenstein-Crowley party in 1902. The guides, however, knew a hopeless route when they saw one, and quickly turned back.

On May 29, the duke, five of the Courmayeur men, and a number of Balti porters started up the southeast spur. By June 1, they had managed to establish a camp at 18,250 feet, only some 800 feet above the base of the ridge. There, however, the Balti porters saw falling rocks careening down from above and refused to carry any farther. (I can sympathize with those poor guys. They'd never been on terrain like this before in their lives. And the lower slopes on the Abruzzi Ridge feel constantly threatened by falling debris. Even on easy ground, you're always looking up to see if anything is coming your way.)

During the next two days, some of the Courmayeur men, led by the father-and-son guides Joseph and Laurent Petigax, pushed higher. On the harder passages, they left heavy hemp ropes in place—the first fixed ropes ever strung on K2. But it became obvious to the Petigaxes that some of the pitches would be too hard for the Balti porters, even if they could be talked into giving it a go. Without porters, there was no hope of mounting a logistical pyramid toward the summit.

Discouraged, the guides turned back. At the lower camp, the duke accepted their judgment and called off the attempt. The highest point reached by the Petigaxes is uncertain, but it was probably around 21,000 feet. (Incidentally, the Italians retrieved their fixed ropes as they descended—something virtually no subsequent expeditions would ever do.)

Still, the Duke of the Abruzzi was not ready to give up on K2. Now he turned his team toward a reconnaissance of the unexplored western reaches of the mountain. Ascending the Savoia Glacier (which he named after his home stomping grounds in Italy), he tried to gain the high col from which the northwest ridge rises. After a monumental twelve-hour push of step cutting in hard ice and snow, the team reached the col, which they named Savoia Pass, at an altitude they measured at 21,870 feet. But there they found themselves cut off from the northwest ridge by a dangerously corniced crest. Once more, K2 turned the duke back. The mountain would not be climbed from this side until 1991.

The team still had several weeks' worth of supplies stockpiled on the Baltoro. So the duke turned his attention to several lesser peaks. On Chogolisa, he and three of the Courmayeur guides reached an altitude that they measured at 24,275 feet. Faced with dangerous cornices and crevasses, they retreated only 850 feet short of the summit. Still, they had achieved a new record: nobody in the world had ever climbed so high. The record would stand for thirteen years, until the second British expedition to Everest bettered it in 1922.

The duke had perhaps been spoiled by his blithe successes on Saint Elias and the Ruwenzori. It came as a rude rebuff to him to be turned back on K2 nearly 6,400 feet below the summit. And so, once back in Italy, one of the strongest mountaineers in the world declared that he believed K2 would never be climbed.

That malediction took its toll. K2 would not be attempted again for twenty-nine years. In the meantime, seven expeditions did battle with Mount Everest, and six different men turned back (or, in Mallory and Irvine's case, disappeared) above 28,000 feet, within a tantalizing thousand feet of the summit.

By 1938 on K2, no one had succeeded in climbing above 21,870 feet. On neither the 1902 nor the 1909 expedition had anyone really come to grips with the challenge. All the mountain's ultimate defenses remained unknown.

Beginning in the mid-1930s, the American Alpine Club (AAC) repeatedly petitioned the government of Kashmir for a permit for a K2 expedition. In those days, climbing in America lagged far behind the standards set by British, French, German, Italian, Swiss, and Austrian climbers. But in 1936, four young American climbers, all of them graduates of Harvard, joined up with four more senior (and more famous) Brits to make the first ascent of Nanda Devi, a beautiful and difficult 25,643-foot mountain in northern India. At the time, it was the highest summit reached anywhere in the world—a record that would stand for another fourteen years, until the French climbed Annapurna in 1950.

Out of the party of eight, only two—the Englishmen H. W. Tilman and Noel Odell—reached the summit. The strongest American was Charlie Houston, a twenty-two-year-old graduate student at the Columbia University College of Physicians and Surgeons. Despite his youth, Houston had climbed in the Alps as a teenager and was already the veteran of two major Alaskan expeditions, including the first ascent of Mount Foraker, the second-highest peak in the Alaska Range. Houston was chosen for the summit party on Nanda Devi, but the night before the assault he came down with a terrible case of food poisoning, and Tilman took his place.

When permission for K2 finally came through, in 1937, the AAC offered the leadership of the expedition to Fritz Wiessner, a German-American from Dresden who had immigrated to the States in 1929 and gained citizenship in 1935. Wiessner was without a doubt the finest American climber of his day. After putting up new routes on several of the hardest faces in the Alps, he had bagged some of the great prizes in North America, including the first ascent of Mount Waddington, the rugged and intricate peak that is the highest summit in the stormy Coast Range of British Columbia, which had defeated sixteen previous attempts. Wiessner was also the only American with experience on an 8,000-meter peak, as he had served on the 1932 German expedition to Nanga Parbat, where he was one of three climbers to reach a high point of 23,000 feet.

Wiessner ran his own successful chemistry business in Vermont, specializing in the manufacture of ski wax. By the time the AAC got permission for K2, he was too bogged down in business obligations to go to the Karakoram the next summer, so he recommended that the expedition be turned over to Charlie Houston. Oddly enough, that magnanimous referral would be the spark for a lifelong, often bitter antipathy between Houston and Wiessner.

Houston leapt at the chance to lead the expedition. But from the start, he harbored the suspicion that Wiessner had a hidden agenda. The permit the AAC had obtained was good for two years; if the 1938 expedition failed to get up K2, Americans could organize another crack at the mountain for 1939.

Houston's first choice for the team was Bob Bates, a good friend of his from Harvard, himself a veteran of two Alaskan expeditions. In February 1938, Bates wrote a letter to another Harvard crony in which he voiced the fears he and Houston already entertained: "Weissner's [sic] idea, I suppose, is to have us do the reconnaissance + possibly the dirty work + then go in next year and profit by our mistakes. This is pretty surely it, but keep it to yourself."

Houston put together a strong team. Besides Bates, the climbers included Bill House, Wiessner's partner on the Waddington first ascent;

Richard Burdsall, who had reached the summit of the remote and lofty Minya Konka in western China in 1932; and Paul Petzoldt. Houston, Bates, Burdsall, and House were all easterners and Ivy League graduates— the first three had gone to Harvard, House to Yale. Petzoldt not only hadn't gone to college, he was a cowboy from Wyoming. But he was also one of the strongest climbers in the country, having pioneered some of the hardest routes in the Tetons, where he worked part-time as a guide. In terms of rock-climbing skills, Petzoldt was way ahead of his eastern teammates.

The sixth member of the party, invited from afar, was Captain Norman Streatfeild, a British officer living in India who had already been on numerous hunting, mapping, and climbing trips to the Karakoram. Streatfeild was not the mountaineering equal of the five Americans, but he would prove invaluable in terms of logistics and dealing with native porters.

When I was still a teenager, long before I'd climbed any peaks myself, I'd read Houston and Bates's classic *K2: The Savage Mountain,* about the 1953 expedition. I'd loved the book, because it told the story of how adversity transformed a team into an ideal brotherhood; along with *Annapurna, K2: The Savage Mountain* had a lot to do with turning me into a mountaineer. But it was not until Scott and I started preparing for our own K2 adventure in 1992 that I read the book about the earlier American expedition.

Five Miles High is a collaborative effort: five of its chapters were written by Bates, five by Houston, four by House, three by Burdsall—and none by Petzoldt. It's a delightful book, the kind of tale that makes you nostalgic for a vanished era of exploration. It also subscribes firmly to the tradition of keeping the expedition's dirty laundry far from the eyes of the public. There are tongue-in-cheek gibes about certain members' habits and foibles (for example, about how much Petzoldt liked to eat), but you'd hardly know that a harsh word or dispute occurred within the team. And there is not the slightest hint of the Wiessner-Houston tension that would explode inside the AAC after 1939.

Houston admits in the first chapter that the Duke of the Abruzzi's dark prediction still hung over the mountain. "So formidable are the few approaches to its summit," he writes, "that many climbers have felt the ascent to be impossible." Houston also baldly declares that the 1938 expedition was conceived as a reconnaissance:

> Could we determine which route offered most possibility of success, perhaps a later expedition, unhampered by the need of reconnoitering the mountain, might hope to reach the top. Ours then was to be a preliminary attack whose main plan was to find a way for a later party.

But then he coyly closes the chapter:

> We were to examine three main ridges, separated by miles of glacier travel, and to decide which of the three would be most likely to furnish a route to the summit. Finally, given time, weather, and the smile of fortune, we were to try to reach that distant point.

All through the winter and spring before the expedition, the climbers ordered gear and tested food supplies. When you read about the provisions those men took to K2 in 1938, you realize they were closer not only in time but in style to the great Arctic and Antarctic expeditions of the turn of the twentieth century than to our present-day mountaineering jaunts. For instance, the '38 climbers brought along fifty pounds of pemmican made in Denmark. Almost nobody eats pemmican anymore, but it was *the* staple of nineteenth-century explorers. Pemmican is a gooey mixture of dried meat, animal fat, sugar, rice, and raisins. It keeps well in the cold, and it's very high in calories. I have to confess, though, that I've never had a single bite of the stuff. We know now that while pemmican may be great in the Arctic or the Antarctic, it's way too fatty to digest at high altitudes.

The 1938 team tried out dozens of kinds of biscuits and hard bread.

They tested them by dropping them out of a second-floor window and by leaving them out in the rain overnight. They finally chose one brand of biscuit because, as Bates wrote, it "tasted good and resisted moisture, yet needed no sledge hammer to break it." Bates's team also swore by some of the first dried vegetables and fruits available, all of them produced by what their makers called a "secret process." The '38 team's cereals included Cream of Wheat and Maltex. Like all expeditions of their time, the team considered it absolutely essential to bring along large quantities of Klim ("milk" spelled backward)—powdered whole milk, which is almost impossible to find in a market nowadays. On all my expeditions, coffee has been a vital base camp drink. The 1938 climbers brought tea instead (I do drink sweet, milky tea up high), because they considered coffee too much of a nuisance to brew in the field.

When I look over that K2 food list, I'm struck by how bulky and heavy their provisions were. But then I have to remind myself that they were outfitting in an age long before prepackaged dried foods came on the market, or Power Bars or Pop-Tarts, or instant soups, or tubes of high-energy gel. The kinds of lightweight, easy-to-fix meals we relied on in 1992 simply weren't available in 1938. On the other hand, those guys had luxuries we never dreamed of. In Askole, for example, they hired a hefty porter with a huge, straw-lined wicker basket for a backpack, in which he managed to carry twenty dozen fresh eggs to base camp without breaking them!

There's the same historical divide when it comes to equipment. Boots, for instance: in 1938, climbers who wanted the best mountaineering footwear available wore relatively thin leather boots, their soles reinforced with hobnails—little metal cleats affixed to the undersurface. The nails gave you better purchase on ice and snow, but they were a real liability on rock slabs, because your feet tended to skitter off their holds. What's more, at altitude the hobnails conducted cold straight to your feet, contributing directly to the risk of frostbite all early climbers faced in the Himalaya. It would be decades before Vibram rubber soles got invented, not to mention double boots—especially the kind of combination plastic outer shell and foam inner I wore on most of my 8,000-ers. The 1938 team members ordered custom-made boots from England, and they were so finicky that each man chose the precise pattern of hobnails with which his soles would be studded.

Climbing ropes, at that time, were still made out of hemp or manila. Nylon ropes, which are many times stronger and have a stretchiness that absorbs much of the impact of a fall, were still nearly a decade in the future. The ice axes of the day were three to four feet long and had shafts of hickory or ash, with a straight metal pick and an opposing adze for a handle. They looked more like Victorian alpenstocks (glorified walking sticks) than the short, fanged chrome-molybdenum ice tools we used in 1992.

In 1938, the climbers boxed and sealed all their gear and food and sent it ahead by steamer. On April 14, they sailed from New York, bound first for Europe, then for Bombay.

From the start of the trip, there was a cultural gulf between Petzoldt and his teammates. You won't find the faintest hint of it in *Five Miles High,* but the oral traditions of mountaineering have preserved anecdotes about it, and glimpses pop up in the latter-day biographies of Petzoldt and Houston.

Petzoldt was too poor to afford the expedition. Instead, Farnie Loomis—a well-to-do Harvard grad and a member of the Nanda Devi expedition who had climbed with Petzoldt in the Tetons and had recommended him to Houston—paid his way. (Petzoldt was, you might say, the first sponsored climber!) In the perverse logic of the day, that tarred the Wyoming cowboy with a certain unworthiness in the eyes of his Ivy League teammates. And Petzoldt's profession as a guide, just as perversely, could be seen as a detriment on an expedition, not as an asset.

Petzoldt's first biographer was his wife, Patricia, who thus may not be an impartial witness. But in 1953, in *On Top of the World,* she wrote,

> Later Paul discovered that there had been some doubts expressed in the [American Alpine] Club as to whether he would be able to adjust himself socially to the rest of the party. The fact

that he was a professional, a guide, had been questioned; and then of course he was a Westerner and, although he was known to have had some education, he had not attended an Ivy League college.

Houston's biographer Bernadette McDonald insisted in 2007 that Charlie once called Petzoldt "a blue collar guide." That sense of a social gulf may lie behind the fact that Petzoldt was not asked to write any of the chapters of *Five Miles High*.

In his turn, Petzoldt referred to Bates and Houston, behind their backs, as "two Eastern nabobs." According to McDonald, Petzoldt thought that, far from being sneered at as a professional guide, he ought to be paid an extra salary for bringing his expertise to his "amateur" teammates.

Just as serious was the gulf between Petzoldt and the easterners about the kinds of climbing hardware necessary to attempt K2. Houston and Bates had a British disdain for "ironmongery"—the pitons, carabiners, and direct-aid ladders with which European climbers had recently transformed alpinism. Among the expedition supplies, they had included at most ten pitons. Petzoldt, on the other hand, wholeheartedly embraced the new technical gear, without which he could not have forged his Teton routes. On shipboard, a heated argument broke out over this question, but Petzoldt was outnumbered.

Scandalized by his teammates' backward attitude, however, Petzoldt sneaked off during a stop in Paris on the way to India and used his last dollars to buy fifty pitons at the shop of the great French climber Pierre Allain. (Allain, incidentally, had been a member of the French expedition to Gasherbrum I just two years earlier.) Petzoldt then smuggled the hardware into the boxes of expedition gear. On K2, of course, the pitons proved invaluable.

By May 9, the team had reached Rawalpindi. In 1992, to get from there to K2, Scott and the trekkers on his permit took a one-hour flight to Skardu. That's the normal procedure, but the flight was overbooked, and I couldn't afford it anyway, so I ended up scrounging rides in two antiquated vehicles—a journey that I later called "the 26-hour ride from hell." On the first bus, a pregnant Pakistani woman vomited out the window at regular intervals. I barely kept from tossing my own cookies. By the time I got to Skardu, I was covered with soot, dirt, and sweat.

After a few days, we bummed a ride on a jeep to cover the last eighty miles to Askole. It was only in Askole that we would actually start hiking, so it seemed that the expedition really began there. The overland journey from Skardu amounted to little more than an ordeal by bouncing truck, shared by a tightly packed band of sweaty fellow passengers. We glimpsed some amazing scenery along the way, but most of the time we were too busy hanging on or too exhausted to care.

In 1938, there was no road from Rawalpindi to Skardu, and there certainly wasn't an airplane flight. Instead, Houston's team drove to Srinagar, then hiked all the way not only to Skardu but to Askole, crossing high foothills by the legendary trade route over the Zoji La. The Duke of the Abruzzi had made the same journey in 1909, as had Crowley and Eckenstein in 1902. The total distance from Srinagar to Askole is 320 miles, and from there to base camp is another 40. So in 1938, the climbers had to trek some 360 miles just to get to K2. It took them a month to the day.

This, I've always thought, is perhaps the way our modern-day expeditions differ most profoundly from the classic voyages of the first half of the twentieth century. For many climbers today, the hike in is essentially a hassle, a necessary evil in the process of coming to grips with an 8,000er. On the other hand, I like approach marches. Even though the ones we perform today are far shorter than the marathon overland journeys of the 1920s and '30s, those hikes give me a chance to acclimate to the wilderness and to take in the local culture. The trek to K2 from Askole—only one-sixth as long as the approach the 1938 expedition made—is wild, harsh, and dusty. There are no other villages after Askole, but the landscape is starkly beautiful.

My most memorable trek in to an 8,000er was the approach to Manaslu in 1999. My only companions were Veikka Gustafsson, our cook-sirdar, and a handful of porters. There were no teahouses or hotels, like the ones on the way in to Everest from the south; we slept in barns or camped out. The natives often welcomed us into their farmhouses to share a cooking fire and a meal. It was rustic yet relaxing, and there were no hordes of trekkers like the ones on the way in to Everest.

Granted, technical skill on steep rock and ice has risen dramatically since 1938. But those early climbers were tough in ways that we moderns aren't. I've never made a continuous overland journey by foot of anything like 360 miles. My personal record is just shy of 150 miles of cross-country skiing on Baffin Island with John Stetson in 2007. True, we were each man-hauling 220-pound sleds. On that trip, though, the cross-country journey *was* the expedition. That's quite different from having to travel 360 miles just to get started, as the team did in 1938.

What's maybe even more impressive is that the '38 climbers seemed to treat the overland trek not as an unavoidable chore but, rather, as a voyage full of both tribulations and delights in its own right. In just getting to the mountain, they had a rich adventure before the real adventure even began. In *Five Miles High,* Bates devotes four chapters to the trek from Srinagar to base camp, and they contain some of the most lyrical passages in the book.

At Srinagar, Houston's team met the six Sherpa they had hired out of Darjeeling. As all-purpose high-altitude porters, the canny Sherpa had been vital to all the Everest expeditions since 1921. This was, however, the first time they were used on K2. These six had come personally recommended by the British Himalayan veteran H. W. Tilman. The most accomplished of them was Pasang Kikuli. Among his previous expeditions was Nanda Devi in 1936, when he and Houston had formed a close bond. Pasang was, in fact, the team member with by far the greatest Himalayan experience: besides Nanda Devi, he had been on four expeditions to Kangchenjunga and one to Everest.

It seems like a quaint practice today, but in the 1930s it was normal for each "sahib" to be assigned his personal Sherpa. Houston's was

Pasang Kikuli, who was also the Sherpa sirdar, or head man. The whole relationship between Sherpa and Westerner was modeled on Victorian colonialism, particularly that of the British. Even though they often performed heroically on expeditions, the Sherpa were infallibly regarded as servants. Bates was not being particularly racist when he wrote, "Though slight of build, they are strong, willing, and above all filled with enthusiasm for mountaineering. To them an attempt on a high mountain is a pilgrimage and the white climber almost a holy man." Bates was simply reflecting the attitude of the day.

Unfortunately, that condescension persists even in the twenty-first century. At best, Sherpa are described as simple people, childlike, superstitious, and perpetually grinning. But if something goes wrong on an expedition, the Sherpa usually get the brunt of the blame. I can't count the number of times I've read articles about Himalayan ascents in which the Europeans who reached the summit are all named, and then a phrase such as "and three Sherpas" gets tacked onto the end of the sentence. Sometimes even when Sherpa die on an expedition, they go unnamed in the official accounts.

To get from Srinagar to Skardu, the team hired porters, who carried the expedition's goods on their backs and on the backs of their ponies. In the nomenclature of the day, these hired hands were usually called "coolies." An even greater condescension colors expedition accounts of the porters' contributions to the march. Bates could never have imagined just how politically incorrect the following passage would sound in 2009—he simply thought he was painting an amusing scene:

> Often the natives would give each of us bouquets of flowers and then beg for the honor of being allowed to help our Sherpas smooth the ground and put up our tents. Then came the real struggle. Several coolies would plead for the privilege of being allowed to blow up the sahib's air mattress, and if his Sherpa permitted it, the victorious coolie was overjoyed. He would puff and strain away, often blowing for a good five minutes with the valve

shut if the Sherpa in charge didn't watch him closely. Next each Sherpa himself would lay out his sahib's sleeping bag, diary and toilet kit, and then come up with a change of shoes and personally take off his master's marching boots, if he would let him.

In all honesty, I can't say that I wish we had had to hike 360 miles to get to K2. But in rereading Bates's chapters, I realize that we moderns have lost some of the richness of the full expedition experience. Today it seems that we want to race to base camp just to start our climbs, and we forget to savor the approach journey, with its valuable transition from modern society into mountain wilderness.

Just reading Bates's evocations of the landscape makes me envious:

> The rest of the march to Kharal lay along rocky hillsides marked infrequently across the river with terraced villages shaded by cool groves of apricot and mulberry trees. Brilliant green fields of barley soothed our eyes, even as in our imagination the shade of the trees cooled our bodies.

A standard snafu on classic expeditions is the porter strike. Without warning, in the most inconvenient spot possible, the "coolies" will throw down their packs and refuse to go a step farther, unless their wages are doubled or tripled. At this point, in the Western author's eyes, the cheerful natives become "rogues" or "rascals." Rare is the climber who recognizes that the porter strike is just another form of bargaining, an integral part of native culture.

Still, a porter strike can cripple an expedition. I've been pretty lucky, in that among all thirty of my expeditions, the worst porter strike I had to face was hiking in to Broad Peak in 1997. Several days up the Baltoro, the porters stopped and demanded higher wages. We had agreed on set wages at the start on the trip, but after a few days that didn't seem to matter. Our only option was to call their bluff. We told the porters we would send them back unpaid, while a couple of us would return to

Askole and hire new porters. Somehow that convinced them to keep going.

The 1938 team was lucky, too, in that the only porter strike they had to deal with came quite late on the trek, midway between Skardu and Askole. On May 27, 279 miles out from Srinagar, at the tiny hill village of Yuno, the team paid off their pony men and tried to hire local "coolies." But two "trouble makers" (Bates's phrase) held out for a wage of four and a half rupees per man for the 44-mile carry to Askole, rather than the two rupees and eight annas (about 95 cents) the climbers were willing to pay. The disagreement almost turned into a brawl, as sixty Yuno men "yelled and surged forward." The Sherpa seized their ice axes and brandished them as weapons, pleading, "Let us at them, sahibs. We do not like these men."

Rather than give in to the natives' demand, the team concocted a solution that, I think it's safe to say, no other expedition to the Karakoram has ever resorted to. Bob Bates and Norman Streatfeild decided to *raft* back to Skardu to hire better porters than the Yuno "scoundrels."

To get from Yuno to Skardu, the men would have to navigate twenty-eight miles of river, first through the raging rapids of the Shigar, then along the powerful current of the Indus. The craft of choice was a *zok*. It consisted of twenty-eight inflated goatskin bladders covered with a framework of slender poplar poles. The whole thing weighed only a hundred pounds. In a photograph reproduced in *Five Miles High,* the *zok* looks incredibly flimsy.

All the work was done by local boatmen, as Bates and Streatfeild sat in the middle and hung on. Bates recounts this watery adventure almost as a lark. The boatmen, he says,

> spent the time alternately grounding us on sandbars, spinning us round and round in the swift water, and examining our shoes. When we approached rapids in the river they put down their poles and prayed loudly, while we spun and tossed and held on grimly; but the raft seemed unsinkable and we soon agreed that

as long as it didn't turn over we were safe. . . . Most of the time one or two of [the boatmen] would be blowing up the leaky bladders or splashing water on the raft to keep the sun from cracking the skins. The lung power of these fellows was amazing, for with perfect equanimity they would blow up the very ones we were sitting on, even while the *zok* was being tossed violently by the waves.

Where the Shigar entered the Indus, the boatmen had to make a desperate paddle to cross the big river to the Skardu side. The current was so strong that the *zok* reached the bank two and a half miles below the town. But it had taken only seven hours to raft those twenty-eight miles. The cost of the wild ride was eight and a half rupees, or $3.15.

Bates was evidently a handy man with a raft. In 1935, at the end of an epic five-month traverse of the Saint Elias Range in subarctic Canada and Alaska, he and two teammates had run into the Alsek River, which they had hoped to ford and which they had to cross to get to civilization. Instead, the river was in spring flood, far too deep and swift to wade. Unfazed, under Bates's direction the trio improvised a raft out of driftwood logs, two air mattresses, and two pairs of skis, and, using another ski as a paddle, they pulled off the dangerous crossing.

Apparently for the boatmen, a ride downstream from Yuno to Skardu was all in a day's work. After they had arrived, they took the *zok* apart and carried it in pieces back to their home village.

In Skardu, after consulting with the *tehsildar,* or local governor, Bates and Streatfeild quickly solved the porter crisis. By May 30, the whole expedition was back on the trail. The perils of the trek were not finished, however. Above the village of Hoto, the whole caravan had to cross a two-hundred-foot-deep gorge by means of what Bates called a rope bridge. "Rope," however, was too fancy a term: the contraption was made entirely of willow twigs twisted and braided into cables. At regular intervals, the bridge was stabilized by branches jammed crossways between the two handrails.

Bates admits that the crossing of this native bridge was terrifying. It "creaked like an abused wicker chair" underfoot, and as they tiptoed gingerly along the middle cable, the climbers recalled the Balti maxim "No rope bridge should be repaired until it is broken."

By 1992, the willow-twig bridge was long gone. In the years since Pakistan had won its independence from India, the approaches to the Karakoram had become a region of military importance, so the primitive trail the 1938 climbers had hiked was now a good paved road, and sturdy bridges crossed the gorges. Right out of Skardu, for instance, you cross a giant metal suspension bridge. In the jeep on which we'd hitched a ride, the journey was basically routine.

On June 3, 1938, Houston's team reached Askole, by their reckoning precisely 323 miles from Srinagar. So far, the worst mishap the team had suffered was Burdsall's bad blisters. But now a new crisis struck, as Petzoldt came down with a fever of 104 degrees. Houston, the twenty-four-year-old medical student serving as expedition doctor, could not determine the cause of the illness, which lasted for days. (It was later tentatively diagnosed as dengue fever.)

Whatever tensions might have existed between the Wyoming cowboy and the Eastern "nabobs," they seemed to have dissolved by the time the party reached Askole. As Petzoldt's fever raged on, the team made an excruciating decision. Houston, though the leader of the expedition, would stay in Askole to minister to his patient. The other four climbers, the six Sherpa, and the porters hired in Askole would forge ahead toward the Baltoro Glacier and base camp. If Petzoldt did not recover soon, that could mean the end of the expedition for Houston and himself. "If he dies," Houston joked to his departing comrades, "I'll bury him and go on to meet you. If he recovers, we'll both try to catch up with the expedition."

I've never met Charlie Houston, but I've admired him ever since, as a teenager, I read *K2: The Savage Mountain*. And that decision is one of the things for which I admire him most. No matter how headstrong he may have been, he was incredibly loyal to his teammates. He supported them to the utmost on the expedition, and praised them to the skies afterward. Mountaineers—especially good ones—can be pretty coldhearted people. But Houston seems to have been full of compassion and empathy. And in a case like this, he was willing to give up a goal he had dreamed about for a year to try to nurse a teammate back to health.

So the rest of the party pushed ahead. For the first time, they marched beneath the savage pyramids of K2's outliers, peaks that somehow seemed familiar, since they had seen them in Vittorio Sella's magnificent photographs. At Paiju, "the last little island of vegetation," as Bates put it, they turned a corner and saw ahead of them "the gray back of the Baltoro Glacier, looking like a huge reptile." In 1992, we found Paiju a bit squalid, since so many other expeditions had camped and left their trash there over the years. When I passed through again in 2003, on the way to Broad Peak, I saw that some Pakistani environmental agency had built outhouses and concrete washbasins in an effort to clean the place up. Still, Paiju will always be a memorable camp for me, because it was here on our 1992 approach that Scott and I took a full rest day, during which we hiked up a wooded hill to a rocky ridge and got that stunning first view of K2.

The 1938 team clambered onto the snout of the Baltoro. The mood of Bates's writing at this point is uncharacteristically gloomy. He describes "the dismal, boulder-strewn surface" of the permanent ice and remarks, "An air of death and decay hung over this part of the glacier." No doubt the men's spirits were dampened by the absence of Houston and Petzoldt, but even today, the lower stretches of the Baltoro make for tedious hiking. You have to wind in and out and up and down through what Bates called "mounds and ridges of loose debris." Oddly enough, although you're on a glacier, the daytime heat is blistering, and the ground is dry and dusty. In '92, we hiked here in shorts, shading ourselves with umbrellas but sweating like dogs the whole way.

Of their first couple of days on the Baltoro Glacier, Bates writes, "For us the uncertain footing was little more than irritating, but for our coolies, with straw or goat-skin moccasins, the passage was severe." Instead of ice axes, each porter wielded a "coolie crutch," a wooden device stout enough to cut steps in the ice which also served as a tripod on which to rest one's load.

On June 8, the team camped at Urdukas, a beautiful grassy oasis just off the glacier on the southern side. For centuries, Balti herdsmen have driven their flocks to Urdukas to graze, but that's as close as most of them ever got to K2, and since you can't see the mountain from that patch of greenery, that may explain why K2 scarcely has a native name. In 1992, it was still a lovely place; you could lounge in the grass and get out of the sun in the shade of large boulders that have come to rest there.

The whole hike in to K2 is utterly different from the approaches to 8,000ers in Nepal. If you're hiking in to Everest on the south side, you pass through villages with tea shops and even restaurants. Your Sherpa take off each night to go visit their cousins, then show up in the morning. The whole thing feels very civilized. On the much more difficult approach to K2, there are no villages—or even isolated houses—after Askole. You're camping out with the porters, most of the time on the glacier. Yet however stark or tedious it may seem at times, that forty-mile approach up the Baltoro is beautiful in its own right.

In 1938, while the men were loafing at Urdukas, Pasang Kikuli suddenly pointed west down the glacier and shouted, "Sahibs, sahibs, look see!" Through binoculars, the two black dots the Sherpa had spotted proved to be Petzoldt and Houston hiking along at a furious pace. "How in the world did he do it?" Burdsall exclaimed.

"Charlie fixed me up," Petzoldt muttered as soon as he had joined his teammates. "How is the food holding out?"

Four days later, the climbers reached base camp. Streatfeild paid off the porters, who were eager to charge back down the glacier as soon as they could, then gave the head man a pouch containing forty-five stones. "Throw away one stone every day," he said. "When they are all gone, come back to meet us."

Now the team had six weeks to reconnoiter K2 and, if there was still time, to try to climb it. But the next seventeen days amounted to a prolonged exercise in futility. The climbers' first views of the Abruzzi Ridge were not encouraging. On a foray up the Godwin Austen Glacier, Bates and Streatfeild had scrutinized the slopes rising above them. They'd reported that the south face proper looked impossible, while the Abruzzi Ridge presented continuously steep ice gullies and rock ribs all the way up to the Shoulder, more than 8,000 feet above the base.

Dividing into subgroups, the team reconnoitered the Savoia Glacier in an effort to reach both Savoia Pass, and thus the beginning of the northwest ridge, and the Godwin Austen Glacier, toward the start of the northeast ridge. On three separate efforts spread across two weeks, various members failed even to get to Savoia Pass, as they were turned back by crevasses and ice cliffs. These were humiliating setbacks—how could a passage that the Courmayeur guides had pioneered twenty-nine years earlier stump some of America's best mountaineers? The men rationalized that conditions must have changed radically since 1909, but privately they nursed the fear that they weren't strong enough to meet the challenge.

One reason for the dogged effort to attack the northwest ridge sprang from an observation first made by the Duke of the Abruzzi. From Savoia Pass, he had seen that the rock strata on the northwest ridge inclined upward, promising staircase-like steps. On the southeast spur on the diametrically opposite side of the mountain, the Italians found just the reverse: downward-sloping slabs and ledges that made for treacherous climbing and insecure campsites.

On the Matterhorn in the early 1860s, the great British climber Edward Whymper had made six attempts on the southwest ridge, failing at increasingly higher points. Finally Whymper attacked the steeper northeast ridge, by which he succeeded in making the first ascent, on July 14, 1865. The difference was entirely due to the angle of the rock strata that composed the core of the mountain: upward-tilting on the northeast, downward-sloping on the southwest.

Whymper's hard-won lesson was famous in mountaineering annals. The Duke of the Abruzzi intended to take the same advantage of the angle of the strata on K2, as did his successors in 1938. But in this case, the mountain fooled everybody. The northwest ridge would not be climbed for another fifty-three years.

During the two weeks of reconnoitering, the weather was consistently stormy. Fortunately, the team had had the foresight to bring willow wands, apparently at Bob Bates's insistence. On previous expeditions in Canada and Alaska—especially his amazing first ascent of Mount Lucania with Bradford Washburn in 1937 and his traverse of the Saint Elias Range two years earlier—Bates had learned just how vital wands could be. The type the 1938 party used was a three-foot-long wooden dowel, one end of which was painted black to about seven inches from the head. After a retreat in a snowstorm on the Savoia Glacier, Bill House wrote, "We were glad we had brought Bates's black-painted wood dowels to mark the trail home, for to get lost on that part of the glacier would have meant a night out or worse."

To add to the woes of these discouraging days, Petzoldt suffered from several recurrences of his fever. Even at base camp, he would shiver for hours, unable to get warm despite wearing all his clothing inside his sleeping bag. The only treatment his baffled teammates could offer was to brew up one hot drink after another and to "take turns rubbing his back."

As their efforts simply to get to the starting points on the northeast and northwest ridges failed, the team members kept studying the Abruzzi Ridge. From certain places on the Godwin Austen Glacier, they could see beyond the 26,000-foot Shoulder to the summit pyramid. It's fascinating to rediscover, in *Five Miles High,* the first description ever published of the massive hanging serac at 27,000 feet that I would nickname the Motivator, the collapse of which would cause so much of the tragedy in 2008. House wrote,

> Partway up this [summit] cone is a great hanging glacier which sweeps the upper part of the northeast ridge as well as one corner of the Abruzzi ridge. Care would be needed in crossing the

plateau from this last ridge, but it looked as though it could be done safely.

On June 28, the team gathered at base camp for what expeditioneers like to call a "council of war." Only two members—Petzoldt and House—favored an attack on the Abruzzi Ridge. Houston and Burdsall argued for yet another attempt to reach the northeast ridge. Bates and Streatfeild were neutral.

During the next several days, the climbers made a couple of very tentative thrusts up the lower slopes of the Abruzzi. On one of them, Houston and House discovered a few wooden sticks, which they realized had to be debris from the Duke of the Abruzzi's boxes. They had reached the highest point to which the Italians had managed to haul supplies, and were now only 500 feet below the cliff where the Courmayeur guides had turned back in 1909. Like the Italians, the Americans recognized immediately that the biggest problem with the Abruzzi was the lack of suitable campsites. As House put it,

> To have found such a long stretch on the ridge devoid of any places where tent platforms could be built and reached by loaded men was serious. It seemed to close up the last avenue of hope we had had for finding a route on K2. On top of this setback, one of our strongest climbers was ill.

One of the things that I most respect about the 1938 team is that after all their setbacks, they didn't simply pack up and go home. By July 2, when House and Petzoldt made the first real stab at the Abruzzi, the party had been in the field for fifty-two days since they had started hiking from Srinagar. They had worn themselves out reconnoitering K2, without as yet deciding which route might go. It would have been tempting to throw in the towel and leave the solution to a 1939 expedition.

There's a memorable passage in one of House's chapters revealing just how far morale had plunged, and how thoughts of home were tugging at each of the climbers:

> The expedition spirits were now at very low ebb. From one side of the mountain to the other we had been unable to find a route. Two weeks had been spent apparently to no other purpose than to convince us that no way we had seen was possible. . . . Every one of us would have liked to be clear of the whole business right then.
>
> Had we been able to spend an afternoon relaxing at the seashore or getting very drunk, we might have realized that two weeks of reconnaissance on a mountain as big as K2 could not possibly be conclusive. . . . At that time, however, it seemed as though each succeeding judgment had been upheld by later checking and that there was no hope at all. Unfortunately the seashore was a thousand miles away and our supply of rum far too slender to indulge in as an escape.

In a letter home written about this time, Houston gave voice to his deep pessimism. "This is a bigger, harder mountain than any of us realized before," he wrote, "and it will take a better party than ours a much longer time than we have left, in order to get anywhere at all."

On July 2, Petzoldt (whose feverish fits alternated with startling recoveries) and House started up the Abruzzi, determined to find a campsite. They had almost given up hope when Petzoldt crawled around a corner and found a tiny but perfect saddle in the ridge, protected from the wind and falling rocks and just big enough for several tents. The next day, the whole team, including the Sherpa, packed loads up to that saddle and established Camp II at 19,300 feet. (Camp I had been placed at the base of the Abruzzi, a bit below the site of our advance base camp in 1992.)

Studying the two photos of Camp II published in *Five Miles High,* I can see why this site looked like a godsend—an oasis of safety in the middle of a vast and dangerous slope. But I don't even remember passing that little saddle on the spur. We didn't pitch our first camp on the ridge until we'd reached 20,000 feet. Starting in the 1980s, climbers realized that the best way to deal with the scarcity of tent sites on the Abruzzi was to pitch camps as far apart as possible. There are all kinds of reasons, some of them psychological, why this wasn't feasible for the 1938 team.

Even before they had really gotten launched on the Abruzzi, the team suffered an absurd but monumental misfortune. At Camp I, they had cached a four-gallon gas can, containing a substantial portion of the team's entire supply of stove fuel. To keep it out of the sun, the men had tucked the can underneath an overhanging rock embedded in the glacial ice. During the next day, the ice melted, causing the rock to topple on top of the can and smash it, spilling the entire contents.

This disaster meant that throughout the rest of the expedition, the climbers would have to be extremely frugal in rationing their fuel. The situation was so dire that Streatfeild, two Sherpa, and the expedition cook decided at once to hike to the base of Gasherbrum I. Streatfeild had been with the French team that had attempted that mountain in 1936, and he remembered that the climbers had left unused gas cached there upon their departure. But he also remembered that after the French had gone home, the "coolies" had returned to scavenge what they could.

If he could find no gas beneath Gasherbrum I, Streatfeild planned to resort to a truly desperate expedient. He would send one Sherpa and the cook all the way down to Askole, a seven-day march, to recruit porters to pack huge loads of firewood all the way back up the Baltoro! "This could be used at our Base Camp and possibly higher," House wrote, "instead of the now precious liquid fuel."

In the end, Streatfeild's splinter group hiked more than twenty miles to the French base camp—down the Godwin Austen Glacier to Concordia, then up the Upper Baltoro and the South Gasherbrum glaciers. At the French camp, which had indeed been looted by the porters, they found not a single ounce of stove fuel. They did scavenge some canned meat and vegetables, which ultimately gave the team's cuisine welcome variety. And, true to his promise, Streatfeild sent one Sherpa, Pemba Kitar, and the cook, Ahdoo, off to Askole to gather firewood. Amazingly, those two returned only eight days later from a trek that normally took fourteen days, accompanied by ten porters carrying massive loads of "fine cedar." Though it was never used above base camp, the firewood solved the expedition's fuel problem.

Meanwhile, throughout the first ten days of July, the climbers pushed the route and carried loads up the Abruzzi. To safeguard the harder passages, the men fixed ropes—lines made of three-eighths-inch-diameter hemp, 1,700 feet of which the team had purchased in Bombay. Here the pitons Petzoldt had smuggled into the expedition gear proved invaluable as anchors for the ropes. Nowadays, on steep terrain, we use *jumars,* mechanical ascenders with which we attach ourselves to nylon fixed ropes. These metal devices slide easily up the rope, but catch and hold fast under a downward pull. In 1938, ascenders were still a quarter century away from being invented. Instead, the climbers tied knots and overhand loops in their hemp fixed ropes, then simply hauled themselves up with their hands.

Descending the steeper passages today, we clip our harnesses to the fixed rope with a figure-eight device and rappel the line. In 1938, the climbers also rappelled, but they did so with the traditional dulfersitz, a simple and ingenious method of wrapping the rope in an S-bend through the crotch, around one hip, up across the chest, and over the opposite shoulder, invented shortly after the turn of the twentieth century by the great German climber Hans Dülfer. On the hike in, Petzoldt had taught the Sherpa how to rappel. Now they employed this vital technique on high-angle terrain above thousand-foot drops with all the aplomb of the Americans.

Throughout this surge, in fact, three Sherpa—Pasang Kikuli, Phinsoo, and Tse Tendrup—played a crucial role, as they carried the bulk of the loads and did most of the work building up tent platforms by stacking loose rocks on sloping ledges.

On July 5, the team established Camp III at 20,700 feet. Camp IV was pitched only 800 feet higher on July 13. For the first time, hope outweighed discouragement in the climbers' hearts.

On my own expeditions, I've always found that it's during the storm days, when you lie around inside your tent and try to kill time, that the tensions among team members tend to escalate. Confined in a small space, elbow to elbow with another guy, you can find that even a good buddy gets on your nerves, let alone a teammate you've already found to be slightly irritating. But when you're climbing hard, those tensions dissolve and you get along better with your partners.

From July 2 on, the 1938 team was pushing hard, with important deeds accomplished every day. And with this activity, morale soared. About one happy camp reunion, House writes, "A hot grog was served up and somewhere an excellent fig pudding was found. Later two chess games started and before we knew it Bates launched into a series of his favorite Alaskan sourdough ballads, startling even the Sherpas, who peered from their tents in awe."

Yet the climbing inevitably produced moments of high tension and even of anger. Since *Five Miles High* adheres scrupulously to the prohibition against airing dirty laundry, those conflicts are only hinted at, in passages whose tone turns semicomic. You have to read between the lines, for instance, to decipher the real antagonism between House and Petzoldt on one dicey traverse. In House's telling,

> I remember in one place trying to enlarge some ice steps with my load on my back and a single finger linked through the head of a piton for balance. Petzoldt, who by now had completely recovered his strength and spirits, unfortunately chose this moment to deliver an enlightening and thoroughly sound discourse on step-cutting, with particular respect to how I might improve my tech-

nique. He admitted later that this was a poorly timed joke, for he
had not realized I was hanging on by my eyelashes.

On July 12, an incident occurred that, thanks in large part to misunderstandings, could easily have killed one or more of the climbers. Camp
III had been pitched in a very dangerous place, directly beneath a steep
slope that was littered with loose rocks. That day, Bates, House, and
Phinsoo had no sooner arrived at Camp III than Houston, Petzoldt,
Pasang Kikuli, and Tse Tendrup started to carry loads above. As they departed, they promised that "they would be as careful as possible with the
loose rock."

The trio who had just arrived at Camp III set to work improving the
tent platforms. Suddenly, from 500 feet above, the first rock fell.

> It came right among us, puncturing the tent we had just erected.
> From then on, at frequent intervals, rocks dropped. Sometimes
> they fell far to one side; sometimes they flew overhead with a
> high-pitched hum; sometimes they crashed right into camp,
> bursting like shrapnel as they hit the slope. There was no escape.

The three men in the line of fire were terrified—and furious. They
screamed at their comrades above. But, as House explains, "A high wind
was blowing so the climbers could not hear our shouts and thought the
rocks were bouncing harmlessly out to the sides." By the time the four
men in the lead had almost returned to camp, their three teammates
were "wild," unable to suppress "bitter remarks." As they arrived, Houston, Petzoldt, and the two Sherpa found "their cheery greeting followed
by a dead silence. One look at the holes in all three of the tents was
enough to tell them what had happened."

I can completely sympathize with those guys' predicament. No one
was really to blame—the true cause of the potentially fatal accident was
the bad placement of Camp III. But given the logistics of the day, that
placement was unavoidable. What else could Houston and Petzoldt have

done? They weren't happy with the location of Camp III, but they had to climb. From 500 feet above, you can't tell where the rocks you knock loose are landing. And on that kind of sketchy terrain, it's almost impossible to avoid dislodging rocks.

But in *Five Miles High,* House gives the dispute a happy ending:

> While we sat and sulked, seeking the most effective way of voicing our great displeasure, [Houston and Petzoldt] rummaged through the food supplies. A short time later they brought humble offerings of jam, dates, and hot tea hastily conjured out of sun-melted snow. With such companions ill-humor could not last long, and soon we were laughing sheepishly at what we had let ourselves in for.

So the official expedition narrative sticks to its formula of tucking the dirty laundry out of sight. But in her 2007 biography of Houston, Bernadette McDonald published excerpts from Houston's letters home that, when I first read them, puzzled me. "Petzoldt has turned out to be a gem," Houston wrote early on in the expedition. The tension between the cowboy and the nabob seemed to have vanished. It was instead Bill House of whom Houston was critical. "He is continually complaining about the lack of food," Houston wrote around June 27, "and demands much more than we are able to provide. He is a very fine climber, but his choice of routes is poor and he takes far too many chances. In addition, he has frequent depressed spells during which is very bad company."

These strictures are all the more surprising in view of the fact that House led many of the hardest pitches all the way up the Abruzzi Ridge to just below the Shoulder, including the indisputable crux of that 8,000-foot ascent. As I mentioned earlier, the nearly vertical 80-foot rock fissure at 21,500 feet has been known ever since as House's Chimney. On July 14, with Bates belaying, House tackled the cliff.

The team had pitched Camp IV only 75 feet below that cliff, but the ice leading up to it was so hard that it took the two men a full hour to chop steps to reach the base of the chimney. Bates set up a belay by drap-ing a loop of rope over a prong of rock, then passing the rope behind the prong. That technique harkened back to Victorian times, but by today's standards it seems pretty marginal. If House had fallen off the cliff, the hemp rope might well have severed as it came tight on the sharp rock.

House's lead was a desperate struggle, as it took him two and a half hours to surmount the 80-foot pitch. He managed to drive a good piton near the base of the crack, but 40 feet higher, as he stood on a tiny ledge and tried to place a second piton, "the metal only crumpled up after pen-etrating a half-inch of rock." (The soft-iron pitons of the day, the best available, were all too liable to bend into useless spikes under a hammer blow. It would not be until the 1960s that chrome-molybdenum pitons vastly improved on the old hardware.)

To inch his way up the fissure, House got into classic chimney posi-tion, feet flat against one wall, back against the other. Abruptly, however, he realized that he had left his crampons in his pack. The metal spikes dug into his back and caught on nubbins of rock. Only by thrashing his way brutally upward could House gain ground. "I felt I was pretty close to my margin of safety," he later wrote, "but there were no piton cracks and I thought anything would be better than climbing down without some protection from above."

Out of sight around a corner below, shivering with cold, Bates shouted up to urge that House retreat. "It was a suggestion I certainly would have liked to follow," House joked in retrospect. Instead, he struggled onward, at last emerging on top of the cliff.

The importance of House's brilliant lead can hardly be overestimated. In that long band of cliff at 21,500 feet, there's no other weakness, so no alternative to the chimney. If the climbers had not been able to get up that pitch, their attempt on the Abruzzi Ridge would have ended then and there.

In 1992, after Scott and I drew straws and I won the lead, I got up the fissure not by chimneying inside it but by stemming outside, my feet and hands spread-eagled on rock holds on either side. Unlike House, I wore my crampons all the way up. I was able to clip in to a couple of pitons already in place—"fixed pins" left by some previous expedition. It's almost impossible to rate pure climbing moves on a big mountain, but I'd say the chimney was only about 5.4. (The decimal scale of difficulty in use today ranges from 5.1, the easiest, to 5.15, the hardest. In the 1960s, when pitches harder than 5.9 started to be performed, climbers could think of no way to rate them except by calling them 5.10, then 5.11, and so on.)

On the other hand, I found the crack half-choked with ice and snow, into which I could kick a few footholds, which I'm sure made the pitch easier than it was for House. No matter what, as Peter Boardman remarked in 1980, House's Chimney was far harder than anything that had been climbed on Everest by 1938.

The climbing had so worn out Bates and House that they decided to pitch Camp V only a little bit higher, a mere 500 vertical feet above Camp IV. They had reached the foot of the Black Pyramid, a steep, triangular buttress made up of mixed rock.

By now Burdsall, though he had gamely carried loads to the lower camps, had dropped out of the team pushing higher on the route. At forty-two, he was the oldest of the five American climbers and the least skilled technically. Streatfeild had already withdrawn from the advance guard, as he'd performed his fuel-searching mission to Gasherbrum I, then turned his attention to surveying unmapped parts of the surrounding peaks and glaciers.

The climbers still pushing high were reduced to Bates, House, Houston, and Petzoldt—as well as the three strongest Sherpa. Among those three, Pasang Kikuli was the stalwart, performing as well as the four Americans.

In 1992, after I'd strung a good fixed rope down House's Chimney, it was a routine business to rappel down that pitch and jumar back up it. Not so for the guys in 1938, who, carrying twenty-five-pound loads up the chimney, had to haul themselves hand over hand as they hung on the loops they had tied in the fixed rope.

From July 15 to 20, as the weather held almost perfect, the climbers frenziedly pushed the route higher and higher. Houston and Petzoldt made some daring, exposed leads as they forced their way through the Black Pyramid. The team established a Camp VI at 23,300 feet, and then Camp VII at 24,700 feet. On the afternoon of July 19, Petzoldt and Houston broke through the 25,000-foot barrier. Only a relatively low-angle snow slope stood between them and the Shoulder.

There's a line of Houston's about this gutsy push that makes me chuckle: "After a restful cigarette, which seemed especially welcome at these high altitudes, we turned again to our task." These guys, in the shape of their lives, were smoking all the way up the mountain!

That evening, with everyone ensconced in Camp VI, the team held another council of war. Bates had calculated that the men had only ten days' worth of food and fuel left. Worried about an eventual descent in bad weather, the party decided to err on the side of caution and send only two climbers up to push the route to the highest possible altitude. Without even putting the question to a vote, the team chose Houston and Petzoldt, as Bates and House magnanimously stepped aside.

On July 20, all four men made the last carry to Camp VII. They decided that the Sherpa had "reached the limits of their climbing ability" and so should be left behind; but at the last minute Pasang Kikuli begged to be included, and the "sahibs" relented.

That evening, Petzoldt and Houston settled into their sleeping bags at Camp VII, restless and eager for the final push the next morning. Houston had already concluded that there was no hope of reaching the top; it would be achievement enough simply to scope out a route through the summit pyramid that might show the way for some future party to make the first ascent of K2. In light of subsequent events, Petzoldt apparently did not agree.

And then the pair made a dismal discovery: they had forgotten to bring matches with their loads! Without matches, there would be no way to light the stove; without the stove, no way to melt snow into water. Houston later wrote,

This was a catastrophe. In my pocket I found four safety matches and five strike-anywhere matches, all of dubious value. The latter, brought all the way from New York, carefully dried in the sun at many of the lower camps, had persistently failed to function well above 20,000 feet, and only with extreme care and preparatory rubbings with grease did they even glow. The safety matches, on the other hand, were made in Kashmir and were very fragile.

It took three matches to light the stove for dinner. The men melted pot after pot of snow, and even slept with a pot full of water wrapped in their clothing and placed under their feet, so that it would not freeze during the night.

In the morning, it took three more matches to light the stove to cook breakfast. The two men were off as soon as the sun's rays struck their tent. Roped together 60 feet apart, Petzoldt and Houston slowly plodded up the snow slopes leading to the Shoulder, often plunging in to their knees. In an era before down jackets, each man wore four Shetland sweaters over his flannel shirt, with an outer windproof suit and two pairs of wool mittens, but they still felt the cold acutely.

On that last push, the Wyoming cowboy came into his own. "Petzoldt was feeling strong and moving rapidly," Houston later admitted, "but I had a curious weakness in my legs, so that every upward step was an effort requiring several breaths." By 1:00 P.M., the two men had not only topped out on the Shoulder but had traversed its easy ridge to a point only 900 feet short of the slope that leads up to the Bottleneck couloir.

The men ate a quick lunch, then unroped, hoping to dry the coiled line by laying it out in the sun. Petzoldt continued in the lead. Houston later recalled,

I could see him ahead of me working steadily upward, pausing now and then to take bearings. My progress was ludicrously slow. Every inch I gained in altitude was an effort. My legs were so weak I was forced to rest every five or six steps, and soon fatigue made me forget all danger from above. I struggled on—why I do not know.

At last Houston gave up and sat down with his back against a large boulder, trying to warm himself in the sun. Petzoldt plugged onward. He reached a point several hundred feet higher than his partner before turning around himself. At 26,000 feet, Petzoldt was still 2,250 feet below the summit.

All his life, Houston inclined toward the mystical. Of that high point on K2 he later wrote,

> I tried to look ahead years into the future so as to cement firmly in my mind recollections of these great moments on our mighty peak. There were other emotions too deep to be expressed. I felt that all my previous life had reached a climax in these last hours of intense struggle against nature. . . . I believe in those minutes at 26,000 feet on K2, I reached depths of feeling which I can never reach again.

The two men started down at 4:00 P.M., reaching their tent as dusk turned to twilight. They had a desperate craving for hot tea, but there were only three matches left. Houston recalled:

> With infinite care we waxed one of the matches, dried it as much as possible, and struck it. It fizzled and went out. A safety match broke off at the head. Paul in a gesture of bravado struck our last one. It lit and we were assured of our warm supper. Too tired for much talk, we melted water for the morning, snuggled in our sleeping bags, and drowsed off to a dreamless sleep.

The climb was over, but not the expedition. It took three more days for the team to climb carefully back to base camp, retrieving gear (but not the fixed ropes) as they went; six more days to hike with their porters back to Askole; and eleven more days, some of them on horseback, to return to Srinagar by a shorter route than the one they had taken on the way out. All told, from Srinagar to Srinagar the expedition lasted ninety days.

Exhausted though the men must have been after their effort on K2, they regarded the retreat from the Karakoram as simply the final stage in a three-month lark. For all six of the "sahibs," the expedition had been one of the greatest adventures of their lives. In the last pages of *Five Miles High,* Burdsall sums up the team's sense of satisfaction:

> Behind us were unforgettable days—days on the march, and days on the peak, whose memories we would not exchange for any-thing. No harm had come to us or to any of our helpers. In a few days we must say farewell to our Kashmiri and our faithful little Sherpas. . . . Later we sahibs too must part to go our separate ways, but we knew that our bond of friendship would last as long as life itself.

Alas, the aftermath of the 1938 expedition to K2 would turn out not to be quite so clean and pure. It's always seemed to me that one of the saddest things that can happen in mountaineering is for teammates to get along well during an expedition, only to have a falling out afterward. One of the best-known examples is the partnership of the Austrian Peter Ha-beler with the Tyrolean Reinhold Messner. During the 1970s, they set the climbing world on fire, with such astounding deeds as the ascent of the Eiger Nordwand in a then-record time of ten hours. In 1978, Ha-beler and Messner pulled off their greatest feat when they climbed Ever-est without bottled oxygen, despite widespread predictions that climbers would die or suffer irreversible brain damage in such an attempt.

Messner and Habeler apparently got along fine on Everest. The trou-ble came afterward, in the discrepancies between the books the two men wrote about their adventure. (Messner, who always had an outsized ego, seems to have resented the fact that Habeler would write a book at all.) The media seized upon the conflict, and the two former best friends began a feud that lasted a quarter century. To their credit, these two great mountaineers finally patched up their quarrel and even climbed together again.

After K2, Paul Petzoldt stayed on in India for several months. His initial intention was simply to sightsee, but he soon fell under the spell of a very odd duck named Dr. Johnson. The man was a retired physician from California who had come to India as a Baptist missionary, repudiated his faith, and set himself up as a guru of a mystical Buddhist cult. Petzoldt was so taken with Johnson (whose first name he could not later recall), that he arranged to have his wife, Patricia, join him at Johnson's compound in the village of Dera Baba Jaimal Singh.

On January 25, 1939, gathering tensions within the Johnson household exploded. The only published versions of this bizarre event appear in the two biographies of Petzoldt, and they disagree in many details. Since the first biography, *On Top of the World,* was written by Patricia herself, who was present at the time, it may be suspect, because her agenda would have been to exonerate her husband of any wrongdoing. But even the more reliable account, in Raye Ringholz's 1997 *On Belay!,* depends entirely on Petzoldt's own story of what happened.

In this telling, Johnson's wife, who is portrayed as a depressive paranoiac, suddenly seized a shotgun and tried to shoot Petzoldt with it. Petzoldt grabbed the stock of the gun, struggled with her for several moments, wrenched the weapon out of her hands, and threw it out a window. In the melee, Dr. Johnson had hurried into the room. As Petzoldt fled into the courtyard, he accidentally knocked Johnson down. The guru's head struck the stone floor and he was instantly killed.

(In the 1960s, in climbing circles, the scuttlebutt told an utterly different story. In this version, Petzoldt had ended up in a fistfight with a porter on some sort of trek and had killed him with a single blow to the head. Like most Wyoming cowboys, Petzoldt had honed his skills as a brawler and bar fighter. The climbing gossip had it that Petzoldt was allowed to leave India only after promising that he would never return to the country.)

In Ringholz's account, Petzoldt and the other witnesses to the accident fabricated a bogus version of what had happened. Even so, Petzoldt was charged with manslaughter and underwent a three-day trial before he was acquitted. By then, he was flat broke. The American consul took him under his wing and communicated with Charlie Houston, who was back in the United States. Houston shared the news with Bates and House. The four men scrounged up $550, which they wired to Calcutta. The money paid for both Petzoldts' passage home by steamer.

Yet according to Ringholz, Petzoldt never realized that his teammates had come to his financial rescue. "I never knew that they sent the money there," he told his biographer. "If they sent money to the consul, I never got it."

After interviewing those former teammates, Ringholz wrote:

> Unfortunately, the $550 has been the source of ill feeling among the members of the K2 expedition for almost sixty years. Houston, House, and Bates claim it was difficult for them to scrape up that amount of money in those days when they were young and not established. They expected, and contend that Petzoldt promised them, that on his return to the States the loan would be repaid.

Houston's biographer Bernadette McDonald comes to a similar conclusion:

> Back in the United States, Charlie received an urgent cable from the Consul General requesting money. Together with his father, he quietly made the necessary arrangements for Petzoldt to return. Charlie never completely forgave Petzoldt for not thanking his family for helping him out in this moment of need. Petzoldt claimed ignorance on the source of the money, but the friendship subsequently withered.

Whether or not this event caused the estrangement between Petzoldt and Houston, there seems to have been another source of lasting rancor between the men. Houston always felt that his team had done the very best it could on K2. To have reached 26,000 feet on the first real attempt on the great mountain was more than anyone could have hoped for. But Petzoldt evidently thought the team could have done better.

A little-known fact about the 1938 expedition is that the members took along a movie camera, with which they shot footage not only on the approach to the Baltoro but all the way up to Camp III on the Abruzzi. In 2004, sixty-six years after the expedition, Houston had the best footage remastered and put on a DVD. A DVD disk was inserted in a plastic sleeve in each copy of McDonald's *Brotherhood of the Rope*.

There's some amazing footage from that expedition. For me, the most moving scene was shot as the climbers packed up their camps in a gathering storm to head down the mountain. The camera catches a tent flapping wildly in the wind, in front of which Bob Bates is grinning as he sings his head off—perhaps some Alaska sourdough ditty or one of the railroad ballads, such as "The Wreck of the Old 97," that he had memorized and would sing at the drop of a hat for the rest of his life. There's no sound track on the film, but in the voice-over that he supplied in 2004, Houston narrates:

> We have done what we came to do. We have found a route to the summit cone, and we're very happy and ready to go home. . . . As the storm thickens, it's clear that we must start for home as soon as the weather clears. In a few days it does clear, and we go on down to base camp, arriving there two days later, very excited, very happy. We have accomplished far more than most people expected we would. We have found a route up the mountain, and we enjoyed every minute of our success.

That formula summarizes Houston's lasting feelings about the 1938 expedition. But Petzoldt's lasting feelings were different—and less happy.

A friend of mine met Petzoldt in 1963, when he took a job as an assistant instructor at the Colorado Outward Bound School near Marble. Petzoldt, who was then fifty-five, was serving as one of the school's senior guides. My friend, who was only twenty, was completely in awe of the great man. But one day he got up the nerve to ask Petzoldt about reaching their high point on K2 in 1938. Petzoldt said simply, "I wanted to go on. Charlie decided to turn back."

Asked the same question by Raye Ringholz for her 1997 biography, Petzoldt responded more vehemently. "Jesus Christ," he said. "We weren't turned back by bad weather. We made up our mind not to climb the mountain. If we'd have brought up a little bit more food and planned to get to the summit, we could have gone back as conquerors of K2!"

Well, that's how memory works. In hindsight, it's pretty hard to congratulate yourself for making the right decision and turning back. I know that's been a key to my own success on the 8,000ers—turning around and coming back to fight another day, even when it means giving up the glory. There's no doubt in my mind that in 1938, Houston and Petzoldt made the right decision. They reached the highest point they could, while still allowing the whole team to get safely down.

But the anguish of that "what might have been" seems to have gnawed away at Petzoldt for the rest of his life. For whatever reasons, he never went back to the Himalaya or the Karakoram. The final word—and the saddest—on the gulf between Petzoldt and Houston came at the Telluride mountain film festival in the late 1990s. Both men were on a panel celebrating K2. The chairperson was Rick Ridgeway, who in 1978 had been one of the first four Americans to climb K2. In *Brotherhood of the Rope,* Bernadette McDonald replayed the scene:

> [Petzoldt] said that he had been opposed to the decision to go down, and that the decision had been taken because Charlie wasn't feeling well. Ridgeway looked over at Charlie and raised his eyebrows. Charlie said nothing. He was hurt and angry, but he didn't respond.

As far as I know, Petzoldt never claimed that if Houston hadn't decided to turn around, the two of them (or Petzoldt solo) could have reached the summit on July 21. Petzoldt's declaration at the Telluride festival implies that he felt the team hadn't built up enough supplies or pushed their deadlines hard enough to make a legitimate try for the summit. It's just possible that he harbored a private fantasy that he could have gone for the top alone on July 21, as Hermann Buhl would do on Nanga Parbat in 1953. But it wouldn't have been realistic.

Look at our own 1992 expedition. Vlad, who was a really strong climber, and who had the advantage of more than half a century of improvement in gear and knowledge of the mountain, left his camp on the Shoulder at 3:00 A.M. with a strong partner. He didn't reach the summit until 9:00 P.M., after eighteen straight hours of climbing. Then he had to bivouac on the way down.

Houston and Petzoldt didn't reach the upper end of the Shoulder until 1:00 P.M. on July 21. By that point they were already worn out from the climb from Camp VII. Even if Petzoldt had been strong enough to go all the way to the top, there's no way he could have gotten there before nightfall. My God, in 1938 they didn't even have headlamps—just flashlights they'd hold in one hand! And with the clothing they wore, I doubt that either Petzoldt or Houston could have survived a bivouac above 26,000 feet. And even if they had survived, they might have suffered debilitating frostbite.

In no sense should the 1938 expedition ever be regarded as a failure. It was, instead, a true breakthrough. When the summits of the fourteen 8,000ers were finally reached for the first time, between 1950 and 1964, only a single one—Annapurna—was climbed on the first attempt (and that at the cost of Herzog's fingers and toes and Lachenal's toes). K2 would finally be climbed only on the fourth attempt (or the sixth, if you count the 1902 and 1909 expeditions).

One of the things I admire about the 1938 expedition is that all the serious climbing was carried out by a team of only four, aided by three brave Sherpa, including the indomitable Pasang Kikuli. Whatever went on between them after the expedition, those four men became good friends on the mountain as they worked together with clockwork precision. Their effort was a far cry from the kinds of huge militaristic expeditions countries would launch against the 8,000ers in the 1950s. I suppose that in a sense, Houston and his teammates carried an American banner to K2, but their expedition had nothing to do with nationalism. Ever since I first read *Five Miles High,* that 1938 team has served as a model for me of what a small group working in harmony can achieve on an 8,000er. By pioneering the route by which K2 would eventually be climbed, and by getting to 26,000 feet, they pulled off a magnificent achievement.

4

THE GREAT MYSTERY

The deepest mystery in K2 history is what happened on the 1939 expedition. All the other major campaigns on the mountain produced not only "official" books but articles and chapters in memoirs by the principal climbers. From the 1939 expedition, the only English-language publications to see the light of day were a dutiful and unilluminating article published in 1940 in *The American Alpine Journal* and a more illuminating (but still brief) account by the leader of the expedition that appeared seventeen years later in *Appalachia,* the journal of the Appalachian Mountain Club.

Yet no K2 expedition—not even the vexed first ascent in 1954—ever provoked a storm of controversy comparable to the one that engulfed the 1939 climbers on their return home. As Galen Rowell writes in *In the Throne Room of the Mountain Gods,* his personal account of a star-crossed American attempt on K2's northwest ridge in

1975, the 1939 expedition produced "the most bizarre tragedy in the history of Himalayan mountaineering."

As is seldom true in climbing, the controversy was deeply enmeshed in the politics of the day. And the troubles that would afflict the 1939 team were set in motion even before the members left the United States, as Fritz Wiessner assumed leadership of the party.

In the winter of 1937–38 (as mentioned in the previous chapter), while he tried to assemble his K2 team, Charlie Houston suspected that Wiessner had deliberately put off his own expedition until the summer of 1939, in hopes that Houston's party might pave his way with a thorough reconnaissance of the mountain. Whether or not Wiessner's motives were so Machiavellian, that was exactly what happened, for in reaching 26,000 feet on the Abruzzi Ridge, Houston and his partners had demonstrated that K2 would best be climbed by that route.

Houston's irritation was ratcheted up a notch when he began to suspect that Wiessner had already exacted pledges for the 1939 expedition from some of the best American climbers. In a letter to Bob Bates, Houston fumed,

> Wiessner has asked him to go next year and Bill [House] thinks that would fit in better with his career. Bill makes number three that is not coming with us because Wiessner has extended hope of next year to him. I am so damn mad at Wiessner I have been aching to write him a fiery letter all day, but hope to restrain myself.

In the end, of course, House joined the 1938 team, which, ironically, meant that Wiessner's friend and partner from the first ascent of Mount Waddington was not available for K2 in 1939.

The tragedy that would unfold that summer had everything to do with the makeup of the party. Besides Bill House, Wiessner hoped that Paul Petzoldt would be able to return to K2, but the fatal accident in India involving Petzoldt made that impossible. Through the winter of 1938–39, Wiessner doggedly lined up potential teammates. At one point, four very strong climbers were on board. Bestor Robinson had met Wiessner at the foot of Waddington, as part of a team of strong California rock climbers who had their own designs on the mountain. Wiessner had magnanimously given the Californians the first crack at Waddington. He and Bill House had made the first ascent only after Robinson's crew turned back 600 feet below the summit. Back on the glacier after their defeat, Robinson hiked over to Wiessner's camp and said, "It's all yours. We're just not ready for it." In the process, the two men became friends.

Al Lindley, a Yale graduate from Minnesota, had made the second ascent of Mount McKinley in 1932; he was also an expert ski mountaineer. Sterling Hendricks had perfected the art of lightweight assaults on remote and little-known mountains, particularly in western Canada. Roger Whitney, yet another Yalie, had learned to climb in the Alps, and had made first ascents in Alaska, Canada, and the Tetons.

On paper, then, Wiessner's party boasted plenty of skill and experience. At various times through the spring of 1939, however, all four of those strong teammates backed out of the expedition. Some of Wiessner's critics later tried to see those defections as rooted in a distrust of Wiessner's leadership, but I don't buy it. In those days, nobody could make a living from mountain climbing. All those guys had jobs they couldn't sacrifice: Whitney was a physician, Hendricks a biochemist, and Lindley and Robinson were lawyers. Then, as now, an expedition to K2 was an expensive undertaking. Climbers often back out of such trips after they've made a tentative commitment to them. Look at our own K2 team in 1992: Scott went from having so many teammates lined up—that he had to put me on the waiting list—to heading off to Pakistan with only me as a partner.

In the end, Wiessner had to scrounge among casual friends he had met climbing or skiing. And he was swayed to include relatively inexperienced candidates whose deep pockets could help pay the cost of the expedition. The pivotal figure in this roster was Dudley Wolfe, a near millionaire from Boston. After graduating from Harvard, Wolfe had become an expert in long-distance sailing races, as well as a competent skier. But he had taken up climbing only in 1936. By 1939, he was over-weight and forty-four years old. According to Andrew Kauffman and William Putnam, the authors of *K2: The 1939 Tragedy*—published in 1992, it remains the only book-length chronicle of the expedition—Wolfe "required more than one guide [in the Alps] to haul his large bulk to the summits. . . . He was not accustomed to making decisions in the mountains and could move over difficult terrain only with the guidance and help of others." Wolfe's funding may have been the chief reason why Wiessner invited him to K2, but on the mountain, against all odds, he would perform better than all the other Americans (except, of course, Wiessner himself).

Forty-two-year-old Eaton ("Tony") Cromwell was also a blueblood with access to money. Like Wolfe, he had climbed mostly with guides. As Kauffman and Putnam sardonically put it, Cromwell's "main climbing qualifications for candidacy on the 1939 expedition consisted of the longest, but not most distinguished, list of mountain ascents of any member of the American Alpine Club; and there is some reason to believe that no one ever attempted to surpass this record, much less to boast of it." Cromwell, in other words, was what we climbers dismissively call a "peak bagger."

In the 1930s, forty-four and forty-two were pretty advanced ages for climbers attempting K2. But Wiessner, at thirty-nine, was at the top of his alpine game, and that summer he was, by his own report, in the best shape of his life. He had reached 23,000 feet on Nanga Parbat in 1932, and his record of technical first ascents in Europe and the United States was unmatched by any other American.

The party was rounded out by two Dartmouth students. Chappell Cranmer had shared part of a single season with Wiessner in the Canadian Rockies, but the bulk of his experience consisted of weekends on New England crags and slogs up easy peaks in Colorado. His classmate George Sheldon was even less experienced, with only two seasons in the Tetons under his belt, during which he seconded routes led by more accomplished climbers. Both Dartmouth boys were only twenty years old.

As the team sailed for Europe in March, it must have been obvious to Wiessner that he was the leader of perhaps the weakest team to that date ever to attempt an 8,000er—much less the formidable K2. Executives of the American Alpine Club, which officially sponsored the expedition, were so apprehensive that at the last minute they recruited a sixth man, Jack Durrance. A twenty-six-year-old Dartmouth medical student, Durrance had become a first-rate rock climber in the Bavarian Alps after his family had moved to Munich. Back in the States, he worked three summers as a guide in the Tetons, where he compiled a record of first ascents in that spiky range that was second only to Petzoldt's. His finest climb was the first ascent of the north face of Grand Teton—with Petzoldt and Petzoldt's brother, Eldon. On that daunting route, Durrance led the hardest pitches.

Durrance should have been a powerful addition to the party, but for strange reasons, it would not work out that way. He caught up with his teammates in Genoa, where they all boarded a steamship for India. And from that moment on, things started to go wrong.

Wiessner had not been notified of the addition of Durrance to the party. In Genoa, he was expecting to meet Bestor Robinson, who had backed out only after the other five climbers had sailed for Europe. Greeting Durrance, Wiessner could not suppress his shock and dismay, and Durrance was badly hurt by his leader's reaction. In his diary, Durrance wrote a few weeks later, "Can't quite forget Fritz's look of disappointment at finding insignificant Jack filling Bestor Robinson's boots."

On all thirty of my expeditions to 8,000ers, I don't think I ever joined a party as weak as that 1939 team. There were plenty of feeble performers among the Americans in 1992 on K2, as I kept complaining to my diary, but we also had enough strong guys—particularly Scott, Charley Mace, and Neal Beidleman—to put together a decent summit effort. In 1939, Wiessner was the only member of the team who had ever previously been on a mountain in the great ranges, whether in Alaska, the

Andes, the Himalaya, or the Karakoram. It's hard for me to say, particularly given the half-century gap between Wiessner's era and mine, but I think that if I had found myself part of a party with as little collective experience as that one, I'd have backed out. And if I'd been the leader, I might have called off the whole endeavor.

Inexperienced teammates can get you in trouble on a serious mountain. John Roskelley, the best American high-altitude climber of the 1980s and my teammate on Kangchenjunga in 1989, had an ironclad principle that he would never jumar up a fixed rope that had been anchored by someone else. He didn't trust any teammate to fix those anchors the way he trusted himself. (I'm not so adamant about this myself, but I respect Roskelley's stubborn self-reliance.)

Inexperience among the teammates on the 1939 expedition would contribute directly to the tragedy. But there's no evidence that Wiessner ever thought of calling off the show. For one thing, he had an ace up his sleeve: he had recruited nine Sherpa in advance. Five of them were returning from Houston's expedition of the previous year: Pasang Kikuli, Phinsoo, and Tse Tendrup, who had all carried loads high on the Abruzzi; Pemba Kitar, who had performed the extraordinary errand of dashing down to Askole to recruit porters to carry firewood up to base camp; and Sonam. Rounding out the Sherpa contingent were Pasang Lama, who would play a pivotal role on the '39 expedition, Tsering, Dawa Thondup, and Pasang Kitar.

If the American team was weak, the nine Sherpa amounted to as strong a cast as had ever signed on for an expedition to an 8,000er. It is no exaggeration to say that in 1939, Pasang Kikuli was the most experienced high-altitude climber in the world, with six previous expeditions to 8,000ers (seven if you count Nanda Devi, which is just under 8,000 meters). Kikuli had seen tragedy before, on Nanga Parbat in 1934, when eight climbers died after getting trapped in a storm high on the mountain. (That and the equally catastrophic 1937 Nanga Parbat expedition were, in the words of historian James Ramsey Ullman, "as sheer horror stories, unmatched by anything in the history of mountaineering.") The dead in 1934 included the team's leader, Willi Merkl (the finest German Himalayan mountaineer of his time), two German teammates, and five Sherpa. Kikuli narrowly escaped the same fate but suffered serious frostbite. It's a testament to what a powerful and devoted climber Kikuli was that he continued to go on so many dangerous expeditions. In 1939, he was the sirdar again, as he had been in 1938, and he became Wiessner's "personal" Sherpa, just as he had been Houston's the year before.

The 1939 team faced the same 360-mile hike to base camp from Srinagar that Houston's party had performed. But before the Americans even left the Vale of Kashmir, Wiessner arranged for eight days of acclimatization, during which the members practiced skiing on the nearby hills, combined with cushy living in houseboats in that colonial paradise. It was an ideal warm-up for the expedition. Describing the outing in a letter to the AAC treasurer, Wiessner was full of enthusiasm:

> Our party is really exceptionally congenial. We have lots of fun.
> I am terribly pleased with it. Today's ski ascent seemed exceptionally easy to everybody, and it makes me very happy and hopeful to see that the physical condition of the party is so good.

On May 2, the team left Srinagar. The overland journey proceeded smoothly, as the caravan averaged fifteen miles a day. The climbers' letters home (many of which are quoted in Kauffman and Putnam's *K2: The 1939 Tragedy*) report continuously high spirits. The members' sense of participating in an extended lark matched that of their predecessors the year before. On May 6, George Sheldon wrote,

> You probably want to know how we individually are getting along.
> Fritz, despite an enormous amount of work, is doing nicely. We

have named him Baby Face Sahib. Chap, wise and silent as the owl, is brown as a berry. Jack and his lusty sense of humor, which once in a while draws howls of disapproval, is the acting doctor because he is considering the medical profession. Tony, or Pop Sahib, is the Voice of Experience and doing very well at it. He came out with this amazing statement today; "Climbing is fun."

Two days later, Wiessner wrote to the AAC executive:

The boys are such a nice lot, taking everything from the easy side and hitting hard when necessary, it is fun to be a member of such a congenial group. Sometimes they may be a little too carefree but one word suffices to make them do their duty and work hard. I feel quite certain they will do well on the mountain.

Without mishap, the team reached Askole on May 21. From that last village, having hired 123 porters—forty-eight more than the 1938 team had employed—the expedition marched eastward, camping at Paiju and Urdukas, then on the Baltoro Glacier. Even before reaching the glacier, Pemba Kitar came down with a mysterious and persistent illness and had to be sent all the way back to Skardu to see a doctor. Though he would rejoin the team, the Sherpa who had played a critical role in 1938 would play none in 1939.

A pair of short-lived porter strikes (the second caused by a shortage of snow goggles) delayed the team slightly, but by May 31 they were installed at base camp. In terms of schedule, they were two weeks ahead of the 1938 expedition.

The agreement crafted with the porters as they were paid off and sent back to Askole would turn out to play a vital part in what went wrong on the expedition. Kauffman and Putnam summarize the exchange:

Absent new instructions, [the porters] were to return on July 23 for the homeward journey. This gave the team fifty-three days in which to ascend the mountain, ample time Fritz believed; by then someone would have reached the top or the attempt would have been abandoned.

So far on the expedition, nearly everything had gone well. But no sooner had the team settled in to base camp than Chappell Cranmer came down with a serious illness. His temperature rose to 102 degrees, and, as Durrance wrote in his diary, "He coughed profusely and expectorated quantities of phlegm & slime." Durrance gave the young man various medications, but his condition only worsened. By 6:00 P.M. on June 1, Cranmer had severe diarrhea and was still spewing mucus. Durrance was so alarmed that he gave his patient artificial respiration for two hours.

The symptoms sound like those of pulmonary edema, but they could also fit any number of other illnesses with pulmonary symptoms. If you combine traveling through a third-world country with the plagues of high altitude, you can come down with all sorts of maladies that people have rarely heard of. I've had to deal with teammates who were suddenly afflicted with pulmonary edema, though usually at much higher altitudes—Gary Ball at 26,000 feet on K2, for instance. Cranmer had succumbed at an altitude of only 16,500 feet. On the other hand, pulmonary edema has been known to strike victims at altitudes as low as 10,000 feet. The odd thing about the condition is that it can happen to anyone—previous experience on high mountains seems irrelevant. So does the kind of shape you're in. J.-C. Lafaille got it in 2003 as we summited on Broad Peak and had a really hard time getting down the mountain. Only two weeks before, we had climbed Nanga Parbat together, and J.-C. had also reached the summit of Dhaulagiri just before that. I thought that on Broad Peak he would have been so well acclimatized as to be basically immune to altitude-related illness, but that's not how it works. I'm just lucky that neither pulmonary nor cerebral edema has ever laid me low.

In 1939, pulmonary edema was virtually unknown. Durrance diag-

nosed Cranmer's malady as either pneumonia or "cardiac decompen-
sation." There was little he could do for his patient except hold his
head, keep him warm, try to clean him up, and give him such medi-
cines as phenobarbitol, a sedative. We know today (as Durrance could
not) that the most important thing to do to save the life of a victim of
either kind of edema is to get him at once to a lower altitude. If that's
not possible, all you can do is put the victim on supplemental oxygen.
Even if the 1939 party had known about the importance of getting to
a lower altitude at once, it would not have been an easy task. Descending the glacier, they would have lost altitude only very gradually.
Cranmer could not walk, so the men would have had to improvise a
litter.

Cranmer slowly recovered, but he was essentially out of action as the
team started up the Abruzzi Ridge. Meanwhile, the five healthy climbers
and the strongest Sherpa began to build a logistical pyramid of well-
stocked camps. By June 21, the team had established its Camp IV just
beneath House's Chimney. Learning from their predecessors' frighten-
ing experience, Wiessner's crew avoided camping on the 20,700-foot
platform where the 1938 party's tents had been bombarded by rocks
kicked loose from above. Instead, the 1939 team used that nook only as
a supply depot.

Wiessner always claimed that he had made a real effort to get along
with Durrance from the start. In 1984, he told a writer:

> I knew Jack as a great sportsman, and I knew he was strong. He'd
> done some climbing in Munich when he lived there, and he had
> good climbs in the Tetons. But I also knew he was very compet-
> itive, which might cause troubles. Actually, at that time I liked
> Durrance, and hoped he could do well.

But tensions between the two men began to spark only a day or two
after the team reached base camp. To the same writer, Wiessner recounted an unhappy conflict:

On our first trip up the glacier, I wanted to check a little bit on safety and roping. We had two ropes. Soon Jack's rope started to put up speed, trying to go faster than the others. Cromwell and Wolfe said to me, "What's up? Do we have to do this running?" When we got back to base camp, I gave a long talk. I said, "Look, fellows, I can tell you right now, we will never climb this mountain if there's competition between the members. Get it out of your head. We have to work really hard and work together." Jack didn't say anything, but seemed to agree.

After the expedition, and ever since, Wiessner was criticized for his style of leadership. Certainly his notion of his role as leader differed from Houston's. In 1938, nearly all the decisions were made by consensus; though officially the leader, Houston was uncomfortable with that very label, referring to himself instead as the team's "organizer."

Wiessner was far more dictatorial, and sometimes condescending, as in the letter quoted above in which he referred to the other climbers as "the boys" (even though Cromwell and Wolfe were older than he was) and praised them when they were able to "do their duty and work hard." But it's here that the politics of the day—both climbing politics and the international antagonisms that were about to explode in World War II— get all tangled up with what happened on K2 in 1939.

Because he was German-born, Wiessner was all too easily stereotyped as having a "Teutonic" character and style of leadership. Writing as late as 1992, Kauffman and Putnam lapse again and again into that kind of ethnic caricature. According to them, Wiessner had a "heavy personality." He was "hard in body, Spartan (but not invariably), stoic in outlook, ready for sacrifice, and dedicated to the achievement of what became his life's ambition." Even more explicitly,

German by birth and upbringing, Fritz had been reared in the school of absolute obedience to authority that characterizes much of the Teutonic ethos: the leader leads, and the troops obey, whatever the situation. He may have been ideally suited to command a German venture, but his background did not lend itself to directing Americans. . . .

Fritz was no humanist. Rather he preached Darwinian naturalism with its emphasis on survival of the fittest. The weak must perish so the strong may live—such was his philosophy. . . .

To my mind, this stereotyping is completely unfair, and the qualities that Kauffman and Putnam ascribe to Wiessner had nothing to do with what happened in 1939. In *K2: The Story of the Savage Mountain,* the English historian Jim Curran offers an eloquent rebuttal:

It is . . . all too easy to fall into the trap of racial stereotyping. Undoubtedly Wiessner was a rigid, single-minded, humourless and authoritarian figure. But these are by no means exclusively Teutonic characteristics—it is not hard to think of British, French and Italian climbers who have over the years displayed the same qualities and earned themselves huge accolades in the process.

To understand the climbing politics of the 1930s, one needs a bit of background. Mountaineering was essentially invented in the Alps at the end of the eighteenth century. The first great deed was the ascent of Mont Blanc in 1786. Throughout the nineteenth century, British climbers were in the forefront of the game; Americans didn't really take it up until the beginning of the twentieth century. By the 1930s, both Brits and Americans had adopted a conservative, rearguard approach to the pastime. The debate over "ironmongery"—the use of pitons, carabiners, and other metal devices—was a hot issue of the day. In disdaining those aids in 1938, Charlie Houston was subscribing to the Anglo-American view, while Paul Petzoldt had a more European outlook.

In the 1930s, the most technically advanced climbers in the world were Germans, Austrians, Italians, and French. The debate crystallized dramatically around attempts to climb the north face of the Eiger in Switzerland—the "last great problem" of the Alps, as many called it. The leading contenders were Germans and Austrians, and the face was so dangerous that eight out of the first ten men who tried it died in the effort.

The campaign on the Eiger provoked a virulent reaction in England and America. In 1937 Colonel E. L. Strutt, president of the Alpine Club, called the Eiger climbers "mentally deranged," adding, "He who succeeds first may rest assured that he has accomplished the most imbecile variant since mountaineering began." In the United States, the writer and mountaineer James Ramsey Ullman deplored how "perverted nationalism can infect even the most unpolitical of human activities."

The Eiger Nordwand was finally climbed in the summer of 1938 by two Austrians who teamed up with two Germans. Although the climbers themselves insisted that their passion had nothing to do with politics, Hitler gave them medals in a public ceremony before a cheering throng. This only reinforced the Anglo-American conviction that the best climbers in the Alps were Fascist maniacs throwing away their lives for *Führer* and *Vaterland*.

Although Fritz Wiessner had immigrated to the States in 1929 partly to escape looming Fascism and had become an American citizen six years later, he was regarded by some of the more conservative higher-ups in the AAC with the kind of suspicion that had attached itself to the German and Austrian Eiger climbers. And that suspicion deepened after the 1939 tragedy on K2.

Through the first three weeks of June, various members, including the Sherpa, carried loads up to Camps II, III, and IV (Camp III being the supply depot exposed to rockfall). But only Wiessner seemed capable of leading. With the exception of a few hundred feet of steps chopped in snow and ice above Camp II by Pasang Kikuli, Wiessner led every pitch from base camp to House's Chimney. That inequality would persist through the rest of the expedition: from Camp IV through Camp IX and even higher, Wiessner led every single foot of new ground.

Just how incredible a performance that was is hard to grasp. When

I've been at my fittest, I've been on expeditions where I did a lot of the leading. But never anything like every foot of the route—except for my solo attempt on the north side of Everest in 1993, when I reached 25,000 feet. Breaking trail in deep snow is one of the most exhausting chores in mountaineering, even on Mount Rainier, let alone on an 8,000er. Normally you're only too glad to turn the job over to a teammate after you've plowed a few hundred feet upward. From the Bottleneck to the summit of K2 in 1992, Scott, Charley, and I regularly swapped leads because of the exhausting snow conditions.

In 1939, Wiessner didn't take the lead time and again out of some egomaniacal need to be in the vanguard. The problem was simply that nobody else was up to the job. Yet in *K2: The 1939 Tragedy,* Kauffman and Putnam take Wiessner to task for being out front all the time. Their criticism is founded on an expedition theory that doesn't make a lot of sense to me. As they explain it,

> Until recent times . . . virtually all large expeditions had an official leader whose task consisted of coordinating and supervising major activities from before departure until return. On any such expedition, in modern times or earlier, the leader has by far the most important duties. But these are usually thankless ones involving drudgery, hard work, dedication, and constant attention to detail. . . .
>
> In addition, someone, usually the fittest and most experienced member of the climbing team, is selected point man (the military term), or lead dog (the Eskimo term). This is the person who takes care of the actual climbing problems on the mountain. The expedition leader and deputy cannot be expected to take over the role of point without seriously endangering the flow of supplies and support.

Basically, Kauffman and Putnam argue that the lead climber cannot also be the leader of the expedition. And so, armed with a theory whose rationale they never justify, they insist that in doing exactly that, Wiessner endangered the whole expedition:

> But Fritz failed to select anyone to serve as point, and at Base Camp it became increasingly clear that he was reserving that position for himself, either because he didn't trust his companions' abilities, or because he had always been in the habit of going first. . . .
>
> In short, it was Fritz who had to go first. And with his heavy personality it was natural that he would want to be in the position of making all decisions. Fritz was also brought up in a culture in which no one ever questioned the orders of a higher authority—a far different environment from that of the New England town meeting.

Well, I'm sorry, but this just doesn't cut it for me—even if I ignore that last sneer about Teutonic culture. There have indeed been expeditions on which the leader never intended to go to the summit, choosing instead to stay in the middle of the pack and organize logistics. A good example is the 1953 Everest expedition, whose leader was John Hunt. Hunt designated four other climbers to try for the top—Tom Bourdillon and Charles Evans on the first attempt, Tenzing and Hillary three days later on the second. (On the other hand, by his own admission, Hunt wasn't in the same league with those four as a technical climber.)

But on some of the expeditions I most admire, the man officially in charge of the assault led from the front all the way. In 1950 on Annapurna, Maurice Herzog was always out in front, and in some ways he was also the strongest climber on the French team. In 1938, Charlie Houston led from the front all the way to 26,000 feet on the Abruzzi.

For that matter, David Breashears, the leader of our 1996 IMAX expedition to Everest, had a reputation for being a dictatorial leader. Some people actually said to me beforehand, "How can you work with that guy?" But David was always out front, and he worked harder than anyone else. I knew when he hired me that he expected a lot from me. But if you did your job, you never heard any criticism from David. That's leadership: lead by example, lead from the front, inspire people to follow your lead. That's why, despite the difficulties of our own mission to get the IMAX camera to the top of Everest while filming ourselves, and despite getting caught up in the tragedy that unfolded that May, our expedition was a success. That's why David's *Everest* is still the highest-grossing IMAX film ever made.

In my opinion, a much worse situation develops when the official leader attempts to lead from the rear, watching the climbers through binoculars and ordering their movements over the radio. It's all too easy to sit on your duff at base camp and tell people up high what they should be doing. The one time I had to put up with that sort of nonsense, I felt like radioing back to the leader, "Hey, dude, why don't you get your ass up here and try it yourself?"

Whether or not Wiessner was overbearing and dictatorial toward his teammates, the logistical plan he came up with, although it necessitated a large number of load carries, strikes me as a brilliant one. Every camp was to be equipped with three sleeping bags and air mattresses, as well as stoves and gasoline and plenty of food. As Wiessner explained in 1984, "I believe that if you climb a mountain like this, you want to be sure, if something goes wrong or somebody gets ill, you can hold out for at least two weeks in any camp. If a man had to come down in very bad weather, he ought to be able to just fall into a tent, and everything would be there."

The problem that developed on the 1939 expedition, starting at Camp IV, was due almost entirely, I think, to the physical weakness or psychological faintheartedness of all the "sahibs" except Wiessner and Wolfe. On June 21, Wiessner, Wolfe, Sheldon, and five Sherpa were established at Camp IV, with plenty of food and fuel. Wiessner was looking forward to leading House's Chimney in the morning. Instead, a violent storm arrived in the night. With only a brief lull, the storm lasted through the next eight days.

At Camp II, 2,200 feet lower, Durrance guessed that the peak gusts of wind reached eighty miles an hour. At Camp IV, temperatures as low as minus 2 degrees Fahrenheit were recorded. Even Wiessner was daunted by the conditions. In a 1940 article in *The American Alpine Journal,* he would write, "To describe these days and nights of storm and cold is not within my power. They were terror-inspiring."

It was at this point that George Sheldon seemed to have had his fill of K2. In Camp IV, he suffered frostnip of the toes. When the storm finally broke, on June 29, he descended with three Sherpa, eventually going all the way to base camp. Sheldon would make only one more load carry on the mountain. During the rest of the expedition, he and Wiessner would not see each other again.

Meanwhile, on June 30, after nine days at Camp IV, Wiessner started up House's Chimney. The fixed ropes left by the 1938 party had frozen into the slope, and in any event, Wiessner was not willing to count on them. (Even in a single year's worth of freezing and fraying in the wind, fixed ropes—especially the old hemp ones—become dangerously fragile. I've never completely trusted ropes left on 8,000ers by parties from previous years.)

So Wiessner led the pitch the same way his old partner Bill House had the year before, and it took him two hours (only half an hour less) to gain those critical 80 feet. In *The American Alpine Journal* article, he later saluted his friend's 1938 effort: "I can only commend House for his ability in having originally led up this piece of difficult rock climbing."

On top of the cliff, Wiessner strung a new fixed rope. Then, with the aid of strenuous hauling on the climbing rope, he got both Pasang Kikuli and Dudley Wolfe up the chimney. Wiessner was a slight man, wiry and only five feet six inches tall. Kikuli was also slight, but Wolfe was a big hulk of a fellow, and a clumsy climber to boot, so it must have taken a prodigious effort even for two men to drag him up the nearly vertical cliff. The trio pitched Camp V at 22,000 feet, reusing the platforms built up by the 1938 party. Then they waited out two more days of storm.

In this way, the team started to fragment. Down below, the Dartmouth students, Cranmer and Sheldon, of whom Wiessner had expected great things, had effectively thrown in the towel. Cromwell, whom Wiessner had appointed to the rather nominal role of deputy leader, had been intimidated from the start by the difficulty and the danger of the climbing on the Abruzzi. Now he declared that under no condition would he go above Camp IV. Only Durrance, among the American climbers below Camp V, still had any heart for the ascent. But he had been hampered all along by having to use old, lightweight boots, after a custom-made pair ordered from a Munich store had failed to arrive. When the new boots finally made their surprise appearance, carried up to base camp along with the mail by porters from Askole, Durrance was overjoyed. But thereafter, despite numerous attempts, he found it impossible to acclimatize. Even at only 20,000 feet, he would have to stop and pant desperately, crouched over with his hands on his knees. During the rest of the expedition, he would never climb higher than 600 feet above Camp VI, which was at 23,400 feet, below the Black Pyramid.

On our own K2 expedition in 1992, we had team members who seemed to lose heart for the project after they'd been on the mountain for a month. It's all too easy to let one's initial gung-ho enthusiasm evaporate in the face of storms and setbacks. In its place, a powerful longing to get the hell out of there and head for home takes over. That's why I've always (and especially on K2) psyched myself up beforehand, to the point where I was willing to spend as long as it took on the mountain to get a chance to climb it. By June 30, the 1939 team had been at base camp or above for exactly one month. Already Sheldon, Cranmer, and Cromwell were, it seems, ready to go home, and it would not be long before Durrance was of the same mind.

So the two halves of the party began to separate—a disconnection that would have everything to do with the coming tragedy. Later, Wiessner would be severely criticized for allowing a communications gap to develop between the climbers up high and those waiting below. Some "experts" would fault him for not bringing along radios. But the 1938 team had had no radios, and it would be several years before these de-vices really became practical on mountains like K2.

Kauffman and Putnam admit that in 1939, intercamp radios were both exorbitantly heavy and unreliable. But they react to Wiessner's later state-ment that he had chosen to do without radios "for ideological reasons" with yet another piece of armchair second-guessing: "Should ideology have been allowed to play a dominant role in a life-and-death situation, such as an assault on the world's unclimbed, second-highest, and most formidable mountain?"

The inability or unwillingness of four of the Americans to climb high put a huge amount of pressure on the Sherpa. Not only did they take the brunt of the load hauling, but as the weeks passed, they moved between camps more and more while unaccompanied by any "sahibs." In 1938, as much as Houston trusted Pasang Kikuli, he never let him climb solo between camps. The Sherpa were always paired with at least one of the four leading Americans. Pretty much the same routine had been the norm on all the British Everest expeditions since 1922.

In 1939, the Sherpa also became message carriers. Rather than climb up to a high camp to confer with Wiessner, Durrance, since he was un-able to acclimatize, would write a note to the leader and entrust it to a Sherpa. This sometimes unreliable communication system created its own confusion.

To Wiessner, the responsibility of the climbers lower on the mountain was simple and obvious: get those camps supplied! The whole logistical pyramid depended on a chain of well-stocked camps leading all the way up the Abruzzi Ridge to the Shoulder. That makes perfect sense to me, and I know that if I'd been in Durrance or Cromwell's shoes, I'd have done my damnedest to get those loads up the mountain. If that's the agreed-upon plan, you stick to it. But Kauffman and Putnam, as well as other critics, fault Wiessner at this point for not giving clear orders to the troops in the rear.

What else could Wiessner have done? If he hadn't been out front pushing the route, nobody would have done it. Sheldon and Cranmer were out of action; Cromwell refused to go above Camp IV; Durrance could not adjust to the altitude; and Wolfe, though game and strong, didn't have the skill or nerve to lead.

As they researched *K2: The 1939 Tragedy,* Kauffman and Putnam won the trust of Jack Durrance, who was eighty years old by the time the book was published. And they made a great breakthrough when Durrance let them read and quote from his 1939 diary—a privilege he had granted to no previous journalist. Those diary entries add a wealth of new information about the expedition, and Kauffman and Putnam's use of them goes a long way toward exonerating Durrance from his role as the villain of the 1939 K2 saga, a view some of Wiessner's defenders (and Wiessner himself) long held.

Yet in many ways, Durrance's diary only deepens the mystery of what went wrong on the mountain. Its passages, which vacillate between hopefulness and despair, between enthusiasm and misery, do not neatly support any of the latter-day theories about what caused the tragedy. One thing the diary does document, however, is just how disheartened and homesick the four rearguard Americans had become even before the end of June. On June 26, Durrance wrote, "The most discussed topic is what we shall do when once again in civilization—a week's stay in Srinagar—sightseeing in India (Taj Mahal, etc.)." As Kauffman and Putnam acknowledge, at this relatively early stage of the assault, with the scheduled return of the porters from Askole still almost a month in the future, "Eyes turned away from the hardships of K2 and toward the comforts of home."

There's a term some mountaineers use for this phenomenon. It's called "crumping." To *crump* is to let the hardship and danger of expedition life drain you of all your mountaineering ambitions, so that all you want to do is get the hell out of there. (It's not a piece of jargon I grew up hearing, but after a climbing friend defined it for me, I thought it was pretty appropriate.) By the end of June, the four Americans lower on the mountain had crumped. It happens a lot on expeditions. And after crump sets in, you've psychologically thrown in the towel: you care only about going home, and you'll make up all kinds of excuses as to why it makes sense to hike out early.

Meanwhile, Wiessner, Wolfe, and the best Sherpa were pushing hard to establish higher camps. On July 5, carrying heavy loads, Wiessner, Pasang Kikuli, and Tse Tendrup placed Camp VI at 23,400 feet. The next day, Wiessner smoothly led up through the Black Pyramid to 24,500 feet, only a 900-foot traverse away from the slope where the 1938 team had pitched their highest camp.

As impressive as Wiessner's leading virtually every foot of the route was another of his achievements. After June 21, when he had established Camp IV just below House's Chimney, except for one very quick trip down to Camp II and back up, Wiessner would spend twenty-four straight days at or above 21,500 feet. Most climbers would simply fall apart under such a regimen—we all need to descend regularly on 8,000ers to recuperate at base camp or slightly higher. The longest continuous stretch I've ever spent above 21,500 feet was ten days on the north side of Everest. But Wiessner just seemed to get stronger as he moved higher on K2.

Dudley Wolfe's performance surprised almost everyone. He was a clumsy enough climber that both Cromwell and Durrance expressed their doubts as to whether he belonged on the mountain at all. But when paired with Wiessner, Wolfe kept chugging upward. He had none of the problems acclimatizing that so afflicted Durrance, and up high, he seemed to have none of the fears that had made Cromwell vow never to go above Camp IV. Storms and cold fazed him very little. Wiessner would later characterize Wolfe as "the most loyal of my comrades."

While Wiessner had been pushing the route up to 24,500 feet on July 5 and 6, Wolfe had rested in Camp V. Expecting his teammates to arrive from below with loads to equip the higher camps, he was first puzzled, then annoyed when no one showed up. On each of three consecutive days, Wolfe climbed down to the top of House's Chimney and called out to Camp IV, only a few hundred feet below. No answer came. Where *was* the rest of the team?

On July 10, Wiessner took matters into his own hands. Leaving Wolfe and the Sherpa who had carried loads up high in Camp V, he dashed solo all the way down to Camp II—yet another herculean effort. Rallying his troops and the rest of the Sherpa, Wiessner got the supply train moving once more. Two days later, Durrance made his best effort to go high. With Wolfe, Wiessner, and two Sherpa, he struggled all the way up to Camp VI, but only 200 feet above the tents, he collapsed. With fixed ropes in place, it was a simple matter for him to slide back to Camp VI while the others forged ahead. As Durrance and Wiessner parted, the leader assumed his teammate would wait at Camp VI for more supplies, try to recuperate, and eventually push higher.

Despite Durrance's continued problems with the altitude, Wiessner still considered him the most skilled of his teammates, and hoped the two would reach the summit together. Only gradually did he shift his plans and substitute Wolfe for Durrance in the summit party. But the third climber going for the top would be Pasang Kikuli, whose talent, experience, and courage Wiessner deeply admired. Had Wiessner climbed K2 with a Sherpa, it would have set a glorious example, one not realized until 1953 on Everest, when John Hunt, recognizing Tenzing Norgay's vast experience and bold ambition, paired him with Hillary for the May 29 assault.

On July 14, Wiessner led four men—Wolfe, Tse Tendrup, Pasang Kitar, and Pasang Lama—all the way up to 25,300 feet, where they established Camp VIII. The going was very hard, as Wiessner broke trail through knee-deep snow covered with an icy crust, but as usual, he stayed in the lead the whole day. At last the team had solved the Abruzzi Ridge and reached the lower edge of the Shoulder. Wiessner planned to place one more camp at the upper end of the Shoulder, at or above 26,000 feet, and go from there for the top. After so many stormy spells, the good weather was holding splendidly.

Thus the stage was set for one of the most astounding performances in the history of mountaineering—and for the all-but-inexplicable disaster into which it would evolve.

———

Sadly, Pasang Kikuli was no longer at the front. On the push to Camp VII on July 12, he had suffered a recurrence of the frostbite that had first afflicted him on Nanga Parbat five years earlier. That evening, he stayed in Camp VI with the exhausted Durrance.

Having reached the lower edge of the Shoulder and set up Camp VIII on July 14, Wiessner sent Tse Tendrup and Pasang Kitar back down to Camp VII, where the team had already stockpiled "eleven loads of supplies." Staying at Camp VIII were Wiessner, Wolfe, and Pasang Lama—after Kikuli, the strongest Sherpa on the mountain. There followed two days of light snow as the men rested. Then the weather turned fine again. On July 17, the three men set out carrying a tent, their sleeping bags and air mattresses, and food and fuel for seven days. Their goal was to establish a last camp at the upper end of the Shoulder, then launch the summit bid from there.

The going was agonizing, thanks to two days' worth of new, soft snow that had piled up on the Shoulder. As he led, Wiessner sank into the powdery stuff up to his hips. Only 250 feet out of camp, the trio approached a *bergschrund*—a crevasse where the rocky core of the mountain is separated from the glacial mass that lies on top of it. Here the slope steepened, and though the crevasse itself was crossable on a snow bridge, the texture of the snow grew even softer and less stable. The snow bridge covered a gap of only twenty vertical feet, but it would take all the strength and skill Wiessner had to tame it. He would write in 1956:

> After two hours of the hardest conceivable work I succeeded, almost by swimming, in getting up across the snow-bridge and then treading out a belaying stance on the steep slope above the bridge. . . . Pasang Lama followed in my trench but almost disappeared in the snow before he reached me; he too needed an

hour. Now came Wolfe, by far the heaviest of us three. He was not able to master this place and suggested that he return to Camp VIII, only 100 steps away, and follow us with one or more of the supporting party the next day, when the tracks would have become firmer.

As Wolfe returned to Camp VIII, the other two men continued above, always with Wiessner breaking trail. Worn out from floundering in the deep snow, the pair pitched a temporary camp at 25,700 feet. The next day they pushed on. Wiessner had taken careful note of the "great ice cliff" that hangs over the Bottleneck couloir and the Shoulder, and he did not like the looks of it. On July 18, he and Pasang Lama crossed a field of scattered ice blocks—avalanche debris that had fallen from the cliff, the very same serac that would collapse in 2008. So Wiessner angled upward toward the left, leaving the Shoulder as he headed toward a band of rock cliffs, out of the line of fire of what I would later call the Motivator. By late that afternoon, the two men had pitched their tent on a solid snow platform, protected by the rock bands above. By Wiessner's estimate, they were at 26,050 feet. The camp was even a little bit higher than our Camp IV in 1992. Wrote Wiessner later, "The view from this spot was inconceivably magnificent."

By now, he was confident of success. On July 12, when Durrance had turned back to Camp VI, he and Wiessner had explicitly discussed their plans for the following days. There was no communications gap. As Wiessner later summarized the plan, "On July 14 Durrance was to attempt to climb to Camp VII with four Sherpas and if possible join us again higher up; in case he should not feel well he had only to send the Sherpas on up." The agreement between Wiessner and Pasang Kikuli was equally clear. Since the best Sherpa could no longer hope to reach the summit, "his wish now was only to oversee the final support operations between Camps VI and VII."

At Camp IX, 2,200 feet below the summit, Wiessner and Lama had six days of food and plenty of fuel. Beneath him on the mountain, Wiessner assumed, was a continuous string of well-stocked camps, the logistical pyramid he had designed from the start.

But things had not gone quite as planned. Still suffering miserably from the altitude at Camp VI, Durrance had decided to go down on July 14. And for some reason, he took Pasang Kikuli with him, as well as the other three Sherpa who were supposed to make critical carries to stock up the camps above. In the end, Durrance and Kikuli descended past Camp IV and all the way down to Camp II. The only concession to Wiessner's plan came at Camp IV, where Durrance dropped off two of the Sherpa with instructions to ferry loads higher during the following days.

Durrance's diary fails to explain why he took Kikuli down with him. Kauffman and Putnam interpret the action as springing from concern over Kikuli's frostbite. But if so, why take the other Sherpa down as well? Even in his demoralized condition, Durrance must have realized that his precipitous descent with four Sherpa was sabotaging Wiessner's plan.

Why did Kikuli accede to Durrance's request? Wiessner drily wrote years later, "He was unhappy not to be given this job as planned." "This job" was to stay at Camp VI and superintend the ferrying of loads higher on the mountain. Even though Kikuli was vastly more experienced than Durrance, the latter was still a "sahib"—and Sherpa took orders from sahibs even when they disagreed with them. But the best explanation for Kikuli's heading down is that Durrance was by now in such bad shape that the Sherpa may have doubted whether he could make the trip by himself. Kauffman and Putnam partially agree: "Dawa [Thondup] and Kikuli, the latter with what appeared to be serious frostbite of his toes, because of which he could not stay high, had almost carried [Durrance] down the 2200 feet from Camp IV."

At Camp II, Durrance found, in Kauffman and Putnam's words, "three beaten men surrounded by unwashed pots and pans filled with the remnants of a 'horrible stew concoction.' . . . Rather than touch it, Jack threw it all out." One of the three was Tony Cromwell, the by now almost useless "deputy leader."

K2 from Windy Gap—
the 1909 photo, shot
by the Duke of the
Abruzzi, inspired
several generations
of mountaineers to
attempt the peak.

Vittorio Sella's classic
view of K2 from the
Godwin-Austen glacier,
taken in 1909. © Vittorio
Sella, Fritz Wiessner
Collection

Charles Houston, leader of the 1938 and 1953 American expeditions to K2. © Charles Houston, expedition photograph

Bob Bates crosses the Braldu River on a rope bridge near Askole, 1938. © Charles Houston, expedition photograph

The ice traverse just below Camp VII, 1938. © Charles Houston, expedition photograph

Fritz Wiessner, leader of the 1939 American K2 expedition. © Fritz Wiessner Collection

Pasang Kikuli climbing toward Camp V, 1939. © Fritz Wiessner Collection

BELOW: Pasang Kikuli at Camp VI, 1939. © Fritz Wiessner Collection

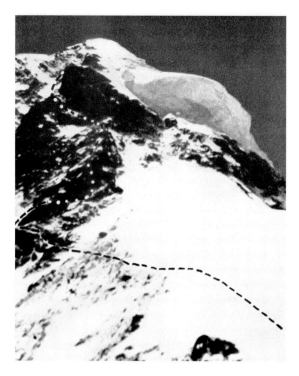

The route led by
Fritz Wiessner on his
astounding first attempt
on the summit pyramid
in 1939. © Fritz Wiessner
Collection

One of the most
remarkable photos in
climbing history.
Carrying a huge pack,
Pasang Lama uses a
shoulder belay to
secure Wiessner on the
steep and difficult
rock-and-ice band at
27,000 feet, 1939.
© Fritz Wiessner Collection

ABOVE: Team members and Baltis cross the Braldu River on a zok, a raft made of inflated goatskin bladders covered with a framework of poplar poles, 1953. © Charles Houston, expedition photograph

Hauling loads up House's Chimney with Pete Schoening's A-frame tripod, 1953. © Charles Houston, expedition photograph

Tony Streather digs out Camp III after a storm, 1953. © Charles Houston, expedition photograph

BELOW: Walter Bonatti, hero and martyr of the 1954 Italian K2 expedition. © Walter Bonatti Collection

The telltale photo of Lino Lacedelli on K2's summit, showing the circle of ice particles in the climber's mustache and beard, evidence that he wore his oxygen mask all the way to the top, 1954. © Fritz Wiessner Collection

A composite photo of Lacedelli and Compagnoni's signatures with their route to Camp IX and the summit, 1954. © Fritz Wiessner Collection

At Camp IX, of course, Wiessner was unaware of this breakdown lower on the mountain. On July 19, he and Pasang Lama set out at 9:00 A.M., determined to get to the summit. By today's standards, that's pretty late, but in the 1920s and '30s, nobody realized that the traditional "Alpine start"—getting off in the wee hours to take advantage of every daylight minute and of the predictably better weather in the morning, a practice regularly observed in the Alps, the Tetons, and the Rockies—might also make sense in the Himalaya and the Karakoram. And given the primitive clothing of the day—sweaters instead of down jackets, wool knickers instead of down pants, single leather boots—an Alpine start on a peak like K2 probably seemed too cold to contemplate. On Everest in both 1922 and 1924, no climber ever got started from a high camp earlier than 6:30 A.M.

Rather than traverse over to what would later be called the Bottleneck, menaced from above by that huge hanging serac, Wiessner at once tackled the rock cliffs. The amount of gear the two men carried puts our modern lightweight summit attempts to shame. Wiessner hefted a rucksack packed with pitons, carabiners, food, and extra clothing. Pasang Lama carried both men's pairs of crampons as well as a sturdy "reserve rope," three-eighths of an inch in diameter and an unimaginable 245 feet in length. The pair tied in with a 115-foot hemp rope that was a solid half inch in diameter—much thicker and heavier than any rope we would use today.

In light of what happened in August 2008, Wiessner's avoidance of the Bottleneck looks like pretty canny mountaineering judgment. I suspect, though, that he was simply a lot more comfortable on rock than on snow and ice. As a teenager in Dresden, Wiessner had been part of a gang that put up what at the time were the hardest pure rock climbs in the world (though it would be decades before those men knew it). In the 1920s in the Alps, Wiessner's two great first ascents, on the Fleischbank and the Furchetta, involved much more rock climbing than ice work. On the other hand, Mount Waddington, in British Columbia, of which Wiessner and Bill House made the first ascent in 1936, is a heavily glaciated mountain, some of whose hardest pitches are on "mixed ground"—rock interspersed with ice.

Even so, Wiessner evidently underestimated the difficulty of those rock bands. No one since 1939 has ever climbed them again, so it is impossible to give them an objective rating of difficulty. For nine hours, Wiessner climbed the rock bands, hammering in pitons as he went. Lama belayed him on every pitch. In succession, Wiessner mastered a short couloir of black ice, a short overhang of iced-up rock, and many rope lengths of shattered, friable rock, much of it covered with a treacherous skin of ice called verglas. In the face of several unclimbable obstacles he backed off, traversing right or left to find the way. The climbing was so difficult that Wiessner often had to take off his mittens to seize holds bare-handed; but the air was so calm and the temperature warm enough that he didn't risk frostbite.

Some of the pitches Wiessner later rated as sixth class—as hard as anything that had yet been done in the Alps. All this above 26,000 feet, without bottled oxygen! The climbing on those rock bands was harder by far than anything yet attempted on Everest, Kangchenjunga, or Nanga Parbat. It was harder by far than House's Chimney or the Black Pyramid. It's not easy to judge other people's climbs, but I'd venture to say that nothing of comparable difficulty at such an altitude would be performed by anybody during the next nineteen years, until Walter Bonatti and Carlo Mauri's brilliant first ascent of Gasherbrum IV in 1958.

At 6:30 P.M., with the sun nearing the horizon, Wiessner faced only an easy 25-foot traverse to the summit snowfield. He had reached 27,500 feet, only 750 feet below the summit. The snowfield promised relatively nontechnical climbing. K2 was in the bag.

But as he started to move on, Wiessner felt the rope come tight. He looked down. Pasang Lama smiled almost apologetically. "No, sahib, tomorrow," he said. As a Buddhist lama, Pasang believed that evil spirits hovered about the summit of K2 at night.

For a few moments, Wiessner contemplated unroping and going for the top solo. None of the highest mountains in the world had ever been climbed solo, let alone on a push through the night. But the weather was holding perfect, and a nearly full moon would illuminate the darkness.

Yet he could not abandon his partner. With a heavy heart, Wiessner turned back. He knew, however, that he and Lama had enough gear and food at Camp IX to make a second attempt the next day or the day after. As he had climbed the rock bands, Wiessner had studied the couloir and the ice cliff to the right. The Bottleneck (as it would later be named) now looked well within his capabilities, and the hanging serac seemed more stable than he had initially thought. On the next try, Wiessner would tackle that route, almost all of which was on snow and ice. It was bound to be easier than the 1,500 feet of mixed ground and rock cliffs he had so expertly solved on this first attempt.

Slowly, as night fell, the men rappeled down the complicated route, using pitons Wiessner pounded into the rock for anchors. "Many times during that descent," he later wrote, "I regretted intensely that I had not insisted on continuing over that last traverse."

Wiessner's admirers over the years have argued that if anybody could have pushed on to the summit, reached it after dark, and descended by moonlight, it would have been he. But I disagree. If Wiessner had gone on with Pasang Lama, I think it could very well have turned into another Mallory and Irvine—two incredibly bold and determined climbers vanishing in the mists. If Wiessner had gone on alone, I don't think he would have survived. And left alone on a small ledge at 27,500 feet, unable to descend on his own, Pasang Lama would surely have frozen to death. In turning back, Wiessner made the right decision. And in refusing to abandon his partner, he did the morally responsible thing. I admire him more for that than if he had reached the summit.

Even in the gathering night, the conditions were remarkably benign. It was windless, and at 27,000 feet Wiessner estimated the temperature to be between 23 and 27 degrees Fahrenheit. But the descent was difficult, requiring numerous rappels. (Although Wiessner never explained how the two men negotiated the terrain on the way down, I imagine that their very long "reserve rope" came in handy.) Pasang Lama was far less experienced at this sort of thing than Wiessner, and both men must have been pretty tired. As the Sherpa rappelled down an overhang, the rope running across his back got snagged on the crampons he carried strapped to the outside of his pack. With a furious effort, Lama disentangled the rope, but in the process he dislodged both pairs of crampons. Wiessner watched in dismay as these precious pieces of footgear tumbled into the void. That fluke mishap would make a huge difference during the following days.

The two men reached Camp IX at 2:30 A.M. They had been going for almost eighteen hours straight. To have descended 1,500 feet of difficult ground in the dark without an accident was an extraordinary achievement in its own right.

Wiessner and Lama slept late and took a rest day on July 20. The two men were mildly disappointed that none of the support party had arrived at Camp IX, but Wiessner did not yet suspect any serious disruption of his logistical pyramid. It was so warm in camp that for hours, Wiessner lay naked on top of his sleeping bag, taking what he quaintly called a "sun bath." Unfazed by his setback on July 19, he was eager to make a second attempt the following day. In his 1956 account, Wiessner implied that Lama was equally psyched: "At three o'clock we felt fresh again, so that we decided to go to the summit the next day by the easterly route. I had no doubt of our success." But only two paragraphs later he confessed, "Since the day before [Pasang Lama] had no longer been his old self; he had been living in great fear of the evil spirits, constantly murmuring prayers, and had lost his appetite."

On July 21, the two men got off at 6:00 A.M., a much better start than they had managed two days earlier. Nowadays nearly everyone pitches a Camp IV somewhere directly on the Shoulder. From there the approach to the Bottleneck is a straightforward matter of climbing up the gradually steepening slope. From Wiessner's Camp IX, however, a tricky rightward traverse across the base of the rock bands was the first order of business. If a pair of men are climbing straight up, the leader can safely belay the second simply by taking in the rope. On a traverse, belaying is a much more delicate task. If Lama, coming second, had fallen off, he would have taken a wicked pendulum before the rope came tight to Wiessner. So, as he led, Wiessner had to place pitons at the more difficult moves simply to shorten the length of a potential fall for Pasang Lama. The traverse took a long time, and Wiessner described it in his diary as "disagreeable," "difficult," and "treacherous."

It was still morning, however, when the two men reached the bottom of the Bottleneck. The snow here was so hard-crusted that Wiessner could not kick steps in it. All at once the significance of the loss of the crampons came home to him. As he later wrote, "With crampons, we could have practically run up [the couloir], but as it was we would have had to cut 300 or 400 steps. At these heights that would have taken more than a day." Recognizing the futility of the task, Wiessner and the loyal Sherpa turned back to Camp IX once more.

When they arrived at the tent to find that still no teammates had come up, Wiessner began at last to suspect that something had gone wrong. Even so, he felt that there was still a good chance of climbing K2. Among the supplies being ferried up the mountain were spare pairs of crampons. And the weather was holding perfect.

On July 22, the two men headed down to Camp VIII. Wiessner's plan was to pick up more food and gas and the all-important extra crampons, then return to Camp IX. If no crampons had arrived, Wiessner reasoned, he could borrow Wolfe's to lead the hard pitches up high, then drag his partner up on a tight rope.

Pasang Lama had had enough of the climb, however, and begged to be replaced in the summit team by someone else. Wiessner thought that Wolfe ought to be equal to the task, or perhaps even Jack Durrance, if he had at last overcome his altitude problems. Weissner was so certain of his return to Camp IX that he left his sleeping bag there, while Lama carried his own down. Here the wisdom of Wiessner's logistical scheme seemed to pay its dividends in flexibility. On most Himalayan expeditions to that date, each climber had carried his own single sleeping bag up and down the mountain. But by insisting on stocking each camp with sleeping bags,

Wiessner made it possible, in theory, for the men to shuttle between camps at will with only light loads.

On the steeper slopes above Camp VIII, the loss of the crampons again exacted its toll, for here Pasang Lama took a fall. Wiessner described the accident in 1984:

> Pasang was behind me. I should have had him in front, but then I would have had to explain to him how to cut steps. I had just got my axe ready to make a few scrapes, when suddenly he fell off. I noticed immediately, because he made a funny little noise. I put myself in position, dug in as much as possible, and held him on the rope. If I hadn't been in good shape, hadn't climbed all those 4000-meter peaks in the Alps, I wouldn't have had the technique to hold him.

This account makes Wiessner's belay sound almost routine, but it was a remarkable feat. Even though they were roped close together, Lama fell, out of control, down to his partner's level and an equal distance beyond before the rope came tight with a sudden jolt. Many pairs of climbers the world over have been swept to their deaths in just such an accident.

Arriving at Camp VIII, Wiessner received a bad shock: no one had come up from below. Only Dudley Wolfe was there. The man was overjoyed to see Wiessner but was furious at his laggard teammates lower on the mountain. "Those bastards haven't come yet," he said. Wolfe had run out of matches two days before, and the only water he had drunk was a small pool of snowmelt that he had gathered on a fold of the tent.

"I cannot understand," Wiessner wrote in his diary, "why our Sherpas, [who] had definitely promised to stock up Camp VIII, had not come. I also wondered where was Jack."

Despite a growing sense of alarm, Wiessner was still optimistic. Camp VII, a mere 600 feet lower, had been bountifully stocked even before the team of five had pushed on to establish Camp VIII on July 14. Surely at

Camp VII the men could pick up food and fuel and spare crampons, then head back to Camp IX for yet another summit bid.

After cooking a hot lunch and "celebrat[ing] our reunion," as Wiessner later put it, the three men headed down. Wolfe carried his sleeping bag with him, as did Pasang Lama. For the first time in days, a light fog had crept in. At first, the trio roped up, with Lama going first, Wolfe in the middle, and Wiessner taking up the rear. On a descent of moderate terrain, it was standard practice for the most experienced man to come last, so that he could belay a partner who might slip. But in the fog, Lama kept losing his way, veering too far to the east. (This was exactly what Scott had tended to do as he led our three-man rope down from the summit in 1992.) So Wiessner switched the order, putting himself in the lead and Lama in the rear.

It was here that Wolfe's clumsiness nearly cost all three men their lives. As Wiessner paused in a precarious position, leaning forward to chop a step below his feet, Wolfe accidentally stepped on the rope. The sudden jerk pulled Wiessner off his stance, and he started sliding down the steep slope.

In 1984, Wiessner gave a vivid account of this near catastrophe:

> I immediately called back, "Check me! Check me!" Nothing happened. Then the rope came tight to Dudley, and he was pulled off. The rope tightened to Pasang behind, and he too came off. We were all three sliding down, and I got going very fast and somersaulted.
>
> I had no fear. All I was thinking was, how stupid this has to happen like this. Here we are, we can still do the mountain, and we have to lose out in this silly way and get killed forever. . . .
>
> But getting pulled around by the somersault and being first on the rope, it gave me a little time. I still had my ice axe—I always keep a sling around my wrist—and just in that moment the snow got a little softer. I had my axe ready and worked very hard with it. With my left hand I got hold of the rope, and eventually

I got a stance, kicked in quickly, and leaned against the axe. Then, bang! A fantastic pull came. I was holding it well, but it tore me down. But at that time I was a fantastically strong man— if I had a third of it today I would be very happy. I stood there and I wanted to stop that thing. I must have done everything right, and the luck was there, too.

In the K2 annals—or, for that matter in the history of climbing in the Himalaya or the Karakoram—only Pete Schoening's "miracle belay" in 1953 is more legendary than Wiessner's self-arrest, which saved himself and his two teammates. I'd managed a similar self-arrest in 1992, after Scott got avalanched off and pulled me with him. That was tough enough, but there were only two of us on the rope, not three. And as big as he was, Scott was not as heavy as Dudley Wolfe.

As they approached Camp VII, the shaken men called down to the comrades they presumed were there, but they got no answer. It was dark by the time they arrived. And here the shock became incomprehensible.

Not only were there no teammates installed in Camp VII; the tents sagged, with their doors open. One was full of snow, the other half-collapsed. All the sleeping bags and air mattresses were gone. What was left of the food had been scattered wantonly in the snow outside the tents. It was as if the camp had been attacked by vandals. Wrote Wiessner in his diary, "What had been going on during the days when we were high—sabotage? We could not understand."

Stunned and exhausted, the men cleaned out one tent, repitched it, and crawled inside. In the fall coming down from Camp VIII, Wolfe had lost his sleeping bag. That night the three men shared Pasang Lama's single bag and air mattress. They endured a sleepless vigil that, as Wiessner wrote seventeen years later, "we shall never forget."

It is a testament to Wiessner's indomitable spirit that even after that wretched night, he still planned to go back up the mountain and make a third summit attempt. Surely there would be food and sleeping bags at Camp VI, and Wiessner calculated that there should be at least six Sherpa there as well. In the morning Pasang Lama and Wiessner got ready to go. Wolfe had decided to stay at Camp VII. Wiessner later explained the trio's rationale:

> With only one sleeping-bag we could not stay here in Camp VII, so we decided to go to Camp VI and fetch sleeping-bags from there. One of us, to be sure, could remain up here with Pasang's sleeping-bag, get a rest, and so spare himself the trip down and up. Wolfe suggested that he stay, to recover from the unpleasant night and be in better shape to take a load to Camp VIII the day after tomorrow. As leader of the expedition I, myself, had to go down to Camp VI to get the support operations going again and find the explanation of the unheard-of occurrences. Pasang was to be relieved.

Later, Wiessner's harshest critics would accuse him of abandoning Dudley Wolfe. Even Kauffman and Putnam, looking back from their vantage point of fifty-three years of hindsight, castigate Wiessner on this question:

> The decision now made was to be the major cause of the ensuing tragedy. Fritz split his small party. . . .
>
> A cardinal rule of mountaineering, observed, certainly until recent years, is that under no circumstances does one split a small party if one has any reason to suspect trouble ahead. . . .
>
> Surely this was a time when three ambulatory men should have stuck together rather than separate. Indeed, if by some miracle, all was well below, say at Camp VI, three backs were surely better than two or one to help haul up fresh supplies. . . .
>
> Was this the decision of a leader fully in command of his faculties?

I don't know where Kauffman and Putnam got their "cardinal rules of mountaineering," but this analysis, like their theory that the expedition leader should not be the same person as the "point man," seems cockeyed.

If Wolfe was too tired to push farther down the mountain on July 23, what was Wiessner supposed to do? Sit and wait at Camp VII—three men with a single sleeping bag and air mattress—for help that would never come? Order Wolfe to descend, no matter how wiped out he was? Far from abandoning his teammate, Wiessner tried to spare him a further ordeal. It did not seem possible that Camp VI could have been destroyed as Camp VII had been. To me, what Wiessner did seems perfectly logical.

Wiessner and Lama did not depart until 11:00 A.M. on the July 23. And 700 feet lower, the inconceivable became reality. Not only were there no Sherpa in Camp VI, but the two tents had been taken down and folded up. Some gasoline and a little bit of food were cached there, but the sleeping bags and air mattresses were gone.

"Our situation now became very serious," Wiessner later wrote. The two men had no choice but to continue the descent. At Camps V and IV, still no sleeping bags. The Camp III depot was empty. At nightfall, Wiessner and Lama reached Camp II, which ought to have been the best-provisioned on the mountain. No sleeping bags! Utterly worn out, the two men took down one tent and wrapped themselves up in it while they tried to sleep in the other. Their fingers and toes got frost-nipped, and for the second night in a row, they got no sleep.

In the morning, Wiessner and Pasang Lama staggered down the lower slopes of the Abruzzi Ridge and at last emerged on the Godwin Austen Glacier. Base camp was still several miles away. Wiessner later wrote, "For the last kilometers on the nearly level glacier we could only just drag ourselves along, and often we fell to the ground." Finally, with base camp almost in sight, they saw four tiny figures in the distance—teammates at last. Slowly the gap between those figures and the two utterly spent climbers closed.

This is the great mystery. Why were the tents stripped? While Wiessner, Pasang Lama, and Dudley Wolfe were pushing hard for the summit, what was going on below Camp VIII? What had happened to the other four Americans, and to the rest of the Sherpa?

As the figures on the glacier drew near, Wiessner recognized Tony Cromwell and three Sherpa. The first thing Cromwell said was "Thank God you're alive!"

By now, with his throat desperately sore from breathing thin, cold air, Wiessner had lost his voice, a condition that would last for weeks. But in a rasping whisper, he summoned up his fury: "What is the idea?"

Wiessner later recalled his deputy leader's explanation: "He told us they had given us up for dead. He was just out looking for any sign of anything on the glacier. I said, 'This is really an outrage. Wolfe will sue you for your neglect.'"

In silence, the six men plodded the short distance to base camp. According to Wiessner,

> The cook and the liaison officer came out and embraced me and took me to my tent. Pasang Kikuli and all the Sherpas came and embraced me. But Durrance didn't come for about half an hour.
>
> When he did, I said immediately, "What happened to our supplies? Who took all the sleeping bags down? And why were they taken down?"
>
> Durrance said, "Well, the Sherpas. . . ." It was blamed on the Sherpas.

Wiessner was surprised to discover that the two Dartmouth boys, George Sheldon and Chappell Cranmer, were nowhere to be seen. It turned out that they had left base camp on July 18. After seven weeks on the Godwin Austen Glacier, they were so fed up with the expedition—or simply overwhelmed by K2's challenges—that they did not even bother to hang around to find out what was happening with their three teammates high on the mountain. The pretext for their early departure: a geology side trip back to Urdukas, the pleasant oasis off the side of the lower Baltoro Glacier! Apparently Cromwell had given the young men his benediction to take off.

The porters from Askole had arrived on schedule on July 23. Now they were lingering around base camp, eager to go home. In retrospect, this state of affairs is surprising. Although Askole was a seven-day march from base camp for heavily laden porters, the team had had intermittent contact with that last outpost of civilization. On June 28, for instance, porters had arrived with the mail and Durrance's custom-made boots. As the July 23 deadline approached, with the ascent of the mountain still very much in progress, it ought to have been possible for Cromwell to send a messenger to Askole, delaying the arrival of the porters. After all, in 1938, the cook and one Sherpa had dashed down to that village in only three days, as they organized the team's firewood-gathering mission.

In 1992, we waited until we were finally down the mountain before we ordered our porters. We did not want to risk having them arrive before we were sure that our entire team was done with its attempt. Once the porters return to base camp, the expedition is effectively over. That meant we had to hang around on the Godwin Austen Glacier longer than we might have liked—by the end of August, even I was ready to go home.

The obvious explanation for Cromwell's allowing the porters to show up while three men were still high on K2 is that all the "sahibs" except Wiessner and Wolfe were desperate to get the hell out of there. "Crump" had set in with a vengeance. Cranmer and Sheldon had not even bothered to wait for the porters, they were so eager to leave base camp. It's a scary thought, but you can't help wondering whether Cromwell, having given up for dead the three men high on the mountain, might have pulled the plug on the whole expedition and started hiking out even before Wiessner and Pasang Lama got down to base camp, if he had returned empty-handed from his July 24 search of the glacier for signs of the missing men. Wiessner believed that to be the case. In 1956, with wry irony, he wrote, "At Base Camp, in the firm conviction that Wolfe, Pasang and I had perished, it had been decided to begin the march out on July 25.

This plan had to be altered somewhat when Pasang Lama and I dragged ourselves into camp."

Something very similar to this happened on the 1963 American Everest expedition. The goal of team leader Norman Dyhrenfurth, and of most of the climbers in the nineteen-man party, was simply to make the first American ascent of the world's highest mountain. (In that sense, the '63 campaign was a holdover from the 1950s era of massive nationalistic expeditions.) That goal was accomplished on May 1, when Jim Whittaker topped out with Sherpa Nawang Gombu. Meanwhile, a small contingent made up of the best technical climbers on the team set out to put up a new route on Everest's west ridge. Dyhrenfurth relegated this splinter group to second-class status, directing all the team's logistics and support to the effort on the traditional South Col route. The west ridge group had to bide their time and haul their own loads until Whittaker and Gombu had succeeded. But by then, Dyhrenfurth and most of the climbers on the South Col route were ready to go home.

This rather nasty impasse came to a head on May 9 in a radio exchange between Tom Hornbein, installed high on the west ridge, and Barry Prather at base camp, who spoke for Dyhrenfurth because the leader had developed severe laryngitis. In his classic narrative, *Everest: The West Ridge,* Hornbein replays that exchange verbatim (it had been tape-recorded for use in the expedition's documentary film):

> *Prather:* The porters are coming in on the 21st and we're leaving Base Camp on the 22nd. Over. . . .
> *Hornbein:* O.K., we realize time is running out but we envisioned that there were a few more days beyond the 20th or 21st so far as summit attempts by our route are concerned. . . . How do you read that? Over.
> *Prather:* Only comment is, there are 300 porters coming in here on the 21st. Over.
> *Hornbein:* Well, I guess we'll see you in Kathmandu then.

In the end, Dyhrenfurth relented and supported the west ridge party. On May 22, Hornbein and Willi Unsoeld finished the route, traversed over the summit, survived a desperate bivouac above 28,000 feet, and accomplished a far more impressive deed than the third ascent of Everest by the same route that Hillary and Tenzing had pioneered a decade before. The stellar British climber Doug Scott later called the Unsoeld-Hornbein climb the greatest single feat in Everest history.

At base camp, Wiessner learned for the first time that Durrance, rather than staying on at Camp VI, had descended all the way to Camp II on July 14, taking Pasang Kikuli with him. After that date, on only a single day had any of the four Americans supposedly composing the support team gone higher than Camp II, at only 19,300 feet. Instead, four Sherpa were the only climbers stationed between Durrance and the trio pushing up high from Camp VIII to Camp IX. During the light two-day storm on July 15 and 16, Tse Tendrup and Pasang Kitar had waited at Camp VII. Having descended to IV with Durrance and Kikuli on July 14, Tsering and Phinsoo had then climbed back up to Camp VI to support the lead climbers.

What happened next is an integral part of the mystery. In Kauffman and Putnam's analysis, "The Sherpas' instructions, first from Fritz and then from Jack, were to continue to ferry supplies whenever possible, first to Camp VII and then onward to Camp VIII. They did nothing of the kind; perhaps they had not understood."

The only source for the doings of these four Sherpa between July 15 and 23 is the discussions they had with the Americans at base camp after July 24. Most of the Sherpa spoke Hindustani but not English, so much of the dialogue had to be translated by Chandra, an Indian schoolteacher who had joined the expedition and the only man conversant in both tongues. Misunderstandings must have been rife, and afterward there would be no way of independently checking the Sherpa testimony.

Even Wiessner, who was dumbfounded by the stripping of the camps, eventually accepted the explanation that emerged from the base camp dialogue. He would write in 1956,

On July 17 [Tse] Tendrup and [Pasang] Kitar, who had waited in Camp VII for better weather, came down to [VI], instead of carrying more loads to Camp VII, as I had arranged. As reason for this change in plan Tendrup alleged that Wolfe, Pasang Lama, and I had undoubtedly perished at Camp VIII in an avalanche. P[h]insoo and Tsering, however, were not convinced by this invented story of an avalanche and stayed on in Camp VI.

Descending farther, all the way to Camp IV, the next day, Tendrup and Kitar met Durrance and Kikuli, who were coming up the mountain. Indignant at their defection, Kikuli ordered the two Sherpa to return to the high camps.

Thereupon they climbed back to Camp VI, where P[h]insoo and Tsering were still staying, and on July 19 to Camp VII. There they called up to Camp VIII, which however was beyond calling range. Since they got no answer this gave greater probability to Tendrup's story of the avalanche; we were definitely given up. The two of them now broke up Camp VII, threw most of the stored supplies into the snow, and left the tents open. Only the sleeping-bags and air mattresses were all taken along down to Camp IV. There Tendrup convinced the other two Sherpas that his avalanche story was true, and ordered a descent.

Later on, in Base Camp, the Sherpas called Tendrup a devil, who had deceived them with the avalanche story and wanted to wreck the expedition. I myself suspect that the strong but often lazy Tendrup was tired of packing between the high camps and therefore had invented the avalanche story. . . . At the same time he probably thought the sahibs at Base Camp would praise him for bringing along the valuable sleeping-bags from Camps VII and VI.

This explanation, however, leaves all kinds of questions unanswered. It does not explain why Camps I through IV were also stripped. It does not clarify Pasang Kikuli's role in the unfolding disaster. And it does not begin to address the central question of who bore the ultimate responsibility for leaving Sherpa in high camps with daunting and dangerous tasks to perform, in isolation from all the "sahibs"—a predicament into which Sherpa had never been thrust on any previous Himalayan expedition.

At the moment, sorting out the blunders that had led to the stripping of the camps was of secondary importance. The critical task the men at base camp now faced was to rescue Dudley Wolfe.

It seems almost beyond belief that after what could easily have been a fatal descent, having frostnipped his toes and completely exhausted himself, and having seen his logistical pyramid utterly wrecked, Wiessner still thought there was a chance to go for the summit. But on July 24, the very day he got back to base camp, he wrote in his diary, "The mountain is far away. . . . The weather is the best we have had so far. Will it be possible for me to go up after a short rest with some Sherpas and Jack, if he is in shape, to pick up Dudley and then call on the summit?"

On the one hand, you could call this determination the hallmark of a great mountaineer. Getting up K2 meant almost as much to Wiessner as life itself—as climbing the Matterhorn had to Whymper, or Everest to Mallory. On the other hand, you could call it denial. Wiessner had come so close to the summit on July 19 that perhaps he could not accept the fact that it was now eternally beyond his grasp.

It's also surprising that at this point, while trying to recuperate at base camp, Wiessner told Cromwell to go ahead and start for Askole with most of the porters. Granted, the deputy leader had proved himself useless on the mountain. But faced with the uncertainty of the rescue, didn't the team need every able-bodied climber it had to offer whatever support it could? If Wolfe got down the mountain in a crippled state and had to be carried down the Baltoro by litter, the team could have used all the porters available to take turns performing this desperate evacuation.

It may be that Wiessner was so angry with Cromwell, he just didn't want the man around. And as if to punish him for his "invented" avalanche story, Wiessner also ordered Tendrup to hike out with the porters, further humiliating him among his brethren. Wiessner kept the rest of the Sherpa at base camp.

On July 25, Durrance, Phinsoo, Dawa Thondup, and Pasang Kitar started up the mountain, hoping to reach Camp VII and find Wolfe still alive. The four men climbed to Camp II the first day, to Camp IV the second. By then, however, Dawa had developed a painfully sore throat, and Durrance felt his altitude problems recurring. Both men decided they could not go above IV. Durrance asked the other two Sherpa to push on. Phinsoo was willing, but Kitar balked, believing (quite reasonably) that two slightly built Sherpa could not safely shepherd a possibly stricken man as big as Wolfe down the Abruzzi Ridge. Instead, Durrance asked Phinsoo and Kitar to stay in Camp IV and await reinforcements. In his diary on July 27, plucking at desperate straws, he wrote, "I decided to return to base camp at once with Dawa & get Fritz & Pasang Kikuli to go to the rescue."

Upon the disheartening return of Durrance and Dawa to base camp, Wiessner prepared to head up the mountain himself. But his frostnipped toes and sore throat had troubled him so much that he had slept very little, and that day he was able to climb only a short distance above base camp before he realized that he was too debilitated to make another effort to go up the Abruzzi Ridge. At this point, the sirdar showed true heroism. As Wiessner wrote in his diary,

> Pasang Kikuli seem[s] to feel in good shape and his toes seem improved. He tells me very resolutely that there would be no need for me in my bad condition to go up, he would be perfectly able to handle the situation. . . . Good luck for me to have a man like Pasang left, he is dependable and always does what he plans, I could not do it better.

Early on July 28, Kikuli and Tsering left base camp. What happened during the next six days had to be reconstructed from the testimony of a single witness.

Despite his frostbitten feet, the sirdar and his companion were so fit and committed that they climbed at a rate of almost 1,000 feet an hour— virtually unheard of at such altitudes. In only six hours they reached Camp IV, a gain of 5,000 feet. There, to their surprise, they did not find Kitar and Phinsoo. It turned out that Kitar had overcome his doubts and the two Sherpa left by Durrance at IV had pushed on to Camp VI. So Kikuli and Tsering pushed on themselves. In a single day, they climbed 6,900 feet, from base camp at 16,500 feet to Camp VI at 23,400. Theirs was the strongest single day's ascent performed to that date by any climbers on any 8,000-meter peak.

From base camp, at 11:00 A.M. on July 29, through binoculars, Durrance and Wiessner saw three men climbing a couloir between Camps VI and VII. They were too far away to identify, and soon they passed out of sight. At 5:00 P.M., Durrance and Wiessner saw three figures descending the same couloir. It was impossible to deduce what had gone on.

At noon on July 29, Pasang Kikuli, Phinsoo, and Kitar reached Camp VII. (Tsering had been left at Camp VI to prepare hot beverages.) The three Sherpa found Wolfe lying in his sleeping bag, completely apathetic. He did not even read the note Wiessner had written to him. He had again run out of matches, and had eaten or drunk nothing for days. He had not even gone outside to defecate, so his sleeping bag and the tent floor were smeared with feces. The Sherpa made tea for Wolfe, got him outside the tent, and tried to help him walk, but he could only stagger. Wolfe told the men that he needed another day of rest, and pleaded with them to come back for him the next day.

Kauffman and Putnam write,

> Dudley had spent thirty-eight consecutive days above 22,000 feet, most of them in a tent. Of these, sixteen had been at heights averaging 25,000 feet. In the history of mountaineering to that time, no man—not Noel Odell of Everest, not Fritz himself— has been known to remain at such heights so long—even with oxygen support. And few have done it since.

So the three Sherpa turned back and descended to Camp VI. It is a tribute to their extraordinary devotion that they still did not give up on Dudley Wolfe. They stayed in their tent on July 30, as a minor storm blew through.

On July 31, Pasang Kikuli, Kitar, and Phinsoo started up to Camp VII once more. They again left Tsering behind to brew up tea for their return.

Tsering waited all day, a pot of tea ready, but no one came. He waited at Camp VI all the next day. Finally, on August 2, in a terrified panic, he dashed down to base camp.

We will never know what happened on July 31. It may be that the three Sherpa were avalanched off the mountain between Camps VI and VII, or that one fell and pulled the other two off. In 1939, the survivors thought it was conceivable that the Sherpa had reached Wolfe and rallied him into descending, only to have all four men meet disaster on the way down.

On August 3, with two Sherpa, Wiessner made one more attempt to ascend the route. It took him two full days to, as he put it, "drag myself" up to Camp II. He was incapable of going higher. On August 5 a full-scale storm broke, dumping more than a foot of snow and ending any further hopes of going up the mountain. Two days later what was left of the expedition team started out for Askole.

Dudley Wolfe's body was discovered on the Godwin Austen Glacier in 2002. Curiously enough, ten years earlier we'd stumbled upon what may have been one of Wolfe's hobnailed leather boots, near our base camp. The boot contained the remnants of ankle bones and sock material. But in the aftermath of our rescue of Gary Ball, the boot somehow got forgotten.

In 2002, two documentary filmmakers from a Spanish expedition first came across bones from a leg and a pelvis. That team was led by Araceli Segarra, who had been a key member of our IMAX team on Everest in 1996. Shortly thereafter, the Spaniards found the remains of a canvas tent, tent poles, and a cooking pot. The clincher was a mitten with Wolfe's name written on it in capital letters. The discovery seemed to prove that sometime between 1939 and 1954, the tent at Camp VII, with Wolfe's body in it, had been avalanched off the mountain, and that therefore the three Sherpa had never reached Camp VII on July 31 (or had reached it and had once again failed to persuade Wolfe to descend).

No trace of Pasang Kitar, Phinsoo, or Pasang Kikuli has ever been found.

On the march out to Srinagar, the rearguard party—Wiessner, Durrance, and most of the Sherpa—never caught up to the Cromwell-Cranmer-Sheldon contingent, which had joined forces at Askole. In 1984, Wiessner recalled that hike out:

> We were together every day. Durrance looked after me as if I were a baby. He made pancakes for me. And every day we talked. I just couldn't comprehend what had happened on the mountain. "I don't understand it, Jack," I told him, "why those sleeping bags were taken out after all our agreements." He kept answering, "It was a matter of those Sherpas."
>
> I kept asking him. Finally, he stood there and shouted, "Ah, Fritz! Stop it! Stop it! We have talked about it long enough!"

In Srinagar, Wiessner and Durrance lingered while they painstakingly drafted an official account of the expedition for the American Alpine Club. There they were also interviewed by the American Consul to India, Edward Miller Groth, who, though not a mountain climber, prepared his own analysis of the expedition in a memorandum addressed not to the AAC but to the State Department in Washington, D.C.

It was not until September 20 that Wiessner and Durrance finally separated, as the former boarded a ship for New York. On that day, Durrance wrote in his diary, "Fritz & I part ways, thank God."

Tony Cromwell had preceded Wiessner to the States. Upon disembarking in New Jersey, Cromwell publicly leveled the ridiculous charge that Wiessner had "murdered" Dudley Wolfe. Greeted in New York by reporters armed with Cromwell's claim, Wiessner rashly told the *New York Times* that "on big mountains, as in war, one must expect casualties."

Wiessner had not recovered from the ordeal of K2. In New York City, he entered a hospital, where he was bedridden for six weeks, as doctors treated severe arthritic problems in his knees and chronic back pain. Durrance later came to New York, stayed in a hotel, and sent some of Wiessner's belongings to him in the hospital, but he never paid a visit. The two men would not meet again for thirty-nine years.

In his bed, Wiessner brooded about the stripped camps. He had come to accept that the removal of sleeping bags from Camps VI and VII was due to Tendrup's false report that the three men above must have died in an avalanche. But what explained the stripping of the vital supplies— including thirteen sleeping bags—from Camps II and IV? Had Wiessner found everything in place at Camp IV, he believed, he could still have gone back up the mountain and made a third attempt on the summit. And Dudley Wolfe would not have died—which would have meant that the three Sherpa also would not have died.

As he lay in his hospital bed, rummaging through his personal papers, Wiessner later reported, he came across a handwritten note that he had earlier overlooked. It had been left for him by Durrance at Camp II on July 19. The note, as Wiessner recalled, congratulated him and Wolfe for making the summit, then explained that he, Durrance, had ordered the recovery of the sleeping bags, in anticipation of the expedition's departure and to save valuable equipment. The implication was that Durrance assumed that Wiessner, Wolfe, and Pasang Lama would be bringing their own bags down all the way from Camp IX. When Wiessner had found this note at Camp II on July 23, he had been too exhausted and upset to make sense of it. Now, in the hospital, it seemed to supply the missing piece to the puzzle.

Wiessner later wrote that he deposited this all-important note in the files of the American Alpine Club. When he subsequently tried to relocate the note, it was gone.

In *K2: The 1939 Tragedy*, Kauffman and Putnam devote several pages to what they call the "phantom note." Phantom, because no one else ever went on record as having seen the note. They entertain three hypotheses. The first is that Durrance did indeed write the note, and that it was later lost or destroyed by someone in the AAC. The second is that Wiessner lied, inventing the story of the note. But the third goes a long way toward clearing up the mystery.

The single most important discovery of new evidence made by Kauffman and Putnam comes in an entry from Durrance's diary, written at Camp II on July 18: "Dawa danced up here yesterday aft. with notes from Toni [sic] and Chap: 'Salvage all the tents & sleeping bags you can, we have ample food.' Easier said than done!" Nonetheless, Durrance carried out the command, which surely had come from Cromwell and not from Cranmer (who had played no part in the assault since his early collapse at base camp). The same entry continues,

> Dawa & Pasang [Kikuli] must go aloft and return rather heavily loaded—meanwhile . . . I must pack down 55 lbs. of equipment to [Camp] I and return to-night. The boys are more than willing—so that is precisely what we did. I had some time with my bulky load alone over several icy places and dodging stones in the large couloir. . . . Dawa brought down 65 lbs. and Pasang 75 lbs. from above!! We arrived simultaneously. Big feed!

So the lower camps were indeed stripped on orders from a "sahib"— but that man was Cromwell rather than Durrance. The note Wiessner claimed to have found at Camp II may well have existed and later been lost in the AAC files, but if so, on reading it in his frazzled state, Wiessner had mistaken Cromwell's hand for Durrance's.

The revelation of Durrance's diary entry still leaves questions unanswered. Did no one realize that removing all those sleeping bags and air mattresses, on which the climbers up high completely depended, amounted to (as Wiessner had wondered in his diary) "sabotage"? Cromwell may well have been so witless and so eager to head home that he could issue such a ruthless demand. But why did Durrance and Pasang Kikuli obey it? Surely Kikuli, among all the men on the mountain except Wiessner, best understood the vital importance of that chain of camps so well supplied over the weeks, at the cost of so much labor and risk. Perhaps, despite the note Durrance left for Wiessner, by July 18 all three men had already decided that Wiessner, Wolfe, and Pasang Lama must be dead—though the hastiness of such a conclusion defies credibility.

Kauffman and Putnam argue convincingly that for the rest of his life, Wiessner, whose tensions with Durrance had sprung from the moment they first met in Genoa, blamed the wrong man for the 1939 tragedy. This itself is curious, since it was Cromwell who, as soon as he arrived in the United States, went on the attack and accused the expedition leader of murdering Dudley Wolfe.

If Wiessner had fingered the wrong man, which he did explicitly in his 1956 article in *Appalachia*, why did Durrance not spring to his own defense? A published photocopy of his July 18 diary entry could have solved the question for good. Kauffman and Putnam argue that Durrance was in essence a private person, and that after the expedition he was so soured by its antagonisms that he preferred simply to ignore the controversy. In any event, Cromwell lived for forty-eight years after the expedition, Durrance for fifty-two, without ever committing to print a single line about what happened in 1939.

The ill-starred expedition led by Wiessner had seen the first fatalities ever to take place on K2. In addition, Wolfe's death was the first incurred on any American expedition to the Himalaya or the Karakoram. Tragic those losses certainly were—but the controversy surrounding them would have quickly faded, had it not been for the political climate of the day.

Wiessner was still in Srinagar when Germany invaded Poland on September 1, and when Britain and France declared war on Germany two days later. Within climbing circles, the conservative American and British disapproval of the great breakthroughs German and Austrian climbers were making in the Alps, not only with their "ironmongery" but with their apparent willingness to risk all for glory, had been simmering for most of the decade.

On October 27, shortly after Wiessner had returned from India, the AAC launched an official investigation of the expedition. The club had never done such a thing before; nor was it at all a normal procedure. In 1922, seven Sherpa had been killed in an avalanche on Everest, in an accident that arguably involved real negligence on the part of Mallory and his fellow climbers; but the Alpine Club of London had never considered launching an inquiry. Cynical observers would later suggest that had only Sherpa been killed on K2 in 1939, the AAC wouldn't have lifted an eyebrow. But Dudley Wolfe was a Boston Brahmin, a blue blood from New England—as were many of the AAC's luminaries and officers. And Fritz Wiessner was a German-American, at perhaps the worst time in the twentieth century to be one.

The AAC investigation took months to complete, since the members of the committee had such differing views about assigning blame for the tragedy. The final draft claimed a disinterested motive: to "point the way towards a greater control of the risks undertaken in climbing great mountains." But the report came to some patronizing conclusions. It claimed that the expedition's "human administration seems to have been weak"; that there was "no clear understanding" of plans between Durrance and Wiessner when they parted; that it was an "error in judgment" to leave Sherpa alone in the middle camps; and that an ill climber (Wolfe, who was not in fact ill) should not have been left alone to make his own decisions. The brunt of all these criticisms fell on Wiessner. The committee gave the actions of Durrance and Cromwell an implicit but total whitewash.

A summary of the report was sent to all AAC members. In the accompanying letter, the committee congratulated itself for its "valuable contribution" in the way of guidance "if Himalayan expeditions are undertaken again."

Charlie Houston had declined to serve on the committee. But there was no doubt about his views. On September 28, 1939, he wrote his old Harvard friend and Alaskan teammate Bradford Washburn a letter about the expedition:

> I feel as you do about K-2. The report makes it clear that the party was driven beyond their powers, extended much to[o] far along their line of attack, and very poorly prepared for the very bad luck which they kept enduring. There is no doubt that bad luck is far worse when you aren't prepared to cope with it.
>
> Wiessner is to blame for most if not all of the mishap, and I don't believe I can ever forgive him. I didn't know Wolfe, but I knew and dearly loved Pasang [Kikuli] and P[h]insoo, and what they so gallantly did, *alone,* I can't forget.

Two members of the AAC committee strenuously disagreed with the report and wrote dissenting views. One was Al Lindley, the strong mountaineer who had made the second ascent of Mount McKinley and who had been on board for the 1939 expedition until, at the last minute, he'd had to back out. Lindley argued that Wiessner was being dealt a serious injustice by the report, for the simple reason that "the action of the Sherpas and Durrance in evacuating these camps was so much the major cause of the accident that the others are insignificant." The other dissent came from Robert Underhill, who, though a New England blue blood himself, had applied techniques he had learned in the Alps to bold first ascents in America. Underhill's long rebuttal came to a stirring conclusion:

> What impresses me most is the fact that thruout all the bad weather, the killing labor and grievous disappointments, [Wiess-

ner] still kept up his fighting spirit. Except Wolfe, the rest of the party were excusably enough, finished and thru—quite downed by the circumstances; toward the end they wanted only to get out and go home. Wiessner, with Wolfe behind him, was the only one who still wanted to climb the mountain. Far be it from me to blame the others; I know well that if I had been there myself I should have come to feel exactly the same way, and probably much sooner. But this leads me to appreciate Wiessner the more. He had the guts—and there is no single thing finer in a climber, or in a man.

Bitterly stung by the report, Wiessner resigned from the AAC. The most chilling (and, in retrospect, comically absurd) episode in the backlash against Wiessner came only a few months after he was released from the hospital. Wiessner never publicly spoke about this confrontation until 1984, when he told a writer about it.

One day [in early 1940] my secretary in my New York office told me that two men from the FBI had come by. I went down to the FBI office and met two very nice young chaps—they were both Yale graduates. We sat down and talked. They wanted to know my whole history, and they had the funniest questions. Such as, "You go skiing often in Stowe in the winter, do you not? That's very near Canada, isn't it? Can you get easily over the border?" I said, "Yes. It's quite a distance to walk, but I'm in Canada very often anyway because I have a business in Toronto." And they laughed.

I wasn't very keen on Roosevelt then. And so they said, "You don't like the president? You made some remarks about him." I said, "Well, I wasn't the only one. There are very many people who feel that way!" They laughed again.

They asked about some of my friends. We sat there half an hour, then we just talked pleasantly. On the way out I said, "Now look, fellows, I was pretty open to you. I have my definite suspicions. Would you tell me the names of the men who put you up to this?" They said, "Naturally we can't do that." So I said, "Let me ask this question: was it some climbers from the AAC?" They nodded. They said, "Don't worry about it. You know who we had here yesterday? We had Ezio Pinza, the famous opera singer. It was the same thing, a little jealousy from his competitors. They complained that he was a Mussolini follower."

If Wiessner's story is true—and it seems too bizarre for him to have made it up—it leaves ambiguous the question of whether his AAC detractors simply wanted to harass him or genuinely believed he was a Nazi spy.

Sadly, the criticisms leveled in the AAC report, full of innuendos attributing Wiessner's "mistakes" to his "Teutonic" style of climbing and leadership, became the received wisdom about the 1939 expedition. Kauffman and Putnam rescued from oblivion the memorandum Edward Groth, the American consul in India, had sent to the State Department. It is full of aspersions based on ethnic prejudices. For instance:

> With his German background, also owing to the fact that he possesses a large share of German bluntness . . . it is not remarkable that there should have been a clash of temperaments. Wiessner is undoubtedly an excellent climber and a good leader, but like every German, he is very forceful in giving commands and totally unaware that the abrupt, blunt manner in which the order may have been given might have wounded the feelings of his associates, who in this instance, being Americans, naturally have a different attitude and outlook in matters of this sort.

At its worst, the second-guessing took the form of outright condemnation. In *Abode of Snow,* a widely read history of Himalayan climbing, the British writer Kenneth Mason gave an utterly garbled summary of the events on K2 in 1939, concluding, "It is difficult to record in temperate language the folly of this enterprise."

For the most part, Wiessner ignored these criticisms and got on with his life. In 1955, however, he published a very small book about the expedition in German, titled *K2: Tragödien und Sieg am Zweithöchsten Berg der Erde* (K2: Tragedy and Victory on the Second-Highest Mountain in the World). Miriam Underhill, Robert Underhill's wife, the finest American woman climber of her day and the editor of *Appalachia,* persuaded Wiessner to allow the publication of an English translation of the part of the text that covered events on the mountain between July 9 and August 7. Underhill's introduction ended with a challenge: "If any other member of the expedition disagrees with Mr. Wiessner in any respect, and will send us his version of the matter, we should be very glad to print it." No one responded.

That text for the first time lays out Wiessner's version of the stripping of the camps and makes it clear that this dismantling was what wrecked the expedition and led indirectly to the deaths of Wolfe and the three Sherpa. In a single sentence, Wiessner summed up the personal impact of the tragedy. Had he and Pasang Lama found sleeping bags at Camp IV, he insists, he and Wolfe might have been able "to resume our final attack on the summit of which I felt so confident." Instead, "a cruel fate determined otherwise, and therewith ended the hardest fight, the greatest hope, and at the same time the greatest disappointment of my climbing career."

As few mountaineers ever do, Wiessner kept climbing at a very high level into his seventies and even early eighties, though he turned his talents away from the big ranges and toward rock climbing on smaller crags. Never again did he go on an expedition to the Karakoram or the Himalaya.

Beginning in the 1960s, and accelerating through the '70s and '80s, American climbing underwent a cultural revolution. A new generation, reexamining the 1939 expedition, saw armchair critics such as Kenneth

Mason as reactionary old fogeys, while Wiessner was in effect reborn as one of the greatest climbers in history, his deeds on K2 considered heroic rather than foolish or neglectful.

In *In the Throne Room of the Mountain Gods,* Galen Rowell pithily summed up this reevaluation:

> Leaders don't belong in the first summit team? *What about Maurice Herzog on Annapurna?* Sherpas must not move unsupervised over difficult terrain? *What about the repeated instances on many of the hallowed British attempts on Everest?* Mountain summits aren't worth risking lives for? *Only a rare windless night on May 22, 1963, kept four Americans from perishing in an open bivouac near the top of Mount Everest. . . .* Taking a climber of Wolfe's meager experience on a big mountain was unprecedented? *Andrew Irvine, Mallory's famous companion on Mount Everest in 1924, was even less experienced, but like Wolfe he outperformed those with better records.*

In 1966, Andy Kauffman, Bill Putnam, and several other AAC members persuaded Wiessner to rejoin the club. (It would be decades before Kauffman and Putnam would turn critical of the man they had so long admired and championed.) Soon afterward, in partial expiation of the wrong it had done him years before, the club made him an honorary member for life.

In December 1978, the annual AAC banquet meeting was held in Estes Park, Colorado. The previous summer, my friend Jim Wickwire and his three teammates had become the first Americans to reach the summit of K2. The whole focus of the meeting was to be on K2, and Jack Durrance, who was then living in Denver, was invited to give a slide show about the 1939 expedition. Hearing about this, Wiessner flew back from a meeting in Europe in order to be present.

I wasn't there, but a friend of mine who was later recounted for me the dramatic events that took place. All day long, the rumors flew that a long-delayed confrontation was about to occur. Durrance was finally going to tell "his side" of the story. Meanwhile, Dee Molenaar, who had been on the 1953 K2 expedition, managed to talk Wiessner and Durrance into saying hello to each other. It was the first time they had seen each other since parting in India in 1939. The meeting was curt in the extreme.

A number of AAC old-timers took Durrance aside. They talked him out of making any inflammatory remarks. Whatever dirty laundry remained from 1939, they said, this was not the place to air it. Durrance gave in. His slide show carried the expedition up to base camp, then closed abruptly with a photo of himself in "retirement" in a cabin near the Tetons.

Later, at the banquet, Wiessner was given a special toast in recognition of his years of service to mountaineering. The crowd's reaction was deeply emotional, and the whole assemblage rose to its feet, applauding wildly—except for Durrance, who remained seated, his face fixed in a scowl.

Fritz Wiessner died in 1988, at the age of eighty-eight. During the last decade of his life, Kauffman and Putnam interviewed him at length, as they planned to write his biography. Their book did not come out until 1992. For reasons best known to themselves, the work they published was not a biography at all but an account of the 1939 expedition that its authors hoped would be the definitive record.

Kauffman and Putnam did meticulous research, and they discovered evidence that no one else had been privy to, such as Durrance's diary and Groth's memorandum to the State Department. But *K2: The 1939 Tragedy* was deeply disappointing to younger climbers who had come to see Wiessner as a hero. For some, Kauffman and Putnam's book verged on a betrayal.

I'm not sure I'd go that far, but it is galling to see the same old ethnic stereotypes from the 1930s and '40s recycled in the authors' strictures and interpretations. And it's annoying how Kauffman and Putnam sit in condescending judgment of Wiessner. The authors were good climbers themselves—Kauffman was one of the two men who made the first ascent of Gasherbrum I in 1958, the only 8,000er pioneered by Americans. But their smug second-guessing of an even better climber, Fritz Wiessner, is hard to swallow.

A couple of examples:

> Fritz had a different attitude toward mountaineering from the others. The Americans played for fun, Fritz for keeps. Fritz also adhered to an authoritarian leadership model, whereas the Americans had a tradition of independence, even of rebellion.

> On K2 and elsewhere Fritz Wiessner demonstrated outstanding skill as a climber. But what can be said of his leadership on the 1939 K2 expedition? . . . Did he treat his companions evenhandedly? Did he make allowance for the weaknesses of those less competent than himself and recognize the perils to which these weaknesses might expose the undertaking? Finally, did he overextend his human resources and, at the critical moment, rely on luck?

The upshot of *K2: The 1939 Tragedy* is to blame Wiessner for much of what went wrong on the expedition, and even to implicate him in errors of judgment that led to the deaths of Dudley Wolfe and the three Sherpa. As if in counterbalance, Durrance comes across almost as the hero of the story, constantly solicitous of the well-being of his teammates and doing his best to hold the fragile team together.

It's hard to understand how these two men, who, in the 1960s, had the most to do with rehabilitating Wiessner, who championed his readmission to the AAC and his honorary membership, could write a supposedly "authoritative" account of the 1939 expedition that on almost every other page makes some sly criticism of the leader.

A friend of mine who knew Wiessner well and Putnam fairly well has his theory. He told me recently, "For years Kauffman and Putnam spent day after day with Fritz, recording his memories and listening to him tell his old war stories. Fritz could be pretty imperious, and he probably took for granted that these two guys would hang on his every word. And when you got Fritz talking about K2, his bitterness came to the surface.

"I can imagine that after years of this, Kauffman and Putnam got a little tired of Fritz. They may have started resisting some of the things he told them. And then they befriended Jack Durrance, and got on his good side, until Durrance let them read and quote from his diary. That July 18 entry was a bombshell—it pretty much disproved Fritz's lifelong idea that Durrance was the villain of the expedition.

"So by the time Kauffman and Putnam were ready to write, they had lost interest in doing a biography. But they thought they had instead the true story of what happened on one of the most enigmatic expeditions of all time. And by now, conveniently enough, Fritz was dead. He couldn't answer them from the grave."

My friend used to be an English professor. He explained, "This kind of thing happens a lot in biography. The classic example is Lawrance Thompson's bio of Robert Frost. Frost chose Thompson to be his official biographer, and he lived so long that the research covered decades. Frost was every bit as imperious as Wiessner. There are stories about how he would call up Thompson from his retirement home in Florida and say something like, 'Come on down—I'm ready to tell you about 1913.' By the time Thompson wrote the biography, he hated Frost. In that three-volume life, Frost comes across as a great poet but a monster in human terms. One reviewer called it 'a big fat voodoo doll of a biography, with Thompson puncturing Frost from every angle.' But that's still the public image of Frost, which no amount of later scholarship has been able to undo."

No matter what the ultimate causes of the tragedy were, any climber has to be in complete awe of Wiessner's performance on K2. To lead virtually every pitch of the whole climb, to break trail through the deepest and softest snow every single day, to have established a well-stocked series of camps all the way up the mountain with only minimal support from his American teammates, to have used his ax belay and self-arrest to save the lives of his teammates twice, to have done the hardest climbing so far accomplished anywhere at such an altitude in order to reach a point only 750 vertical feet below the summit, to be ready to go through the night to get to the top—there's really nothing like it in the annals of mountaineering in the great ranges.

And you have to be in awe of the hard work, the loyalty, and the heroism of the Sherpa—particularly Pasang Kikuli, Pasang Kitar, and Phinsoo, who gave their lives trying to save Dudley Wolfe.

I've heard guys say that if Wiessner had reached the summit of K2 in 1939, with or without Pasang Lama, it would have been the greatest accomplishment in mountaineering history. I agree—but in my opinion, that feat would have been nearly impossible. In the years since 1939, such a tour de force has been performed on rare occasions, but more often climbers pushing their limits to such extremes don't survive the ordeal.

I get asked all the time whether I think Mallory and Irvine reached the summit of Everest in 1924. I always answer, "It doesn't matter. It's irrelevant, because they didn't make it back down." That may sound a little harsh, but it's the logical application of the motto by which I lived during my pursuit of the fourteen 8,000ers: *Reaching the summit is optional. Getting down is mandatory.*

What really impresses me about Fritz Wiessner is that, believing that the achievement of a lifetime was well within his grasp, tempted to unrope and go for the summit alone, he listened to the terrified plea of his partner and instead turned back. After K2, Pasang Lama would go on to become one of the greatest Sherpa of his generation. He went on many more Himalayan expeditions, and in 1954 he reached the summit with an Austrian party on the first ascent of Cho Oyu, the world's sixth-highest mountain.

According to Galen Rowell,

> In the middle sixties, an American climber visiting Nepal met
> Pasang and asked him about the 1939 expedition. His eyes lit up
> as he talked about his friend "Fritz sahib," who had saved his life
> by not forcing him to continue to the summit. . . . "Give Fritz
> sahib my good wishes," said Pasang as the American left.

There is no getting around the fact that Wiessner agonized for the rest
of his life about the decision he made at 27,500 feet on July 19, 1939.
As he put it in 1984, at age eighty-four:

> If I were in wonderful condition like I was then, if the place
> where my man stood was safe, if the weather was good, if I had
> a night coming on like that one, with the moon and the calm air,
> if I could see what was ahead as I did then . . . then I would
> probably unrope and go on alone. But I can get pretty weak, if I
> feel that my man will suffer. He was so afraid, and I liked the
> fellow. He was a comrade to me, and he had done so well.

5

BROTHERHOOD

They say that every adventurer suffers from the conviction that he was born too late. When, as a teenager, I read the classic books of polar exploration—like Robert Falcon Scott's diary of his fatal trip to the south pole or the various books about Ernest Shackleton's heroic expedition when his ship, the *Endurance,* was trapped in the ice off Antarctica and sank—I was taken aback by a recurrent theme: those guys were sure they'd been born too late. By 1900, there was no western frontier left to explore, uninhabited by anybody except Indians; no island in the South Pacific waiting to be discovered by a Captain Cook; no source of the Nile still lost in the blank spaces on the map of Africa. Scott and Shackleton and their rivals wondered at times whether trying to reach the poles was too arbitrary a goal. After all, the south pole was simply a spot on an empty, windswept glacial plateau, defined not by a wilderness that could be tamed and settled but by a unique latitude: ninety degrees south. Nobody who ever read Scott's diary can forget his entry on finally arriving there: "Great God! this is an awful place."

But, man! When I read their books, I kept thinking how lucky they were to be exploring in the first two decades of the twentieth century, when nearly all of the Arctic and the Antarctic was still unknown. I was sure that it was I who had been born too late, not Scott or Shackleton. Even the 1950s, when climbers were making the first ascents of the 8,000-meter peaks, loomed for me like a lost heyday. Exploration then seemed simpler, yet more dangerous. Off you went into some little-known region on the map, or toward the top of some unclimbed peak, without being able to send a word back home. You returned home months or even years later. Now we have sat phones, up-to-the-minute weather forecasts, and online dispatches from the field. It seems that we're as much burdened by technology as we are helped by it, and it becomes a crutch to make up for missing skills—just as, for example, the GPS has replaced the compass.

When, as a teenager, I read Charlie Houston and Bob Bates's *K2: The Savage Mountain,* I thought how fortunate those guys were that as late as 1953, the second-highest mountain in the world was still unclimbed. In my mind, there was nothing arbitrary about that kind of goal. Traveling by dogsled, you can't see the north pole from a distance—you have to be almost on top of it before you know what it looks like. Even then, you don't actually "see" the pole. You need to make sextant sightings and triangulate your position before you can honestly say that you are standing on or at least reasonably close to the pole.

But I'd "seen" K2 ever since I'd first opened a book and looked at the famous picture of it from the 1909 expedition: K2 from Windy Gap, looking impossibly big and beautiful, a photo often attributed to Vittorio Sella but actually taken by the Duke of the Abruzzi (see photo insert, between pages 150 and 151). Even as a teenager, I understood that to try to get to the highest windblown point in that glass-plate picture would take all the suffering in the world.

By the time I started climbing in 1977, all fourteen of the highest mountains in the world had long since been ascended. (Shishapangma was the last to fall, to the Chinese in 1964.) All the highest mountains in Alaska and Canada had been climbed. I don't think there was a single summit in the Cascades of Washington State—my first stomping grounds—that hadn't been reached. It was hard not to feel that I'd been born too late.

For Whymper, or Mummery, or Mallory, or even Fritz Wiessner, "mountaineer" was an unambiguous label. Mallory was the guiding force on the first three Everest expeditions, but he was also the best rock climber of his day in Great Britain. Wiessner had been one of the best rock climbers in the world as a teenager, one of the best alpinists in his twenties, and one of the best Himalayan climbers in his thirties. Climbing had yet to be subdivided into specialized disciplines.

By the 1980s, however, that subdividing was well under way, and by now it's become extreme. Some young rope gun at Red River Gorge in Kentucky, trying to put up an 80-foot route that's rated 5.14c in difficulty, knows almost nothing about the Himalaya. And guys who, like me, have specialized in 8,000-meter peaks know very little about Red River Gorge, or Hueco Tanks in Texas, or Mount Charleston in Nevada. We're all still "climbers," but our fraternities (and sororities) are so specialized that we scarcely understand one another's jargon.

In 2009, there are serious climbers all over the world who've never climbed outdoors. Instead, they concentrate on artificial walls in climbing gyms, gearing up for "comps"—competitions complete with referees, stopwatches, and "isolation chambers" (so that one jock doesn't get the benefit of watching another try the route of the day). There's another whole gang composed of those who climb outdoors, but never use ropes. They're into "bouldering"—doing the hardest sequences of moves possible on boulders lying in the woods. Boulderers rarely get more than 30 feet off the ground, and they're secured by buddies spotting them and by springy crash pads laid out on the ground.

"Sport climbers" use ropes, and tackle routes ranging from one pitch to a dozen or more on real cliffs or "crags," but they rely for safety on expansion bolts previously drilled into the rock every six feet or so. These athletes, like boulderers, are into the pure pursuit of difficulty, and the risks they incur are almost nonexistent.

"Trad climbers"—"trad" is for "traditional"—disdain the connect-the-dots bolted routes and insist instead on placing their own protection ("pro," in the jargon of the trade), in the form of nuts and cams wedged into cracks to shorten a potential fall. These climbers think of themselves as purists, in touch with the long legacy of their pastime, and for them risk is a real issue. If your "pro" isn't good, a fall can result in serious injury or even death.

I served my mountaineering apprenticeship as a trad climber. First at Devils Lake in Wisconsin with my high school pal Rich King, and then on more alpine routes in the Cascades of Washington State, I learned the basics of rope work, belaying, rappelling, and placing "pro." All these skills would help me immensely when I turned to the highest peaks in the world.

Trad climbers overlap with "big-wall climbers," who work out long routes on massive cliffs such as El Capitan in Yosemite. Those routes can take several days, but there's also a subgroup of people who are into doing big routes in the fastest possible time. On El Cap, every major route has its speed record, and those times are coveted prizes for the men and women who go after them.

I suppose that true mountaineering begins with "alpine climbing." Alpine warriors set their sights on fiendishly difficult routes in ranges such as the Alps, the Canadian Rockies, and the Fitz Roy Massif of Patagonia. Here, "objective hazards"—everything from avalanches to falling rocks to storms—play a critical role. At the cutting edge, alpinism is a very dangerous sport. (It's somewhere on this spectrum that we stop being comfortable with calling climbing a "sport." We don't know exactly what to call it—a "pastime," a "pursuit," an "adventure"? "Sport" conjures up baseball or golf. Mountaineering is a way of life.)

Alpinists are interested in beautiful "lines" on major mountains, but the height of the mountain above sea level is pretty irrelevant. Some of the scariest and most challenging peaks in the world, like Cerro Torre in Patagonia, are only about 9,000 or 10,000 feet high. And sometimes climbers will complete a difficult new route on an alpine peak but won't bother to go to the summit. The route itself becomes the goal.

Finally you get to my group, which we might call Himalayan or high-altitude climbers. Even within our coterie, there are subgroups. There are guys like the American Steve House, who with one partner climbed the notorious Rupal Face on Nanga Parbat alpine-style, but who's also done very hard new routes on smaller peaks in Alaska and Canada. He's taken the technical skills he's honed on lower peaks and applied them to 8,000ers. I admire House immensely, but I don't have the technical skill or the interest to attack some unclimbed face in the Great Gorge of the Ruth Glacier just south of Mount McKinley. And House has no interest, as far as I can tell, in climbing all fourteen 8,000ers.

From the start, technical climbing per se didn't hold a great appeal for me. I didn't ever pursue it seriously enough to know whether I could have become a top rock climber. But I loved a physical challenge, especially if it involved commitment over the long haul—not just several days but weeks or months. That's why, I think, I gravitated to the 8,000ers, starting with my first attempt on Everest in 1987. That was a huge step, but a logical one, beyond Mount Rainier, where I'd been guiding since 1982. (Some of my fellow RMI guides also turned to 8,000-meter peaks, but they were the exception, not the norm.)

And from the start, I felt instinctively that I wanted to climb those big mountains in as pure a style as possible—without the aid of supplementary oxygen, without the support of Sherpas hauling my loads, and on expeditions that I organized myself. When I go around the country giving slide shows, a lot of people in the audience assume that what I called Endeavor 8000—my quest for all fourteen 8,000ers—was a project I had formulated from the start. Not so: I was three or four peaks into the roster before I could envision a way of completing the whole cycle. And when Annapurna started to seem my "nemesis," as I called it, I would have been willing to walk away with only thirteen under my belt.

Of course, it was gratifying to become the first American to climb all fourteen, and only the sixth mountaineer in the world to do so without bottled oxygen. Maybe I hadn't been born too late after all! I can imagine some young guy in, say, 2025 reading about my era in the Himalaya and the Karakoram and saying to himself, "Damn it, imagine what it must have been like when no other American had been on top of all the 8,000ers. I guess I was born too late . . . ."

I did gain a fair amount of attention after I completed the cycle of 8,000ers, appearing on talk shows such as *Charlie Rose,* the *Today* show, *The Colbert Report,* and *The Daily Show with Jon Stewart.* And my book about the quest, *No Shortcuts to the Top,* generated an unbelievable amount of fan mail, mostly from nonclimbers. But I was first surprised, then hurt when I started to realize that in a certain small portion of the climbing world, there was a nasty backlash against my modest celebrity. I'd hear thirdhand that so-and-so had said, "Big fucking deal. So Viesturs climbed the standard route on Cho Oyu. Why doesn't he try something new or really difficult?" Nobody ever said anything quite like that to my face. So I was sort of left sputtering my answer into the void. I was tempted to say to a critic like that, "Okay, dude, why don't you try climbing three 8,000ers in two months." (That's what I'd done in 1995.) I've never claimed to be anything I'm not. I've never pretended to be a brilliant rock climber. And I've never put other climbers down, or denigrated their achievements.

Some of these critics seemed to operate from a double standard. They'd imply that I wasn't a complete climber if I hadn't done El Cap or led a 5.13 rock climb. Yet they themselves had never set foot on an 8,000-meter peak, let alone climbed one without supplemental oxygen. I've endured risks and hardships on 8,000ers that some other climbers could never imagine.

In the past, one climber would applaud another simply for succeeding, whether it meant putting up a new route or lending his face to an ad for an energy bar. We all pulled for one another to "make it." A lot of the more recent sniping and criticism seems to be based on ignorance, jealousy, or just having too much free time with nothing else to do or talk about.

Mountaineering is too wonderful an endeavor, and too personal a one, you'd think, to be sullied by petty jealousies and one-upsmanship. And yet, from its very earliest years, climbing has been afflicted with intense competitiveness, and has generated the kind of controversy and even mudslinging that, for instance, Wiessner endured after the 1939 K2 expedition.

To mountaineers of the generations before mine, making the first ascent of a mountain was the ultimate accomplishment. The first ascent of Everest, in 1953, is still far and away the most celebrated deed in climbing history. And in my own generation, there were guys (and gals) who focused their passions on finding beautiful unclimbed mountains around the world and figuring out how to get to the top of them. As the 1980s slid into the '90s and then into the twenty-first century, though, these pioneers had to head off to more and more remote ranges—the Tien Shan of western China, for example, or the high valleys of Kyrgyzstan, or the glacial massifs of Baffin Island—to find worthy unclimbed prizes.

That was never my game. In fact, I confess that I've never made a first ascent of a peak anywhere in the world. On the whole, I don't feel that I've missed an essential part of the mountaineering experience by not having done so. I've always thought that even if I'm on a peak that has been climbed before, I'm making my own personal "first ascent." That's the intrigue of adventure—doing something you've never done before.

Yet when I think back to 1953, and imagine Houston and Bates and their teammates setting off for K2, full of confidence that at last they would be the men to make the first ascent of one of the greatest and hardest mountains in the world, a little bit of that teenage envy creeps back. Wouldn't that have been a glorious summer to hike up the Baltoro Glacier? Maybe after all I was born too late . . . . .

From 1939 to 1945, mountaineering pretty much shut down worldwide. There was mountain warfare waged in the Alps—the famous Tenth Mountain Division was hatched as part of the World War II effort, enlisting many of the best American climbers—but scrambling up a steep slope to attack an enemy entrenched on a rocky crest is not the same thing as climbing a great peak "because it is there."

The few exceptions during the war years include some extraordinary adventures. One of the classics of our literature is Felice Benuzzi's *No Picnic on Mount Kenya,* which I read early on in my own climbing career. It's the true story of three Italian prisoners of war interred in a British camp in Kenya. From the grounds, every day they could see Mount Kenya—a 17,058-foot peak that's a serious climb, unlike the more famous Kilimanjaro—towering above them. In January 1943, they escaped from the camp just so they could climb the mountain. They spent eighteen days working their way up its cliffs and couloirs, but were defeated short of the summit. Rather than continue their escape deeper into the African wilderness, the three men hiked back to the British camp and turned themselves in. For their troubles, each of them spent twenty-eight days in solitary confinement.

Even after the war, mountaineering was slow to return to the Himalaya. And the painful separation of Pakistan from India in 1947 made the Karakoram off-limits to outsiders for years. It was not until 1950 that the first postwar expedition to any 8,000-meter peak took place.

Charlie Houston had never gotten K2 out of his blood. For years after the war, he tried to wangle a permit from the government of Pakistan. One huge obstacle was that the battle between India and Pakistan for control of Kashmir rendered the old approach route from Srinagar out of the question for foreigners. Ironically, however, the same struggle turned the sleepy village of Skardu into a military outpost, complete with a modern airstrip. The first postwar expedition to K2 would not have to hike 360 miles to reach base camp but could fly in to Skardu—as virtually all expeditions have done ever since.

Houston was convinced that if Wiessner, at the head of a very weak team, had been able to get within 750 vertical feet of the summit, with only easy terrain above, a stronger team with far better equipment would almost surely succeed on the Abruzzi Ridge. But a permit for K2 seemed so remote a possibility that Houston applied instead to Nepal for permission to attempt Makalu, the world's fifth-highest mountain. (It would first be climbed by a French team led by the great Lionel Terray in 1955.) Yet even as he was preparing for Makalu, Houston finally succeeded, with the aid of the American ambassador to Pakistan, in winning a permit for K2 for the summer of 1953.

In choosing a team for the 1938 expedition, Houston had relied on recommendations from Harvard friends and from colleagues who were higher-ups in the AAC. For the 1953 expedition, he was determined to put together not only the strongest team possible but a group of men who would get along well together. That was a stroke of genius. A team made up of members who like and trust one another will always be more successful than a team built solely on the skills of the climbers. So in 1953 the selection process ended up being more far-ranging and democratic but also more exhaustive than that of any American mountaineering expedition to that date.

There was no question that Bob Bates would be on board. Through the war years, Bates and Houston had stayed the closest of friends, and Bates was as keen for another crack at K2 as was his former Harvard chum. By the summer of 1953, though, Bates was forty-two years old; Houston was thirty-nine. That's not really old in Himalayan climbing terms, and both men were in excellent shape. But to round out the team, Houston and Bates sought younger men.

The AAC put out a nationwide notice soliciting applications for the five remaining slots on the K2 expedition. In the end, Houston and Bates weighed the credentials of more than twenty-five candidates. By 1952, Houston had set up a medical practice in Exeter, New Hampshire. As a rather draconian requirement for consideration for K2, he demanded that every would-be teammate travel (at his own expense) to Exeter to interview in person with the leader.

One of the men who was ultimately accepted was Dee Molenaar, a thirty-four-year-old climber with a solid record of first ascents in the Northwest and the Sierra Nevada who'd also been on the second ascent in 1946 of 18,008-foot Mount Saint Elias, the third-highest peak in Alaska or Canada. (The first ascent, of course, was led by the Duke of the Abruzzi way back in 1897.) In the fall of 1952, Molenaar left his job as climbing ranger on Mount Rainier to accept a new post in Colorado Springs as an adviser to the army's Mountain and Cold Weather Training Command. A modest fellow, Molenaar was surprised when friends urged him to apply for K2.

Dee and I have become really good friends. No one was more supportive of my efforts during Endeavor 8000 than he was. A couple of months after I'd climbed K2, Dee gave me a typed copy of his own K2 diary from 1953, with a really warm inscription to "another Rainier guide who's gone on to higher challenges and with great success."

At the beginning of his typed diary, in an introduction called "K2 Prelude," Dee recalls the tryout process:

> I submitted an application, feeling full well there was really little chance I'd be accepted, in view of the great number of other applicants, most younger and "in-their-prime." . . . Also, because Houston and Bates wanted to personally meet all applicants before confirming any choices—and I couldn't afford a trip East just to be interviewed and meet them. . . . But Bob Craig wrote them and supported my application. And while Craig and I were [later] working at Camp Drum, NY, I had a weekend visit with Charlie and Bates in Exeter, NH, where we hit it off right from the start.

Out of the Exeter screening process a legend was born, to the effect that it was Houston's dog, a golden retriever named Honey, that made the final choices. In 2007, Houston admitted to his biographer Bernadette McDonald, "It's true that our dog didn't like the people we didn't like. But that's as far as it went." Houston's wife, Dorcas, also made sharp appraisals of the visiting candidates. "She had a very good feel for quality people," Houston told McDonald.

Dee did indeed end up being chosen for the team without a tryout in Exeter, on the strong recommendation of his old buddy and fellow Rainier guide Bob Craig, who had already been accepted. By 1952, Craig was a twenty-eight-year-old ski instructor living in Aspen whose 1946 climbs of Devils Thumb and Kates Needle on the Alaska-Canada border already stood as two of the finest alpine first ascents ever performed by an American. George Bell, twenty-seven years old, was a physics professor at Cornell who had been on major expeditions to the Andes. Twenty-six-year-old Art Gilkey, from Iowa, was a geologist who had done hard routes in the Tetons and glacial research in Alaska. Pete Schoening, a chemical engineer, also twenty-six years old, was probably the strongest climber chosen for the team. In addition to numerous first ascents and new routes in the Cascades, he had been a member of the 1952 party that made the first ascent of King Peak in the Yukon, one of the highest mountains in the remote and massively glaciated Saint Elias Range.

Houston and Bates meant what they'd said about valuing the ability to get along above technical skill and ambition. One of the candidates for K2 who was rejected was Fred Beckey. Thirty years old in 1953, Beckey had a more stellar record of first ascents all over the United States and Canada than any other American climber his age. As a nineteen-year-old in 1942, with his seventeen-year-old brother as his only partner, Beckey had made an astounding second ascent of Mount Waddington, six years after Fritz Wiessner and Bill House had made the first ascent. In 1946, Beckey had been the driving force on Devils Thumb and Kates Needle. On his first attempt on the soaring granite spire of the Thumb, Beckey had paired up with Fritz Wiessner, the only time the two men who were probably the country's finest mountaineers of their day shared a rope. But on the approach hike, as he thrashed his way through a fiendish tangle of devil's club, Wiessner twisted and badly injured his knee. He pushed on to the base of the mountain but had to give up the attempt—one of the sorest disappointments of his climbing life. Beckey returned a few weeks later with Bob Craig and a third partner and bagged the first ascent.

No matter how strong he was as a climber, however, Beckey had a reputation as a headstrong, eccentric man with a quick temper. Houston never went on record as to why he turned down Beckey's application, but on the Abruzzi Ridge one day that summer, Pete Schoening would declare that he wished Beckey had been chosen for the team.

Still alive and still climbing at age eighty-six, Beckey today has by far the longest and most distinguished record of first ascents of previously unclimbed peaks of any American ever. And his reputation as a difficult eccentric still clings to him like glue. I don't know Beckey, but I've always admired his climbs.

Rounding out the party was Tony Streather, a twenty-seven-year-old British transport officer who had spent many years in Pakistan and India. Like Norman Streatfeild in 1938, Streather would be invaluable in hiring and dealing with porters. His only previous mountaineering expedition had been with a Norwegian team that in 1950 made the first ascent of 25,289-foot Tirich Mir, the highest peak in the Hindu Kush, the range adjoining the Karakoram on the west. Streather had performed so well that he had reached the summit with several of the Norwegians. On K2, he would climb as an equal with his American teammates.

In Rawalpindi on June 2, the team got electrifying news over the radio: Everest had been climbed by Edmund Hillary and Tenzing Norgay. Many decades later, Houston would tell Bernadette McDonald, "It was thrilling news, but, I must confess, I had a secret unworthy thought that this would upstage any triumph we might have in a few more months." That day, however, Molenaar wrote in his diary, "Good news to mountaineers. . . . Now K2 is the highest unclimbed mountain. We're determined to carry on our plans as before, and without bottled oxygen, which the Everesters had used."

On June 3, the party landed in a DC-3 at the Skardu airport. In the hour-and-a-half flight from Rawalpindi, the team had solved an approach that had taken the 1938 team two weeks and 220 miles on foot. At the airport, the climbers were greeted by cheering Pakistanis carrying banners, one of which read, "We appeal our American friends to solve Kashmir Problem."

In Skardu, the team recruited Balti porters for the hike in to base camp. They also hired ten Hunzas, men from mountain valleys near Gilgit, upstream from Skardu on the Indus River, to perform as high-altitude porters. Six of the best Hunzas were to play the role undertaken by the Sherpa in 1938 and 1939. In 1953, Sherpa were unavailable for K2, because Pakistan would not permit them to enter the country, thanks to the simmering antagonism with India. Because the Hunzas were so much less experienced than the men from Nepal, Houston and Bates decided that no high-altitude porter would go above Camp III, at 20,700 feet. On the hike in to Askole, Molenaar and Craig took time out to run "a climbing school for 8 Hunzas on a nearby boulder."

It took the team seven days, unhindered by porter strikes, to reach Askole. Before the expedition, the seven Americans had known each other other only in pairs—Houston and Bates had climbed together, as had Craig and Molenaar, but in no other pairing had two men shared a rope, and most of them were strangers. But as Craig later wrote in the official expedition account,

> As we approached our mountain, the magic cement that binds men together, the qualities which make unbreakable friendships began to form. Unconsciously, and imperceptibly, we were forming a team. If we had not it is probable that most of us would not have survived the troubles that we were to face.

How sad it is to reflect that that "magic cement" had been so sorely absent in 1939. On the hike in fourteen years earlier, the tension between Durrance and Wiessner had already begun to mount, and the faintheartedness of Sheldon, Cranmer, and Cromwell was already seeping to the surface.

From Askole, it took the team another nine days to reach base camp. At Urdukas, where the climbers thought they could discern the tent platforms hewn out of the turf by the Duke of the Abruzzi's party in 1909, they luxuriated in what Craig would describe as "the last grass we would see for two months." The team's progress, however, was slowed by threats of porter strikes, which Streather solved only by inspired diplomacy. There was also enough petty stealing—boots and ice axes were the objects most coveted by the pilferers—that the Americans began to assign watches over their camps at night.

All his life, Dee Molenaar has been a gifted artist and cartographer. On the hike in to K2, he brought along a watercolor kit, and while his teammates lolled on their air mattresses, he painted the surrounding landscape. (Dee's drawings and maps have been adapted for this book—see pages viii–ix, 217 and the endpapers.) He also paid attention to the character of his teammates, as their quirks and habits slowly revealed themselves. On June 18 he jotted down thumbnail appraisals in his diary. He could not have been more pleased with Houston and Bates:

> Charlie: fine leader, excellent humor and patience, optimistic in most cases.
> Bates: hard worker, cheerful, fine humor, fine organizer, fast walker.

Dee has never been the type to criticize his teammates, even in the privacy of his diary. What faint hints of criticism he allowed himself were tactfully phrased. Of Pete Schoening, for instance, he wrote, "quiet . . . extremely cooperative & hardworking around camp, worries about porters somewhat . . . may tend to make others uneasy due to constant demand for 'something to do.'"

On June 20, the team reached base camp and paid off their 180 porters. They would return on August 10. In terms of the calendar, the 1953 team was thus three weeks behind Wiessner's 1939 entourage, which had reached base camp on May 31. But in allowing fifty-one days before the return of the porters, Houston's team carved out an almost identical span in which to climb K2 or fail in their attempt. (That fifty-three days had not been long enough in 1939 did not seem to give Houston pause.)

One reason for the 1953 team's optimism sprang from the radical improvement mountaineering gear had undergone during the previous decade and a half. Now the climbers had nylon ropes, stretchy and five times stronger than the hemp or manila ropes used in the 1930s. They had rubber-cleated Vibram soles on their boots, instead of the hobnailed leather footgear of the past. Up high, the men sometimes wore rubber boots developed for soldiers in the Korean War. These glorified galoshes provided great insulation, and for a while they became popular on expeditions to really cold mountains. (Climbers started calling them "Mickey Mouse boots" because they looked like the black, oversized feet of the Disney character.) They're pretty clumsy, though, for purchase on rock, and when you strap crampons to them, they tend to twist off.

The Seattle firm of Eddie Bauer had custom-made matching red down jackets for the team, many times warmer and lighter than the layers of sweaters the climbers had donned in 1938. (Another link for me to the 1953 team is that within the last two years, Eddie Bauer has become my principal equipment sponsor. That's sort of fitting, since my first sleeping bag was a green Eddie Bauer model I used on Boy Scout outings.)

The 1953 team also had state-of-the-art down sleeping bags made in Switzerland, each one a nesting pair, a smaller inner tucked inside the larger outer. They were "always warm," the men later testified, and their only drawback was that, weighing seven pounds, they were hard to compress and cram inside a pack. Those packs were of a new steel-and-nylon frame design, far superior to the shapeless rucksacks of the 1930s. And this time around, Houston had no objection to bringing scores of pitons, both rock pins and special ice pitons made for the team by a friend of Houston and Bates's at MIT. (Apparently Houston's old disdain for "ironmongery" had softened over the years.)

Probably the most important gear the 1953 team had that the 1938 team had not was several lightweight walkie-talkie radios. Throughout the expedition, the climbers could usually communicate with base camp, and often from one camp to another. (If Wiessner's party had had such radios, it is possible that the whole tragedy could have been averted. Of course the technology of 1939 had not yet produced lightweight walkie-talkies.) The 1953 team also had a Zenith portable radio at base camp, on which they received the occasional broadcast from as far away as Europe and even, several times, the United States.

The party planned to use, for the most part, the same campsites they had first established in 1938, although they were leery of Camp III, where the rocks kicked loose from above had torn holes through the tents and nearly hit three of the men. There's one detail in Houston's account of camp logistics that I passed right over when I first read *K2: The Savage Mountain* but that on rereading it now gives me pause. The 1953 team planned to pitch a Camp VIII somewhere on the Shoulder, around 26,000 feet. But then, according to Houston, "somewhere in the rocks less than a thousand feet from the summit we hoped to pitch Camp IX, a small bivouac tent with food for two men for three days."

Sorry, Charlie, but that idea sounds a bit odd. Perhaps, though, it derived from how little the team knew about the mountain above 26,000 feet. Evidently, in 1953 the climbers planned not only to follow the arduous 1,500-foot climb up high-angled rock and mixed ground by which Wiessner had made his first attack, but to find a two-man campsite near the top of it! They knew how difficult Wiessner had found those rock bands, and what a good technical climber he was. Why not opt for the Bottleneck and the traverse under the hanging ice cliff? After all, Wiessner had said that if he had had crampons, he could have "practically run" up that couloir on his second attempt.

In the 1950s, the thinking in the Himalaya and the Karakoram was still bound by a dictum from the 1920s and '30s that insisted that camps on 8,000ers had to be placed close together. Just a month before Houston's team started working its way up the Abruzzi Ridge, Hillary and Tenzing had set out for the summit of Everest from a Camp IX at 27,900 feet. Nobody camps there nowadays; instead, it's standard practice to go for the top from the South Col, even though, at 26,000 feet, it's a full 3,000 feet below the summit. Twenty-first-century expeditions place only four camps on Everest, compared to the nine that were used in the 1950s. This certainly makes for longer and harder days, but it drastically reduces the amount of gear that has to be carried high on the mountain just to supply the camps.

Likewise, on K2, Wiessner's party had established nine camps. In 1992, we used only four. Nowadays on K2, nobody camps higher than the Shoulder, which is 2,200 feet below the summit.

The difference between then and now is partly logistical—gear is much lighter today, so loads aren't so heavy. But it's mainly psychological. It took a mental breakthrough to realize that a party could climb Everest or K2 with only four camps above base. It's actually easier in many respects, and safer (fewer camps in precarious places). In 1939, with their amazing push from base camp to Camp VI—6,900 feet gained in one day—Pasang Kikuli and Tsering had proved that such long nonstop hauls were possible for climbers in good shape, even without bottled oxygen. But it would take a while for an economy of campsites to become standard operating procedure.

June 21 was Molenaar's thirty-fifth birthday. It was not a happy occasion. He was ill and weak and "wobbly on legs," as he wrote in his diary. He wondered if he had contracted dengue fever, the malady that had probably been the cause of Petzoldt's recurrent high fever in 1938. Dee added, "Very homesick this evening, wondering how Lee and Patti [his wife and daughter] are, halfway around the world. Charlie also admits much of the same feeling lately; we're the only ones with wives and kids." During the expedition, Dee would often take out his wallet to look at the photos of Lee and Patti he kept there.

On June 27, Bates and Houston set out from Camp I, at the base of the Abruzzi, to find the route to Camp II they had pioneered fifteen years earlier. What must at the time have been a mortifying experience, Houston later treated in print as a comedy of errors:

> For the first two hours we climbed steep scree (loose stone) and snow slopes, crossing a few little ribs, exclaiming "I remember this chimney" or "Do you see that cairn? I'm sure we must be on the old route." . . .
>
> By noon we had to confess that we were lost.

It would take a second effort the next day, and much arguing, to work out the route to the little saddle that Petzoldt had first discovered in 1938, the site of Camp II at 19,300 feet.

In Bates and Houston's defense, I have to say that on the lower slopes of the Abruzzi Ridge, the terrain is so ill-defined that the best route is far from obvious. Today, most climbers follow the tattered remnants of old fixed ropes, which stand out like flags in a sea of gray rock and white snow, to solve the route-finding puzzle of the lower slopes.

At Camp II, the men had a doleful surprise. They found some tins of jam and pemmican, rusty with age, some stoves and a little gas, and "a Logan tent carefully wrapped and sheltered beneath a tarpaulin." These things had been left when Wiessner and Pasang Lama made their desperate retreat on July 23, 1939. It was here that those two shattered men had wrapped themselves in one tent and lain in the other through a sleepless night, as they felt their fingers and toes begin to freeze. Why they—or someone else—had wrapped the Logan tent and cached it under a tarp remains a mystery, since Wiessner never mentions doing so. Most likely, on his last effort to go up the mountain to look for survivors, on August 4, when he managed only to drag himself to Camp II, Wiessner had folded up and stashed the tent in hopes of yet another rescue effort.

Despite such minor setbacks as the route-finding snafu, the team was getting along well. "Morale excellent and no frictions in party," Dee wrote in his diary on June 26. But his homesickness only intensified. "I miss Lee and Patti terribly," he confessed on July 2. "No more lengthy, big-time expeditions for me!"

In 1939, the Dartmouth boys, George Sheldon and Chappell Cranmer, had gotten homesick early on the expedition, and those base camp blues had apparently contributed to the "crump" that left them virtually useless on the mountain. What you have to admire about Dee Molenaar is that despite feeling so down only two weeks after reaching base camp, to the point of vowing never to go on another major expedition (in fact, he would not), on K2, out of commitment to his teammates, he continued to pull every bit of his share of the weight, and to care as much as anyone about trying to get at least two men to the summit. Only a few days after his disconsolate birthday diary entry, Dee led a perilous and poorly protected leftward traverse, much to the admiration of his teammates, who nicknamed it "Molenaar's Madness."

On July 7, the climbers reached the site of the dangerous 1938 Camp III, at 20,700 feet. Intending to use the spot only as a supply depot, as Wiessner wisely had, the climbers were startled when Bates, poking around a corner, found a nook sheltered from falling rocks by an overhanging cliff. It was a major effort to excavate two narrow tent platforms there, but when the men were done, they had a safe and serviceable Camp III. (The brunt of the excavating was done by one of the Hunzas, Hidayat, in "a furious burst of construction." Like the Sherpa, the Hunzas often perform the most backbreaking work on expeditions, and often the "sahibs" are only too willing to sit back and watch them slave away. And sometimes, at the end of the day, the Hunzas or Sherpa are simply stronger.)

The next day, the team got more stunning news, via a radio broadcast received at base camp and relayed by walkie-talkie up the mountain. The great Austrian mountaineer Hermann Buhl had just made the first ascent of Nanga Parbat, the world's ninth-highest mountain, which in the 1930s had cost the lives of so many Germans, Austrians, and native porters. And Buhl had reached the summit solo!

The line in Dee's diary commenting on that achievement is fascinating, because it reflects the suspicion that initially clouded the Austrian's bold deed. Buhl, Dee wrote, "evidently sneaked off from the rest of the party at 3 A.M."

That was the story propagated by the team leader, Dr. Karl Herrligkoffer, who has gone down in mountaineering annals as one of the most autocratic and spiteful expedition dictators in Himalayan history. The true story, which took a long while to emerge, was that Buhl set out from the team's high camp half an hour ahead of his teammate Otto Kempter, who was feeling weak and having trouble getting started. Buhl intended only to break trail until Kempter could catch up, but his teammate lagged behind and finally gave up. So Buhl went on alone, reaching the summit at 7:00 P.M., enduring a standing bivouac on the way down, and later losing toes to frostbite.

Herrligkoffer was the classic example of an expedition boss who always led from the rear. Back in Germany, he claimed Buhl had disobeyed his orders; he even sued his Austrian teammate. But today, mountaineers the world over hail Buhl's ascent as one of the greatest deeds in climbing history.

I admire Buhl's audacity on Nanga Parbat, but I also think he was lucky to have a mild enough night to survive his standing bivouac. A deed such as Buhl's depends on walking the fine line between getting away with a stunning triumph and vanishing in the mists.

On July 9, the team at last reached Camp IV, just below House's Chimney. Here the discovery of yet more debris from 1939 also posed an apparent puzzle. Along with what Houston described as "tents reduced to shreds" and various kinds of food, including "a large tin of Ovaltine half used but still in perfect condition after fourteen years," the climbers found three sleeping bags. They were "frozen and filled with ice," but the 1953 team eventually thawed them out and used them to supplement their own supply of bedding.

Those sleeping bags caused Dee to write in his diary, "Our impression was that this was not an 'evacuated campsite,' as described since 1939 by Weissner [sic]." That's a provocative remark; it may ultimately reflect the bad feelings Houston still harbored toward Wiessner. It implies that the team wondered whether Wiessner's story of his desperate retreat was a lie. If Wiessner claimed he had gone down to camp after camp and found them all stripped of sleeping bags, what were these three bags doing at Camp IV?

Later Dee came to what was surely the true explanation. The bags must have been left by Pasang Kikuli and his Sherpa companions as they climbed back up the mountain to try to rescue Dudley Wolfe.

The same day the team reached Camp IV, Houston, Dee Molenaar, and George Bell tackled House's Chimney. Houston had been thinking about that crux pitch for a decade and a half. He would write in *K2: The Savage Mountain*, with characteristic self-deprecation:

> During the past ten days I had been mulling over different schemes which would put me in position to try this lead myself without being too obviously unfair to my companions. Now the time had come and I hesitatingly turned to George and Dee, both more competent climbers than I. "Would you fellows mind too much if I tried to lead this?"

Molenaar and Bell were happy to turn over the "sharp end" to Houston.

> For the first 30 feet I worked on the face, clutching at tiny holds, and trying not to appear too clumsy to the experts below. More by luck and will power than by good technique, I reached the deep cleft, where I huffed and puffed, all the while pretending to get out pitons, adjust the rope, or blow my nose. The upper section was strenuous, though not too difficult. With considerable elation I reached the top finally, and shouted to the others, "Come on up; I've got you belayed like a house."

That last line was a sly nod to the 1938 partner who had first led the chimney. And Houston's performance must have been more skillful than he let on, because Dee recorded in his diary that it had taken only an hour to lead the pitch—half the time Wiessner had expended on it in 1939.

At the old Camp V, only 300 feet above the top of House's Chimney, the three men found more relics from 1939. "Another smashed tent," wrote Dee, "and letters to Wolfe—including a bill from some laundry outfit back home."

One of the delights of Dee's diary is that it captures—as "official" expedition books rarely do—the homely day-to-day details of life on a big mountain. A few examples:

Backache again, and slight headache—restless sleep, due possibly to Charlie's irregular snoring through night.

Pete, George, and I took loads and set up Gerry tent at IV, lay inside for 3.5 hrs, talking about the Northwest—and exchanging farts.

Problem here: getting stove started and keeping it upright. Also, obeying nature's calls. We urinate in peanut can, and toss it out entrance; defecation requires more guts.

So far, almost everything on the expedition had gone well. The weather had been consistently good, as camps were established and supplies moved steadily up the mountain. Up to Camp III, the Hunzas had performed yeoman work. Houston was tempted to use them higher, but decided against that tactic, on the grounds that the men were simply not experienced enough on difficult terrain. On July 12, as they started back to base camp, the Hunzas parted company for good with the Americans. Wrote Houston later, "Their early cockiness, bred of ignorance, had been succeeded by overcautiousness. . . . After their initial demoralization at Camp I (and what mountain porters have not gone through this?), they had performed splendidly." As the Hunzas receded into the distance below Camp III, they shouted out, "*America zindabad!*" ("Long live America!") and "*Pakistan zindabad!*"

Pete Schoening, the engineer, had designed an aluminum A-frame tripod to which he now attached a pulley. With this device, pulling on ropes fed through the pulley, the men hauled many hundreds of pounds of gear up House's Chimney. "This was hard work, and time-consuming," wrote Houston. "But it was nowhere near as hard as carrying loads up the narrow chimney." In his diary, Dee crowed, "*A-frame big success!*"

Now, however, the weather changed. Beginning on July 14, it stormed on seven of the next eleven days. Houston figured the inevitable delays put the team about a week behind schedule. But the men's spirits plunged with the weather. "Gone were most of the jokes; the banter had become more serious," remembered Houston. "We were more determined now than ever, but the picnic was over; the true struggle had begun."

It's always true on expeditions that when you're stuck in a tent with nothing to do, your thoughts turn to food. Houston wittily recaptured those stormbound vigils:

> We read, we slept. Dinners had become real occasions, because our appetites were still good (they were to fail higher up) and considerable ingenuity was usually exercised by the cook. Sometimes he added Triscuits to the boiled meat bars, or fried raisins to the chicken. Sometimes we had oyster stew (minus the oysters) by mixing Klim, butter, salt, and tuna fish. . . . Bates and I had noticed recently that our companions, heartily sick of our everlasting reminiscences [of 1938], were now again showing interest in these memories, particularly when they involved some of the epicurean dishes then conceived.

I was amused to discover in Dee's diary that everybody's favorite dessert was Jell-O. I haven't taken Jell-O on an expedition since my attempt on the east face of Everest in 1988. There, instead of following the directions on the package, to get a quick gut-bomb of energy, we would mix Jell-O or pudding powder with water in a quart bottle and slug the liquid down before it set. Jell-O may be a great treat for kids, but it's insipidly bland at 20,000 feet, and waiting for it to firm up seems to take an eternity.

On July 20, between storms, Bates and Schoening reconnoitered higher and reached Camp VI. There they discovered the most poignant of all the vestiges of the 1939 expedition. Houston described the scene: "Two tents had been torn to shreds. A stove, gasoline, and sleeping bags, rolled and ready to be strapped to the carrying frames, lay nearby. A small bundle of tea wrapped in a handkerchief lay inside an empty stove box beneath the snow."

On July 31, 1939, Pasang Kikuli, Phinsoo, and Kitar had set out from

Camp VI on their second attempt to rescue Dudley Wolfe, leaving Tsering to brew up tea. The sleeping bags had evidently been rolled up in anticipation of five men descending the Abruzzi Ridge. Instead, only Tsering returned.

Pasang Kikuli and Phinsoo had become Houston's dear friends on the 1938 expedition. Fifteen years later, he saluted them and Kitar movingly: "Whatever their fate, the history of climbing has no braver story, no more generous chapter than theirs. Their sleeping bags, and the pathetic bundle of tea, were sad reminders of their courage."

On July 25, Houston, Craig, and Bell attacked the Black Pyramid. Bell led most of the way, across deceptively tricky terrain: "The rock was solid, steep, polished by icefalls through ages past. The holds were small for hands and feet, and often choked with ice." But, according to Houston, "Bell was in his element here." In 1992 we found the Black Pyramid a challenging and exciting break from the rather ill-defined route work leading up to it. The climbing's not extremely difficult, but until we got it fixed with ropes we were constantly aware of just how exposed it is.

Unlike 1939, when Wiessner, the only strong climber, led virtually every step of the route, in 1953 all eight men—even Tony Streather— took turns advancing the team's push up the Abruzzi Ridge. That goes a long way toward explaining why those men bonded together so harmoniously, and so loyally. I've had my own solid partnerships on 8,000ers, with guys like Veikka Gustafsson and J.-C. Lafaille, but I've only rarely been on an expedition in which as many as eight teammates worked together so smoothly. That's an ideal that many teams aspire to but few achieve.

Camp VII was pitched on a narrow platform hacked out of a steep snow slope at 24,500 feet. It was so marginal a site that on the way up the Abruzzi, only one pair of climbers spent a single night there. But on July 31, during a cold, windy day, Schoening and Gilkey broke through and found a spot for Camp VIII. At 25,500 feet, it was 800 feet higher than the highest camp in 1938.

All the way through the Black Pyramid and up to the lower edge of the Shoulder, the men placed willow wands every 50 feet or so to mark their route—as I did in 1992, but as no one bothered to in 1986 or 2008, an oversight that contributed to both tragedies. Arriving after a tough push through whiteout conditions on August 2, Bates and Streather found their way to Camp VIII. The first thing Bates said to his teammates was "Thank God for your willow wands. We had no idea where your camp was and couldn't see a thing. Your tracks were completely gone above the ice steps."

By August 3, all eight climbers were ensconced in their tents at Camp VIII. ("Some kind of record for an expedition," Dee speculated in his diary.) Houston later recalled, "Morale was magnificent. We were in striking distance of the goal. The summit might still be ours."

The entries in Dee's diary are not so sanguine. The weather during the last ten days had been remarkably cold. Bates and Houston kept remarking on how much colder it was than during the corresponding weeks in 1938. Korean boots or no, most of the climbers had felt the nip of incipient frostbite on their feet. As early as July 25, Dee wrote, "Our experience with frostbite also indicates (happily) that we are thinking more of our fingers and toes than of reaching the summit. Perhaps the altitude is affecting our will to push high at any price." A few days later: "Worried about toes. Craig's are turning white." Soon Dee was deeply ambivalent. "I feel alternately strong," he wrote on July 31, "with good 'eager' days, and then I lose my appetite for taking chances with the weather and personally going much higher—willing now to be in support role rather than attaining the summit myself."

Three days earlier, he had voiced an apprehension in his diary that would prove uncannily prescient: "Bringing an injured man down from K2 would be an *extremely* difficult, if not impossible, task."

On July 31, Dee once more jotted down thumbnail impressions of his teammates and their current states of mind and body. "Charlie continues to push ahead as leader," he wrote, "although I feel he may push himself too hard at times. . . . Gilkey is strong and quiet, probably the only one who really wants the summit badly enough to take a few risks—wants us *all* to make it to the top."

By August 3, however, the team was reconciled to the likelihood that only two men might get a chance to go for the summit. So, democratic to the end, they held a secret ballot. George Bell and Bob Craig were chosen for the first summit team, Pete Schoening and Art Gilkey for the second.

The men kept telling one another that all they needed was three consecutive clear days to give the summit their best shot. But that day a storm swept in over the Karakoram. It lasted for seven straight days. The men sat in their tents, trying to stay warm, burning their precious fuel, and eating their dwindling rations. Houston later recalled the tedium of that vigil:

> Someone tightened the guy ropes on all tents. When we could melt snow, someone had strength to clean and fill the pots, and someone else took tea to those in the other tents. Bob Bates read aloud to us for hours. Dee Molenaar painted. We all wrote diaries; my own was now over 200 pages long.

On August 6, the wind grew so strong that Houston and Bell's tent started to rip apart in the night. The two men gathered up their belongings, waited for a lull, then made a dash for the other tents. Houston threw himself into one shelter, Bell into another. This meant that two of the team's remaining three tents, designed for two men each, had to hold three.

Day by day, the men watched their hopes for the summit slip through their fingers. And then August 7 brought the unforeseeable event that would cancel those hopes completely—and turn the expedition into a survival ordeal.

———

That day began with optimism, as the clouds rose, the sky grew brighter, and the wind diminished. But as Houston would later write,

> We crawled from our tents and stumbled around like castaways first reaching shore. As Art Gilkey crawled out to join us, he collapsed unconscious in the snow. We rushed to him and he smiled feebly. "I'm all right, fellows; it's just my leg, that's all."

His teammates half-carried Gilkey back into his tent. They undressed him so that Houston, the team doctor, could examine the leg. "I've had this Charley horse for a couple of days now," Gilkey said, almost apologetically. "I thought it would be gone by now."

Indeed, Dee's diary for August 2, five days earlier, as the men had pushed up to Camp VIII, notes,

> Craig and I roped together with Art during climb up ice slope, but Art, at lower end of rope, complained of a "Charley horse," untied to keep from slowing us down. But he kept up with us, following the dragged end of the rope up the slope to VIII.

Houston knew at once that Gilkey's ailment was no Charley horse. The man's left ankle was red and swollen. "The diagnosis was all too clear," Houston recalled. "Art had developed thrombophlebitis."

That diagnosis was deeply puzzling to the experienced doctor. Blood clots had formed in Gilkey's left calf. In the best of circumstances, he might lose his leg. But the far greater danger was that as Art moved around, the clots could break off, migrate to the lungs, and cause a fatal embolism, or blockage of a blood vessel. After wrapping Gilkey's leg in Ace bandages and trying to "reassure" him, Houston went from tent to tent to deliver the bad news. "I can't tell you what caused it," he told his teammates. "It's a disease which usually hits older people, or surgical patients. I have never heard of it in healthy young mountaineers."

Worse luck could hardly have struck the team. Thrombophlebitis is so rare among climbers, I've never seen a case of it on any of my thirty expeditions to 8,000ers. But since Gilkey, we all know that the threat exists. Long periods of inactivity when you're stormbound in a tent can cause the blood in your legs to clot. And at altitude, the inevitable dehydration thickens your blood. It's common practice nowadays on 8,000ers to take an aspirin a day to keep your blood thin and, when you're stuck in a tent during a long storm, to periodically get your legs moving to improve circulation. Houston's teammates wanted to believe that Gilkey might simply be out of action for a few days. Bob Bates asked his best friend, "How soon will he get better, Charlie?" Unwilling to burden them with his darkest thoughts, Houston gave them a guesstimate of ten days. Then he crawled back into Gilkey's tent. He later wrote, "I did the best I could to explain his condition, leaving out the complications, taking as optimistic a note as I could, trying to hide my awful certainty that he would never reach Base Camp alive."

Within the team, Schoening, Molenaar, and Craig had the most experience in mountain rescue, so Houston conferred with them about the chances of getting Gilkey down the mountain. The men answered that they thought they could manage such an extreme task, but, as Houston wrote, "Their statements lacked conviction." And:

> I did not believe them. I knew, we all knew, that no one could be carried, lowered, or dragged down the Black Pyramid, over the dreadful loose rock to Camp V, down House's Chimney. . . . My mind's eye flew over the whole route. There was no hope, absolutely none. Art was crippled. He would not recover enough to walk down. We could not carry him down.

In his diary, Dee wrote a laconic assessment: "Situation looks desperate." As if to mock the team's ambitions, that very afternoon the sky in the west started clearing.

Hopeless the rescue might be, but, in Houston's words, "We could try, and we must." Gilkey was placed in a sleeping bag, which was wrapped in a tent, and a climbing rope was tied to his waist. The first effort, however, was a complete failure. The days of storm had loaded the slopes below camp until they were on the verge of avalanching. The lowering was inviting disaster. The men hauled Gilkey only a few hundreds yards before they gave up.

There was nothing to do but return to camp. That took an all-out effort. The snow was too soft and deep for the men to haul Gilkey uphill, so he had to aid the effort by making what Houston called "great leaps with his good leg."

The next day no one could move, as high winds tore at the tents, despite the slowly clearing sky. Gilkey's condition seemed to improve slightly. "I'll be climbing again tomorrow," he told Houston, who knew that this brave promise could never be fulfilled.

By this point, the strongest climbers were Pete Schoening and Bob Craig. On that day, August 8, Craig made a bold proposal. "Charlie," he said, "what about a dash for the summit from here?"

"Or maybe we could move two men up to IX today," Schoening added. "I'm game. We might as well do something while we wait for Art's leg to get better."

If Houston was miffed by his teammates' hunger for the summit, he never said so in print. And he gave them his blessing to head upward onto the Shoulder. In the deep snow, Schoening and Craig managed only some 400 vertical feet before turning back. Dee estimated their high point at 25,800 feet. Thanks to Gilkey's collapse, the 1953 team failed by some 200 vertical feet to match the altitude reached by Houston and Petzoldt in 1938—and by 1,700 feet the high point Wiessner and Pasang Lama had attained in 1939.

On August 9, the storm returned in full force. And that morning, to his dismay, having listened to Gilkey's "dry, hacking cough" through the night, Houston examined his patient and determined that the blood clots had indeed migrated to his lungs. Gilkey had a pulmonary embolism. Houston later wrote in *K2: The Savage Mountain,*

> This was our lowest time. For the first time I thought we might
> all perish here in this pitiless storm. We would never leave Art;

none of us had even thought of it. But we could not move him in the storm; indeed, we could not move ourselves in the storm of that day.

Dee's diary entry for August 9 is equally poignant and honest:

> Charlie came by and asked how our morale was—then informed us that Art probably wouldn't last long. My feelings are hard to put down now. A few moments later, tears are in all our eyes. (I thought I just heard Art laugh in his tent.)
>
> Plans change: Terrible thought that perhaps our getting down safely depends on Art's early passing. (God, spare me from such thoughts!)

Gilkey's courage through this ordeal was extraordinary. He told Houston that while he felt no pain, the nonstop coughing was a "nuisance." Houston recalled, "Art said nothing of himself. He had never talked about his death, though he was too wise not to see its imminence. He apologized for being a burden upon us. He encouraged us, spoke of another summit attempt—after we got him down."

The storm raged on on August 10, but Houston demanded that the men begin the rescue effort that day. "What? Move in this storm?" someone said.

"We've got to," Houston answered. "He'll soon be dead if we don't get him down."

On August 7, after the abortive first attempt to evacuate Gilkey, Schoening, and Craig had gone back out to scout for an alternative route down, one that might avoid the avalanche-prone slopes of the team's ascent route. They returned with the news that a steep rock rib just to the west might serve that purpose. It would take the team across much more difficult ground, but it looked to be safe from avalanches.

On August 10, the men packed up for what Bates would later describe as "the most dangerous day's work of [each man's] lifetime." Gilkey was wrapped in a sleeping bag, with his feet in a rucksack. This makeshift litter was cradled by a network of ropes. Four men, each tending a separate rope—one man above, one below, one on either side—would try to pull and steer the immobile victim down the dangerous ground.

At regular intervals, his teammates knelt close to Gilkey's face to ask him how it was going. "I'm fine," he answered each time, managing a wan smile. "Just fine."

Schoening and Molenaar went ahead to scout the route—a perilous business, in the blinding storm. For able-bodied men to descend in such conditions would have been bad enough. With the burden of their helpless invalid, the team faced an almost impossible struggle. Bates remembered that day in *K2: The Savage Mountain*:

> The wind and cold seeped insidiously through our layers of warm clothing so that by the end of the third hour none of us had feeling in his toes any longer, and grotesque icicles hung from our eyebrows, beards, and mustaches. Goggles froze over and we continually raised them on our foreheads in order to see how to handle the rope. Moving the sick man was frightfully slow.

After hours of grim effort, however, the men had lowered Gilkey to the edge of the rock rib, at about 24,500 feet. Meanwhile, Schoening and Molenaar had located the shallow platform in the steep slope that had served as a dubious Camp VII. Only an easterly traverse of a mere 450 feet separated Gilkey from that campsite. But to haul him horizontally across the icy slope loomed as the toughest maneuver yet.

Shortly before, Craig had been engulfed in a small windslab avalanche and had just managed to keep his purchase. Now he was so exhausted that he could barely tighten his crampon straps, so Molenaar belayed him over to the campsite. There Craig rested for a while before starting to enlarge the tent platforms with his ice ax. Molenaar returned to Gilkey and tied in with a short hank of rope to the invalid's waist loop, hoping to help out in the delicate job of hauling the litter sideways across the slope.

The men were strung out across the dangerously steep terrain in atrocious conditions. Coming last, Schoening had plunged his ax in to the hilt behind a small boulder, using it as an anchor as he looped the rope around the upper shaft and slowly fed it out to lower Gilkey. Bell and Streather were roped together on one rope, Houston and Bates on another. Molenaar stood beside Gilkey's litter, tied in to it close.

As I've often commented, when climbers go to the rescue of someone else, that's when they're most likely to get in trouble themselves. They take risks they wouldn't normally allow themselves, and urgency and adrenaline drive them to desperate efforts. On K2 in 1992, Scott and I got caught in the avalanche that nearly cost us our lives only because we thought we had to do everything we could to help Thor Kieser and the played-out Chantal Mauduit get down. We'd have never been in that place in those conditions if we had been simply climbing from Camp III to Camp IV. And the slope where we got avalanched was very close to where Gilkey dangled on the afternoon of August 10.

It took only a small misstep to trigger the whole chaotic accident. George Bell, who had lost all feeling in his feet, began downclimbing hard ice to aid in the maneuvering of Gilkey. He slipped, lost his balance, and started plummeting down the slope. The rope came tight to Streather and pulled him off his stance. Streather frantically tried to self-arrest but couldn't get any purchase with the pick of his ax.

As the two men careened out of control down the mountain, their rope intersected with that linking Houston and Bates, pulling it tight. With no time to prepare, first Houston and then Bates were plucked off their feet. Four men were now hurtling toward what seemed certain death. Bates later wrote, "*This is it!* I thought as I landed heavily on my pack. There was nothing I could do now. We had done our best, but our best wasn't good enough. This was the end. . . . Only thousands of feet of empty space separated us from the glacier below."

The rope between Bell and Streather next snagged on the short tie-in between Molenaar and Gilkey, pulling Molenaar off his feet with a sudden jerk. Five men were now plunging in a tangled mess of ropes toward the 7,000-foot void. And two more were about to join them.

Dee Molenaar's watercolor sketch of the complex accident of August 10, 1953, that nearly swept seven teammates to their deaths.

From 60 feet above Gilkey, Schoening saw what was happening. He threw himself on top of the ice ax he had jammed behind the small boulder and hung on to the rope with all his strength. The jolt came as Molenaar's fall started to pull the helpless Gilkey down the slope. But Schoening held Gilkey in place, and the short tie-in stopped Molenaar's fall.

Only the fact that the jolts came in a punctuated series kept seven men from being simultaneously swept to their deaths off the Abruzzi Ridge. Schoening held on, clinging to his rope with a death grip, and one by one, each of the falling men came to a halt. By the time the chain of events was over, Bell, the one who had fallen the farthest, lay 250 feet below Schoening. (See diagram, page 217.)

Pete Schoening's "miracle belay" has become a legend. Nothing like it, before or since, has ever been performed in the mountains—one man with a single ax and a grip of steel stopping the otherwise fatal falls of six teammates and of himself. Schoening's deed, which as a superbly trained climber he performed by instinct in a split-second reflex, is, simply, the most famous belay in mountaineering history.

The men were alive. But their predicament would now drain everyone's last reserves.

Bell had lost his pack, his glasses, and his mittens in the fall. As he stumbled, half blind, up toward his teammates, he yelled, "My hands are freezing!" Bates and Molenaar had landed with one on top of the other, sprawled across a rocky outcrop. Before they could even guess what had happened, they heard a cry—probably from Schoening: "Get your weight off the rope!" Still holding his belay in that death grip, Schoening felt his hands starting to freeze, even with his mittens on.

Bates unroped, climbed down to Bell, and offered him a spare pair of loosely woven wool mitts that he had carried in his parka pocket. Bell's fingers, already "an ugly fish-belly white," were so stiff that he needed Bates to put the mitts on his hands.

The worst injured was Houston, whose head had struck a rock, knocking him unconscious. As Bates cautiously worked his way toward the "crumpled figure" below him, he was not sure whether his best friend was alive or dead. Bates touched Houston's shoulder. Houston opened his eyes, then staggered to his feet. "Where are we?" he pleaded. "What are we doing here?"

No amount of explaining from Bates seemed to penetrate Houston's fog. He kept saying, "Where are we?" He had suffered a bad concussion and lost his short-term memory. For the rest of his life, he would be unable to remember the accident. To motivate his friend, Bates brought his face close to Houston's and ordered, "Charlie, if you ever want to see Dorcas and Penny [Houston's wife and daughter] again, climb up there *right now!*"

With a belay from Molenaar, relying on sheer muscle memory, Houston "fairly swarmed" up the rock-and-ice slope. But when he arrived at Molenaar's side, he repeated, "What are we doing here?"

Much of the team's gear had been lost in the fall. The men had only a two-man tent and a smaller bivouac tent. While one man tried to hack out a platform in the steep slope, others set to work frantically pitching the tents, which the wind threatened to rip out of their hands. Earlier, Bob Craig, who had not witnessed the accident, had looked across the slope to see it swept clean of climbers. Then he heard Schoening yelling at him to get an ice ax to anchor Gilkey. Craig soloed across the traverse and planted an ax just above Gilkey's supine body, then tied it to the rope cradle that cushioned the man's makeshift litter. Only then could Schoening release his hands from the rope that had stopped everyone's fall. At once he headed down toward the inadequate campsite, for his fingers, like Bell's, had begun to freeze.

Craig told Gilkey that the team would return for him as soon as they got the tents pitched. Privately, he wondered how the men, in their newly battered state, would ever manage to drag their inert teammate across that dangerous slope. A few minutes later, Streather planted a second ax to improve Gilkey's anchor.

While the men hacked away at their platform, they heard Gilkey, out of sight around a small rock rib, call out several times, but the wind made it impossible for them to understand what he was saying. Bates later wrote, "Gilkey sounded as if he were shouting encouragement, but the wind blurred his words, as it must have muffled our answering shouts to him."

About ten minutes after hearing Gilkey's last shout, Bates, Craig, and Streather roped up and traversed the slope. They turned the rib and moved cautiously toward the victim. "What we saw there I shall never forget," Bates wrote. "The whole slope was bare of life. Art Gilkey was gone!"

As they stared at this blankness, the men noticed a new groove in the ice. The conclusion was obvious: in the time between Gilkey's last shout and the trio's arrival to rescue him, an avalanche had scoured the edge of the rock rib, taking the helpless victim with it. Even the two anchoring ice axes were gone. "It was as if the hand of God had swept him away," Bates later wrote.

The three men returned to camp with the news. As shocking as it was, the team could not dwell on it, for they still faced the ordeal of getting through the night. Four men piled into the two-man tent, with only one air mattress among them; Bates opened his sleeping bag and draped it over the four men like a down comforter. The other three men were jammed even more tightly inside the minuscule bivouac tent.

Houston had suffered not only a concussion but a hemorrhage that blurred the vision in his right eye, as well as cracked ribs that made breathing painful. Molenaar had also cracked his ribs, and had received a head wound and a deep gash in his thigh. Bell was sure that both his hands and his feet were frostbitten, and he was so myopic that he was virtually blind without his glasses. Nobody slept all night.

Houston was out of his head. He became convinced that he had to cut his way out of the tent, or else everyone in it would suffocate. When his teammates physically restrained him, Houston raved, "Leave me alone. I'm a doctor, I know about these things." Later in the night, as if half-returned to his senses, he intermittently blurted out, "How's Pete?" Bates recalled,

> I would say, "He's all right," but Charlie wouldn't believe me. Then I would call across to the tiny bivouac tent, which was swelled to bursting by the three men inside, "Hey, Pete, tell Charlie you're all right."
>
> Pete Schoening would call out, "I'm fine, Charlie. Don't worry about me."

A dozen times that night, Houston repeated, "How's Pete?" Then he would lie quiet for a while, only to cry out, "How's Tony?" And even "How's Art?"

Somehow the men got through the night. They managed to melt snow and brew up tea, which they passed from one tent to the other. The wind dropped, but in the morning the sky was a leaden gray, presaging yet another storm. It would take a dogged effort simply to pack up and start down the dangerous slopes leading to Camp VI.

There was not even an ice ax for every man. The most seriously injured, Houston was still drifting in and out of reality, so Schoening and Craig tied him into the middle of a three-man rope, and Schoening, coming last, belayed Houston on every tricky stretch. The team leader stopped several times, sat down, and, as Bates observed, "put his chin in his hand, and looked around as if to say, 'What are we doing here?'" Schoening would exhort, "Come on, Charlie. Let's go!" Houston would rise wearily to his feet and continue the descent.

Though none of them said a word to each other, each man realized that Gilkey's disappearance had probably saved their own lives. Even more disturbingly, as they covered the ground below their emergency Camp VII, the men climbed past splotches of blood stuck to the snow and the protruding rocks. None of them mentioned this grim memento mori until decades later. But that night, Dee wrote in his diary, "Enroute down, we passed a tangle of ropes and torn sleeping bag that had held

Art, with track of blood speckling snow below, indicating he had died quickly. Poor Art. We all passed by this wreckage silently."

It took the team five days to limp down the mountain. That they pulled off that descent without another accident is a tribute not only to the toughness of those seven men but to the depth of their solicitude for one another. Still, when they reached base camp on August 15, they were a demoralized crew, with the pall of defeat heavy on their spirits and the weight of sorrow over the loss of their teammate even heavier.

On a small ridge above base camp, the Hunzas built a rock cairn as a memorial to Art Gilkey. Over the years since 1953, plaques commemorating other climbers who died on K2 have been added to the cairn. The memorial has become a solemn shrine for all the expedition members who place their base camps on the Godwin Austen Glacier.

I think I was sixteen when I read *K2: The Savage Mountain*. I was so impressed by the story that in a high school class in expository writing, when the teacher assigned us to write a play, I wrote about K2, with the plot revolving around the dilemma of having to leave somebody behind on the mountain. What really inspired me about those guys on the 1953 expedition is how they took care of one another, how they bonded in adversity. Later I would realize that there was a kind of military model for their courage, in the motto "Leave no man behind."

But you can't teach that kind of morality. Those guys were all selfless by nature. They all had high ethical standards. I'm sure their example helped me form my own moral principles, so that much later, when I had to put aside my personal ambitions to go to the aid of another climber in trouble, I did so without hesitation. I know I couldn't live with myself if I didn't try to help out when I had the chance.

In 1992, when Scott and I were climbing above our Camp III toward the Shoulder, we suddenly realized that we were traversing the very slope where Schoening had stopped the interlinked falls of his six teammates and where Gilkey had been swept away by the avalanche. We slowed down as we discussed just how those events must have unfolded thirty-nine years before. The slope was self-evidently a treacherous place, and in that moment, it came home to us just how hopeless it would be to try to carry a completely incapacitated teammate down the mountain.

Houston was right in that grim passage about his thoughts after diagnosing Gilkey's thrombophlebitis: "There was no hope, absolutely none. Art was crippled. . . . We could not carry him down." In 1992, we had gotten Gary Ball, stricken with pulmonary edema, down that same stretch through the Black Pyramid. But Gary was still mobile all the way down to Camp II. We weren't lowering him in a makeshift litter, as the 1953 team was with Gilkey. Gary could still walk, and could hold on to the rope I anchored, using it like a handrail. It was only when we arrived at Camp I, at 20,000 feet, that Gary collapsed and became a litter case. As the American team had with Gilkey, we then wrapped Gary in a sleeping bag and lowered him down the snowy slopes through the night. By that point there were six of us lowering and another climber at Gary's side to steer him onto the right course.

The only time Pete Schoening wrote about K2 was in a small booklet, limited to about a hundred copies and intended only for close friends, which was published after his death in 2004. That work, however, reveals Schoening's lifelong conviction that the team could have gotten Gilkey down the mountain: "It would have taken longer than descending by ourselves and frostbite would have been more severe. But based on experience doing rescues on steep terrain, I believe we could have done it."

Whether or not Schoening's faith in the team's rescue capabilities is realistic, I'm convinced that had Gilkey not collapsed, the 1953 team would have made the first ascent of K2. They had been so successful in getting all eight climbers to 25,500 feet that I believe that, even with the stretch of bad weather that began on August 3, they could have gotten at least two men to the summit.

I also think the 1953 team was accurate in their private realization that Gilkey's death in the avalanche might have saved their own lives.

Decades after the expedition, a provocative theory started to circulate in the mountaineering world, proposed first by Tom Hornbein, Houston's friend and the man who, with Willi Unsoeld, completed the astonishing first traverse of Everest by the west ridge in 1963. Hornbein wondered whether Gilkey, realizing what a fix his comrades were in after the accident, might have "taken the opportunity to disconnect himself from the mountainside to which he had been secured," sacrificing himself to save his teammates.

If Hollywood were to make a movie about the '53 expedition, that would be the crowning touch, the perfect embodiment of what Houston would come to call "the brotherhood of the rope." His teammates had briefly speculated about this possibility shortly after they'd discovered that Gilkey was gone. But Bates and Houston decided that it was very unlikely.

I agree with them. First of all, Gilkey was so swaddled up in his sleeping bag, he might have found it impossible to free his arms. And even if he had had a knife, could he have reached out and cut the rope with it? If he had, the ice axes anchoring him should have still been in place when Bates, Craig, and Streather arrived on the scene. But the axes vanished with Gilkey. Alternatively, it's barely conceivable that Gilkey could have wrenched the axes loose with his hands. By then, however, he was probably too weak to do so, and that morning Houston had given him a dose of morphine to dull the pain.

Dee's diary, written without the benefit of retrospect, is unequivocal: "After the wounded were in tents, Craig, Tony and Bates go out to bring Art in, or make him comfortable for the night. But they found the slope bare—a rock or snow avalanche had taken him down. Art is gone, dead."

At base camp, the men congregated to discuss every last detail of their recollections of what had happened high on the mountain between August 7 and 10, and they captured their discourse on a tape recorder. On the CD called *The Brotherhood of the Rope,* which Houston produced in 2004, you hear the voices of the men speaking in that discussion. Some of the comments are deeply moving.

The seven survivors got back to Rawalpindi on August 28, then went their separate ways. But they stayed friends for the rest of their lives. (There aren't many expeditions that can make that claim.) And in 1978, on the twenty-fifth anniversary of the trip, all seven held a joyful and poignant reunion in the Wind River Range of Wyoming.

In 1993, forty years after the expedition, members of a British team found Art Gilkey's bones on the Godwin Austen Glacier, not far from base camp. During the decades, his corpse had migrated with the ice four miles from the place where he had come to rest after his titanic plunge.

At the Banff Mountain Film and Book Festival that November, Charlie Houston gave the first of what would become a hugely popular series of "armchair talks." Dispensing with the usual slide show, Houston simply sat in a comfortable, well-upholstered chair and answered questions from the moderator, Geoff Powter, who was the editor of the *Canadian Alpine Journal*.

I wasn't there for that talk, but a friend who was later recounted what happened so vividly, I almost felt like I was present. Powter skillfully lobbed his questions so that they covered Houston's long and glorious career as a mountaineer and as the world's leading expert in high-altitude medicine, giving him a chance to tell his war stories. By now, Houston was eighty years old, a living legend, and the audience hung on his every word.

In that audience was Barry Blanchard, one of Canada's best mountaineers. He had been on K2 the previous summer and had participated in the recovery of Gilkey's remains. Blanchard waited through the Q & A period at the end of Houston's talk, until Powter said, "Okay, one more question." Then he stood up, introduced himself, and told the story of finding Gilkey's body. Barry is normally a confident speaker, but his voice quavered as he announced the discovery, which was news to almost everyone in the crowd. He ended by telling Houston that the climbers on the glacier just two and a half months earlier had recovered Gilkey's bones and brought them back to the United States, for eventual burial in a family plot.

Then Barry sat down. It was obvious that he hoped Houston would greet the stunning news of the discovery with an emotion matching his own, and perhaps even express heartfelt gratitude. As Barry had spoken, Houston had stared into the audience in the direction of his voice. By then, Houston was almost blind, so it's doubtful that he could even see the face of the guy who had made the announcement about Gilkey.

For long moments, Houston didn't say a word. The audience held its collective breath. Finally, in a cold, even voice, Houston said, "Frankly, I wish you had left him the way you found him." Barry was devastated.

One reason why *K2: The Savage Mountain* is such a great book, one of the true classics of mountaineering literature, is that Houston and Bates (and Craig and Bell, who contributed a chapter each) tell their story in such a straightforward manner. The very directness of the prose animates the drama of the book. There's no bluster, no bragging, not a whiff of nationalistic bravado in the telling of what, for each of its participants, was the adventure of a lifetime. At the core, all eight of those climbers were modest men.

So even though the expedition ended in failure and tragedy, the lessons it taught several younger generations of American climbers were inspiring ones. "The brotherhood of the rope" that Houston celebrates was no sentimental invention—it was the lifelong bond that their terrible ordeal on K2 forged among its seven survivors. The book affected me hugely. When I first started going on expeditions, I realized that even more important than getting to the summit was the chance to have a great adventure with partners I really liked and trusted. And I found that again and again, with teammates such as David Breashears, J.-C. Lafaille, Rob Hall, and Veikka Gustafsson.

In 1979, Nick Clinch, who led the team that made the first ascent of Gasherbrum I, in 1958 (the only 8,000er first climbed by Americans), and who would later serve as president of the AAC, eloquently summed up the legacy Houston and his teammates had left behind them:

In my opinion, the high point of American mountaineering remains the 1953 American Expedition to K2. The courage, devotion and team spirit of that expedition have yet to be surpassed, and still represent the standards of conduct toward which all American mountaineers should aspire.

6

THE PRICE OF CONQUEST

You would think that after the ordeal of 1953, Charlie Houston would never have wanted to go near K2 again. On the contrary, the tragedy only deepened his fixation on the mountain. His passion for K2 was the equal of Mallory's for Everest. Houston applied for and received a permit to put together yet another expedition in 1955.

In the meantime, however, Pakistan granted the Italians permission for the summer of 1954. After three expeditions, Americans may have come to feel that K2 was "their" mountain, but the Italians had a proprietary stake themselves in the world's second-highest peak. On top of the pioneering effort by the Duke of the Abruzzi's team in 1909, Italy had fielded a massive exploratory expedition to the region in 1929. Led by another nobleman, the Duke of Spoleto, this campaign remains somewhat mysterious. In *K2: The Story of the Savage Mountain,* Jim

Curran calls it a "debacle," and summarizes its history in a few pithy sentences:

> Originally planned for 1928 to mark the tenth anniversary of the end of the First World War, the expedition was also to coincide with one to the North Pole. K2 and/or Broad Peak were to be the objectives but internal strife caused the grandiose project to be modified, and then postponed for a year. In the end it became lamely designated the "Italian Geographical Expedition to the Karakoram," with no mountaineering objectives at all.

The leader of the 1954 expedition was Professor Ardito Desio, a geologist teaching at the University of Milan. (Desio would always insist that "Professor" be prefixed to his name.) Fifty-seven years old that summer, he was a tireless explorer of remote regions who had already led eleven scientific expeditions to Asia and Africa. His climbing résumé was distinctly thin, but, as he bragged in his thumbnail bio in the official book about the 1954 expedition, he was "the author of three hundred publications on geology, geography and paleontology." Desio was also a veteran of the 1929 Karakoram adventure, during which he and a single companion had hiked up the Godwin Austen Glacier to its head, as they carefully studied the Abruzzi Ridge.

When the French team led by Maurice Herzog climbed Annapurna, in 1950—the first 8,000er ever to be ascended—that triumph had a gigantic impact on the people of France. The climbers returned to wild celebrations that diminished not at all over the subsequent months. It is not an exaggeration to say that Annapurna meant to France what putting the first man on the moon meant to America. And the reason for that frenzy had everything to do with France's emergence from World War II as a battered country that had been occupied by the hated Nazis for four and a half years. The victory on Annapurna gave a whole nation an incalculable boost of self-esteem.

In its own way, Hillary and Tenzing's ascent of Everest in 1953 had a comparable impact on the British public, especially when (thanks to a brilliant system of couriers and coded messages organized by the *Times* reporter James Morris) the news arrived back in England just in time to be announced in the middle of the coronation of Queen Elizabeth II. (One wag later called it "the last great day of the British Empire.")

The 1950s were an intensely nationalistic decade, and the politics between countries inevitably crept into the world of sports. I wasn't born until three years later, but some of my elders had vivid recollections of the 1956 Olympics, when the Russians and the Hungarians tried to kill each other in their water polo match.

Like France, but for different reasons, Italy was a battered country after World War II. Everyone old enough to have lived through it would never forget the sting of losing the war, climaxed by Mussolini's body being hung upside down on a meat hook from the roof of a gas station in Milan. Professor Desio was thus fully aware of the potential value in national pride should Italians make the first ascent of K2.

But Desio was a geologist first and foremost, a mountaineer second. So once he was put in charge of the 1954 expedition, he conceived it as a joint scientific and climbing mission, with completely separate goals to be carried out simultaneously. Along with eleven mountaineers, a cameraman, and a medical officer, the K2 expedition would assemble five scientists, whose disciplines ranged from anthropology to petrography.

Making arcane discoveries about the rate of flow of a certain glacier or the linguistics of Balti hill tribes was obviously not going to stir the blood of the Italian public the way getting up K2 would, but Desio was adamant about his scientific program. In *Ascent of K2,* the professor acknowledged that many observers were skeptical of his two-pronged attack on the Karakoram:

> Its programme caused some bewilderment in mountaineering
> circles, where it was felt that so much scientific activity might seriously interfere with the work of the climbing party. That I refused to be deflected from my course was due to my conviction

that success could be achieved above all by careful preparation and by an appropriate distribution of the tasks of the two teams in space and time.

That passage gives the flavor of Desio's writing throughout the book. It's hard for me to think of any "official" account of a dramatic expedition that's as boring as Desio's *Ascent,* or as chock-full of pompous posing and self-congratulatory slaps on the back.

An old tradition, with roots in the Victorian age, argues that exploration for its own sake is simply self-indulgence, and that every adventure in the wilderness should have a scientific purpose. The most poignant example of that faith in science that I know of comes from Robert Falcon Scott's last expedition. When his teammates finally discovered Scott's last camp on his return from the south pole, eight months after the leader and his four brave comrades had starved and frozen to death, they found more than thirty pounds of rocks—geological specimens—still loaded on Scott's sledge.

By 1954, however, that tradition was almost obsolete. Certainly Houston's and Wiessner's expeditions to K2 had made no pretense of carrying out any scientific work (unless you count Cranmer and Sheldon's little "geologizing" jaunt to Urdukas, which was likely nothing more than an excuse to flee base camp).

Desio took his science so seriously that he ends *Ascent of K2* not with the climbers' triumphant return to base camp and thence to civilization but with two chapters called "The Work of the Scientists" and "Summary of the Expedition's Scientific Researches." While the climbers were struggling up the Abruzzi Ridge, the "professors" were puttering about the glaciers, doing things like taking magnetic observations and collecting "fauna" found above 13,000 feet. (In 1992, the only fauna we saw at base camp were goraks—huge, black ravenlike birds—and mice, and I sure didn't feel like collecting any of them.)

Of the latter effort, Desio observes, with his habitual smugness, "I personally took part in this work, the results of which will repay study on the part of specialists." And he closes the book not with a line like Herzog's famous "There are other Annapurnas in the lives of men" but as follows: "Only when the fruits of our labours are enshrined in the five volumes scheduled for eventual publication shall we be able to say that the expedition's work is done." I wonder how many people have read those five volumes—assuming they ever got published.

The professor was not only a scientist; he was a born generalissimo. On the mountain, the climbers would obey his orders to the letter, or else. Desio justified the militaristic organization of his team in a memo he sent to all the potential expedition candidates beforehand. He quotes it in full in *Ascent of K2*. It's not a document that many climbers I know of would have been happy signing off on:

> The need for rigid discipline will become apparent to every man once he has grasped the essential fact that everything must be subordinated to the attainment of the final goal, which is the conquest of K2. This discipline will be created by the spirit of genuine brotherhood and mutual understanding and confidence which must prevail among the members of the expedition.

Man, that's about as far from Houston's concept of "brotherhood" as you can get! You can't *order* "genuine brotherhood and mutual understanding" to exist: it has to evolve among men, like the climbers in 1953, as they get to know each other on the mountain. In the end, the 1954 expedition would generate the polar opposite of brotherhood among the principal climbers.

That kind of military approach to the 8,000ers, however, was far more common in the 1950s than it is today. John Hunt, the leader of the 1953 Everest expedition, was selected by the Himalayan Committee of the Alpine Club for his military background. On the mountain, however, he exercised his skill not by ordering climbers around like toy soldiers but by keeping firm control over the team's complex logistics. And Hunt never led from the rear, as Desio would. He carried loads all the way up to 27,350 feet and even contemplated trying for the summit himself. In general, an expedition chief who leads from the front and by example inspires his team.

In 1950, before they left Paris, the French climbers bound for Annapurna were required by the Club Alpin Français to swear to an oath of complete obedience to their leader, Maurice Herzog. Such freethinkers as Gaston Rébuffat and Louis Lachenal were taken aback at this demand, but they mumbled the oath anyway, knowing they had to in order to get a crack at Annapurna. On the mountain, however, Herzog constantly sought the advice of his teammates, and he led from the front all the way from base camp to the summit.

There's no doubt that Desio was keen to climb K2. He just didn't want to do any of the climbing himself—and at age fifty-seven, with so little alpine experience, he probably made a wise decision. In the end, despite spending ninety-one days on the Baltoro and Godwin Austen glaciers, aside from a single jaunt to Camp II, aided by fixed ropes, Desio never set foot on the Abruzzi Ridge.

But the generalissimo was nothing if not thorough. Before he even learned the outcome of Houston's expedition, and before he knew whether his own permit for 1954 was approved (no done deal, since a number of other countries had also applied), he planned his own reconnaissance of K2 for the late summer of 1953. In Rawalpindi, Desio overlapped for a couple of days with the Americans, fresh from their defeat. They generously shared all the information about the route that Desio could have wanted.

With a single Italian companion, Desio flew to Skardu in September 1953 and undertook a thirty-two-day mini-expedition of his own, hiking with porters all the way in to the base of the Abruzzi Ridge and back out again and making several side trips along the way. The companion was Ricardo Cassin. Forty-five years old that summer, Cassin was the greatest Italian mountaineer ever to that date, and one of the greatest in the world. In the 1930s, he had led the teams that had made the first ascents of two of the classic six north faces of the Alps—the

Piz Badile and the fearsome Walker Spur on the Grandes Jorasses, near Chamonix.

Yet in *Ascent,* Desio says nothing about Cassin's contribution to the reconnaissance. And his identification of his partner is laconic in the extreme: "To accompany me on this preliminary reconnaissance I had chosen Ricardo Cassin, a climber, to whose travelling expenses the Italian Alpine Club had generously contributed."

Upon the return of the two men to Italy, and with the official granting of the permit to Desio in October, it was universally assumed that Cassin would be the climbing leader of the 1954 expedition. The reasons for Desio's coolness in print toward his recon partner would eventually emerge—though only if you read between the lines.

With eighteen members from Italy, comprising both climbers and scientists, Desio's extravaganza would amount to one of the most massive expeditions ever launched in the Himalaya or the Karakoram. A comparison with the American effort the year before puts this in perspective. The Americans hired 180 porters to get their gear to base camp; the Italians would end up employing 600, and the total baggage those native porters hauled amounted to sixteen tons of food and gear. The budget for Houston's team in 1953 was exactly $30,958.32 (the 1938 expedition had cost only a little over $9,000); although Desio never discloses the final figure, the cost of the Italian expedition was well in excess of 70 million lire, or about $108,000 in 1954 currency. That figure calculates out to $821,000 in today's dollars—an astronomical sum, any way you look at it.

The most expensive expedition I ever went on was Jim Whittaker's International Peace Climb of Everest in 1990, because we Americans footed the bill not only for ourselves but for the Russian and Chinese climbers as well. Far more typical of my expeditions, though, would be one like my last attempt on Annapurna, in 2005. With only three climbers on the team—Jimmy Chin, Veikka Gustafsson, and myself—that trip cost us only $18,000, even though we indulged in the luxury of helicoptering in to base camp.

Another sign of the times, and of just how nationalistic an enterprise K2 was for the Italians, emerges from the fact that a substantial part of their budget was raised by the Club Alpino Italiano (CAI), which solicited contributions from its members. That kind of appeal sure wouldn't fly today! If I'd hit up AAC members for contributions so I could go to Annapurna in 2005, I doubt that I would have found very many checks filling my mailbox. On the other hand, in 1954 there was no such thing as a climber being sponsored by equipment companies. Nowadays, we're on our own when it comes to raising money for an expedition—we're no longer carrying the banner of the good old U.S. of A.

By late autumn of 1953, Desio and his cronies in the CAI had made a list of twenty-three climbers to be invited to audition for the expedition. Desio chose his scientists by word of mouth, but the climbers had to undergo a much more rigorous screening. In the winter of 1952–53, Houston had whittled his roster of applicants down from about twenty-five to five, but his process, while relatively stringent, had required only a brief interview in Exeter, New Hampshire (and, as mentioned in the previous chapter, Dee Molenaar didn't even have to fly east to get chosen). Desio instead organized a pair of winter mountain training runs in the Alps, which doubled as tryouts. In *Ascent* he solemnly ticks off the qualities sought in the candidates: "good health and physical fitness, strength of character and iron determination, mental preparedness and a readiness for the task at hand based on recent mountaineering experience. All other qualities were of secondary importance."

The candidates first assembled in mid-January on a glacial plateau near Cervinia for a ten-day camp. The men, as Desio reported, were put through their paces as they found themselves "taking part in various climbing exercises on rocks and ice, practis[ing] setting up tents on the western spur of the Little Matterhorn, conveying packages along a specially-constructed light rope-way, communicating with one another by portable radio, etc." At the end of the ten days, some doctors hiked up to the plateau to administer "psycho-physical tests." Afterward, a panel of thirteen self-styled experts cut two of the candidates from the list.

To me, the whole thing sounds both brutal and ridiculous. It's pretty tough to forge brotherhood when you're competing with the guy on the other end of the rope for a place on the team. You can't build an effective team based only on the skill levels of the climbers, and mutual respect and trust can't be dictated from on high. Near the beginning of my climbing career, from 1980 to 1982, I tried out with Rainier Mountaineering, Inc. (RMI) in hopes of landing a job as a Rainier guide, and I got hired only on my third attempt. But RMI handled the whole business in a pretty humane way; the veterans explained that they were seeking a combination of people skills and mountaineering talent. Just because you were a phenomenal climber didn't mean you would make a good guide. You had to be a patient teacher and show compassion for your clients. All of that made sense to me.

By the 1990s, no American expedition to an 8,000er had ever run its candidates through a training mill like the one Desio concocted. On the other hand, to this day the Russians—despite the collapse of the Soviet Union—maintain an equally Spartan tryout procedure. They'll get a bunch of climbers together in the Caucasus and tell them to race one another up some mountain. The fastest six or so make the grade: "Okay, you guys get to go to Kangchenjunga." As for brotherhood, the Russians are told, "You *will* get along."

It sounds absurd, but you wouldn't believe how hard the Russians fight for those slots. In the USSR, the top climbers got the title of "Master of Sport," as well as such additional perks as a free apartment and a car.

From February 16 to 26, 1954, the CAI ran its second tryout camp on Monte Rosa, after Mont Blanc the second-highest peak in the Alps. The team was then whittled down to the eleven men who supposedly performed the best, but before they could count on going to K2, each man had to pass ear, nose, throat, and dental exams as well as receive a "prescribed course of vaccination."

Only one of those eleven would go on to be a truly world-class mountaineer. That man was the youngest of the eleven, twenty-four-year-old Walter Bonatti, who earned his living as a hutkeeper near his hometown of Monza. Despite his youth, Bonatti already had a better record than any of his teammates on cutting-edge routes in the Alps. On K2, he would end up as the pivotal figure in the dark controversy that would forever tarnish the Italian triumph—a controversy that would still burn half a century later.

One shocking result emerged from the tryout camps. Ricardo Cassin, the greatest climber in Italy in 1954, was rejected. The official explanation was that he had failed a medical test, but climbers all over Italy knew better. Fifty-two years after the expedition, and five years after Desio's death at the astonishing age of 104, one of the principal K2 climbers, Lino Lacedelli, set the record straight:

> Desio's version was that Cassin was unable to take part for health reasons. Varicose veins were mentioned, amongst other things. But that wasn't the real reason. If Cassin had come, all the newspapers would have focused on him rather than Desio. To me that was obvious. Cassin never got over it. He's still upset today. For us climbers, having Cassin along would have been really great.

In his own way, Cassin took his revenge for being snubbed. In 1958, he played a crucial role in the first ascent of Gasherbrum IV in the Karakoram, as Walter Bonatti and Carlo Mauri reached the summit, setting a new standard of difficulty in the Karakoram and the Himalaya. And in 1961, at the age of fifty-two, he led the first Italian team to climb in Alaska since the Duke of the Abruzzi in 1897, as they tackled the unclimbed south face of Mount McKinley. Despite incurring serious frostbite, all six members reached the summit. The beautifully direct route, known today simply as "the Cassin," is the most storied line on North America's highest peak. In January 2009, Cassin himself turned one hundred years old.

———

Rereading *Ascent of K2* today, I was struck by how completely unaware Desio was of the semicomic consequences of the gargantuan logistical effort required to keep his marching army in motion. From Skardu to Askole, for instance, the 500 porters so far employed by the Italians consumed 1,100 pounds of flour *per day*. There wasn't anything like that reserve of grain in the region, so other porters had to hurry ahead to lay in depots of flour at Askole.

I've seen this happen on even smaller expeditions. You end up needing porters to carry the food for the other porters, who are in turn carrying food and gear for the Europeans. This makes for a huge logistical headache, but it's unavoidable on long approach hikes. If, as is often said, an army marches on its stomach, these massive caravans are in constant danger of grinding to a halt.

At Urdukas, appalled by the wintry conditions of early May, the porters at first refused to go on. This delay meant that the team immediately needed another thousand pounds of flour, so Desio sent porters back to Askole to haul up the reserves that had been stocked in previous weeks. The caravan finally got going again, but it was no surprise that the porters called an all-out strike at Concordia. Unless the team could get its sixteen tons of stuff up the last ten miles to base camp, the expedition was doomed. Desio sounds dumbfounded by this "desertion" on the part of the porters: "Thereupon they dumped their loads and, uttering hostile shouts and singing religious songs, returned that same evening the way they had come. I was perplexed and disconcerted."

It took the intervention of the liaison officer (the same Pakistani who had served admirably on Houston's expedition) to sort out the mess and, in effect, bribe enough porters to carry the loads the rest of the way to base camp. It was only because the team had left Italy so early in the season that, despite all the delays en route from Skardu, they were well established at base camp by May 29.

As the 1953 American team had done, the Italians hired Hunzas from Gilgit to serve as high-altitude porters. Those thirteen men would play a far more essential role on the Abruzzi Ridge than did the Hunzas in '53, who never went above Camp III. Two of the Hunzas would go as high as the Italian Camp VIII, at 25,300 feet, and one of them, Amir Mahdi, would perform a heroic deed that would lead directly to the team's eventual success and to the bitter controversy that spun out of it. Yet Desio's narrative credits the Hunzas' work only in the most cursory way.

One measure of how tedious *Ascent of K2* is as an account of the expedition is that the reader doesn't get to Skardu until page 94, to base camp until page 122—more than halfway through the 239-page book. And rather than seem the slightest bit embarrassed by his party's logistical overkill, Desio revels in it. That's a very 1950s attitude: the more gear and food, the more porters, the author implies, the more serious the expedition. It would take another couple of decades before a lightweight approach to the world's highest mountains would start to seem purer and bolder than a massive army-style assault.

Desio also revels in his role as generalissimo. Before leaving Skardu, the leader took a flight around K2 in a plane flown by Pakistani pilots. There was absolutely no need for that flight for reconnaissance, since the climbers knew they were going to tackle the Abruzzi Ridge, about which they had learned everyting they needed to know from the Americans in Rawalpindi. But Desio devotes eight humdrum pages of his book to this joyride. It all falls vaguely under the heading of "Science" with a capital "S." As Desio sums up this aerial diversion,

> Unfortunately, the responsibility of guiding the pilots, coupled with the extremely high speed of the aircraft, prevented me from collecting all the information I would have liked regarding the orographical structure of the region and above all the relative positions of the various glacial basins. But a patient and scientific examination of our films and photographic surveys may well lead to the discovery of many hitherto unsuspected geographical features.

When I first read that paragraph, I had to look up "orographical." It means "having to do with the branch of physical geography dealing with mountains." I rest my case.

As early as May 26, four climbers started up the Abruzzi, hoping to discover the site of the Americans' Camp II. (The launch of the climb that was the expedition's central focus does not appear until page 138 of the book.) Before they could get started, though, the mountaineers were required to digest a route guide their leader had prepared.

That guide, reprinted in full in *Ascent,* represents a classic case of micromanaging from the rear. The leader at base camp, with his binoculars or telescope, thinks he can direct the climbers on the route better than they can themselves. A sample:

> *Camp VI to Camp VII.* A rise of 1,640 feet. After negotiating a series of steep, difficult rocks, necessitating the use of several pitons, the climber is confronted with a dangerous eastward traverse of some 590 feet over ice which slopes at an angle of 45°.

Whether or not Desio got the idea from Pete Schoening's A-frame tripod, which the Americans had used to haul loads up House's Chimney, the Italians brought along a thousand-foot-long steel cable and constructed a pair of windlasses, crank-operated hauling devices. This apparatus would serve to lug vast quantities of gear over stretches as long as a thousand feet, all the way up to Camp V, at 22,000 feet. On June 2, Desio found a small saddle on the Godwin Austen Glacier; from there he supervised the first attempt to use a windlass to get loads to Camp II. "All went well," he reported.

Slowly the climbers and the Hunzas got camps established and huge piles of gear ferried and winched up the route. And as the distance between them and base camp grew, the climbers allowed themselves various small acts of resistance to the iron mandates of their dictator down below.

This was not easy. Every day, Desio typed out—on an actual typewriter hauled all the way to base camp—the orders for the day, then had them carried by the Hunzas or radioed up to the climbers. In 2003, when he was interviewed by an American journalist, Lino Lacedelli recalled one such command: "Order 13: 'Who will not obey my orders will be punished with the heaviest weapon in the world—the press.'

"We called him 'Il Capetto' [the Little Chief]," Lacedelli reminisced. (Desio was shorter than all the climbers, some of whom stood no more than five foot five.)

In one critical respect, the 1954 Italian plan for K2 differed from those of all previous expeditions to the mountain: up high, the climbers intended to use bottled oxygen. Those bottles themselves would become a major cause of the enduring controversy.

Desio was such a control freak that long before the climbers got high on the mountain, he had decided on the precise movements to be carried out on the summit assault. The memorandum of instructions for that assault is also reprinted verbatim in *Ascent of K2*. A sample:

> *Second day.* B, C, and possibly also A, the group-leader, will move up to Camp IX together with F and G. A, B and C will each carry an oxygen-mask complete with cylinders and sufficient food for two days. F and G will carry oxygen-masks in addition to a *Super K2* tent and two small cylinders filled with propane. B, C and possibly A will spend the night at Camp IX, while F and G will return to Camp VIII.

You cannot, of course, dictate these kinds of troop movements on an 8,000er. Everything depends on the weather, the snow conditions, and the relative strengths of different climbers, so up high you always have to be flexible and ready to improvise to meet the challenges thrown at you. Desio just didn't seem to get this fundamental truth about mountaineering.

The oldest among the eleven climbers, at age forty, was Achille Compagnoni. A guide and ski instructor, he had a decent record as an alpin-

ist but was not the equal of several of his teammates, including Lacedelli
and Bonatti. Nevertheless, early on Desio appointed Compagnoni as his
climbing leader. This choice didn't sit well with some of those teammates. Lacedelli wrote in 2006, in *K2: The Price of Conquest*:

> More than anything Desio preferred those who agreed with him.
> Most of us were not happy with this. We were not the sort of
> characters to flatter the expedition leader. We did what we had
> to and that was all. . . .
>
> [Compagnoni] flattered Desio and vice versa. This annoyed
> us a lot, particularly later on when Desio made him leader of the
> first climbing group [for the summit assault]. None of us felt he
> deserved this.

The mutual ass-kissing between Compagnoni and Desio leaves its
traces in the pages of *Ascent*. Desio lavishes almost no praise on the other
climbers in the team, but Compagnoni is "a man endowed with great
strength of both body and mind," of whom on more than one occasion
the leader stands in admiration: "I had a long conversation that day with
Compagnoni, and at the end of it I was left with the unshakable conviction that he was a man of iron will who would let nothing deflect him
from his main purpose."

Then, on June 21, with the team no higher than Camp IV at 21,500
feet, a sad event took place that could well have wrecked the expedition.
Three days before, Mario Puchoz, a thirty-six-year-old guide from Courmayeur, had carried a load to Camp IV, but on returning to II complained
of a throat infection. As his condition worsened, the expedition doctor
put him on antibiotics and bottled oxygen. At 1:00 A.M. on June 21, in
Desio's telling, "the sick man—who had appeared to be sleeping—
suddenly passed away after a very brief agony."

The doctor had diagnosed Puchoz's condition as pneumonia, but I
wonder if it wasn't yet another case of pulmonary edema. In a difficult
maneuver, several climbers managed to lower Puchoz's body all the way

to the foot of the Abruzzi Ridge. He was then buried by his teammates "in a grave carved out of rock" near the cairn erected the year before in honor of Art Gilkey. Ever since, that cenotaph has been known as the Gilkey-Puchoz memorial.

There seems to have been no thought among the team members of canceling the expedition. But, as Lacedelli later wrote,

> When we returned to the camp after burying Puchoz, Desio immediately said, "Tomorrow you need to go back up!" That started a big argument because we wanted to be left alone for at least a day, after all we had lost one of our colleagues. But Desio was immovable. He wanted us to leave the next day. We went away very upset.

When a climber dies in the early stages of an expedition, the whole team has to decide whether to call it off and go home or to continue with the effort. In the latter case, the teammates always justify the decision with a phrase like the one Lacedelli used: "We must get to the summit for Mario."

Desio's rationale for forging onward was more grandiose: "It was our duty, then, to continue the ascent with renewed energy, that we might the sooner be able to inscribe on Puchoz's grave-stone the date of the feat with which his name would be forever associated."

I'm really fortunate in that I've never had to face that kind of decision. In fact, I've never lost a partner on a climb. In that situation, I don't know what I'd do. It's a complicated dilemma. If there's a single determining factor in making that choice, it seems to be the size of the expedition. The larger it is, the more likely the members are to decide to go on with their campaign and climb the mountain in honor of their fallen comrade.

In 1963, the American Everest expedition lost Jake Breitenbach, one of their youngest and most skilled members, early on, when a serac collapsed in the Khumbu Icefall, crushing him beneath tons of ice. One of the two teammates who was roped to Breitenbach and witnessed the collapse described the debris as "the size of two box cars, one atop the other." It was obvious at once that there was no hope of even searching for the man's body. Breitenbach had had one close buddy on the team, Barry Corbet, but he'd scarcely known most of the other climbers. That impersonality within a large expedition seems to allow the members to go through a mourning ritual, but then gird up their loins and head back into battle.

On the other hand, on Chris Bonington's eight-man attempt on K2's west ridge in 1978, Nick Estcourt was killed in an avalanche after the men had spent only twelve days on the mountain. Those guys were among the toughest and most ambitious mountaineers of their day, but they were all good friends of Estcourt's and had shared previous expeditions with him. After a futile search for his body, the survivors sat down to discuss what to do. They were divided right down the middle, but since only three climbers (including Bonington) wanted to go on, they all gave in to the wishes of the other four and called the expedition off.

Yet in 1952, on the French expedition to Fitz Roy in Patagonia, with a team as small and close-knit as Bonington's, Jacques Poincenot was drowned on the approach march in a botched attempt to ford a dangerous river. Lionel Terray, one of the greatest expedition mountaineers in history, later wrote in his autobiography, *Conquistadors of the Useless,*

> [Jacques] was a perfect companion and a prodigious climber, and his sudden disappearance dealt us a cruel blow. For forty-eight hours, indeed, we debated seriously whether to pack up and go home. After a few days we recovered our spirits and carried on, seriously weakened, however, by the loss of one of our best members.

More than a month later, Terray and Guido Magnone made the first ascent of that beautiful pyramid of granite and ice. The team named a handsome nearby peak Aiguille Poincenot, in homage to their lost comrade.

As the Italians worked their way up the Abruzzi Ridge, they found a vast range of enthusiasm and usefulness among their Hunza high-altitude porters. Only five of the thirteen seemed fully up to the challenge of carrying loads above Camp III. Of the others, Lacedelli recalled, "With them you agreed one thing and then you didn't see them again. You would go back down and discover that they were still in the tent sleeping. It would drive you mad."

Desio, too, complained about these slackers: "The language difficulty, the indiscipline of the Hunzas and the capriciousness of certain among them . . . frequently led to misunderstandings which it was not always easy to clear up." Disciplinarian to the end, Desio eventually ordered "the dismissal of three men and the return of the five delinquents to their posts on the Abruzzi Ridge."

Fifty-five years later, it's hard to guess what was going on with the Hunzas. The language barrier must indeed have played its nefarious part. Since the Karakoram region had for so long been part of British India, some of the Hunzas spoke a smattering of English. But they certainly didn't speak any Italian. Desio could probably get by in English, but mountain guides such as Compagnoni, Lacedelli, and Bonatti, who had never traveled far from northern Italy, didn't comprehend a word of that language.

It may be fortunate that the less courageous Hunzas were scared out of their minds on the Abruzzi Ridge. Houston's team had wisely decided that the Hunzas' meager climbing skills made them a liability above Camp III. Desio, however, expected them to carry loads all the way up to the Shoulder at 26,000 feet. Hunza terror on steep terrain may well have looked to the Italians like mere laziness. It's also possible that these high-altitude porters bridled every bit as much as Lacedelli and his disaffected teammates did under Desio's stern dictatorship.

One incident barely mentioned in Desio's text reveals the true courage some of the Hunzas were capable of. On July 6, one of the climbers, Cirillo Floreanini, started to descend from Camp III. For security, he held on to a fixed rope left from the American expedition the year before, but he had no sooner put his weight on the rope than the anchor popped loose. Before the horrified eyes of his teammates, Floreanini rolled and then bounced 800 feet before stopping on a narrow ledge. Lacedelli ran to his aid. Writes Desio, "Bruised and bleeding, he was then hoisted on to the shoulders of a Hunza, who, helped by his colleagues, carried him down to Camp II."

I've participated in a number of rescues on the 8,000ers, but I sure as hell have never carried another climber on my shoulders down steep terrain! That's an almost unimaginable feat. But Desio doesn't even bother to mention the gutsy Hunza by name. Just one more job the men from Gilgit were expected to perform.

As they crept higher on the Abruzzi, the climbers' frustration with Desio's autocratic leadership mounted. Typically, Compagnoni would radio down to base camp after each day's effort. He and Desio would discuss the day's events; then the leader would dictate the next day's orders over the radio. Compagnoni relayed the command to his teammates.

A minor mutiny eventually erupted. As Lacedelli remembers it,

> For a while we played along, but then we told Compagnoni it wouldn't work. We said that the orders had to be based on the needs of those on the highest rope party. . . . "They know best what they need," we said, "not Desio, not even you." "I'm sorry," Compagnoni would say, "but Desio has spoken." "We couldn't care less," I said eventually.

No one worked harder on the mountain than Walter Bonatti. And no one cared more about getting to the summit than he. But as the youngest member of the team, he knew it was unlikely that Compagnoni or Desio would choose him for a summit attempt. Throughout the expedition, moreover, relations between Bonatti and Compagnoni were cool at best.

Despite the tensions between the climbers high on the Abruzzi and their leader typing out orders from base camp, a chain of well-stocked camps crept up the mountain. Logistical overkill can work on a mountain, in the simple sense of getting men and gear and food in place. The Italians were skilled climbers, technically perhaps a bit better than the Americans of the previous year. (Most of the Italians worked at least part-time as professional guides in the Alps, which gave them a steady climbing regimen. The Americans all had jobs or graduate school programs, from which they could escape only on weekends and holidays to hone their mountain craft.) And two of the Hunzas, Mahdi and Isakhan, performed as well at altitude as the Italians.

On July 18, four men, including Bonatti, first reached the Shoulder, where they chose a site for Camp VIII. It was not until ten days later, however, that that camp was installed. At 25,300 feet, it stood only 200 feet lower than the Americans' Camp VIII of the year before, where Art Gilkey had collapsed with thrombophlebitis.

So in a few days the stage was set for what ought to have been one of the proudest accomplishments in twentieth-century exploration. Instead, what developed high on K2 during the following days would turn into a feud so sordid, bitter, and long-lasting that it has few parallels in mountaineering history.

On July 28, Desio made radio contact with the climbers at Camp VII. But then, during the critical days that followed, the leader at base camp lost touch completely with the high camps. The Little Chief was vexed.

> As time went on we became more and more anxious. We were sorely tempted to set out in a body for the ridge, but on second thoughts we decided that it would be wiser to remain in camp with our ears glued to the radio-set, ready to intervene as and when circumstances required. We had set up the radio out in the open, on a "glacier table" [a flat rock perched on a pedestal of ice], and we tried to contact our colleagues at half-hourly intervals.

To no avail. Just what sort of intervention Desio planned if he did make contact, only he would have known.

Fifty-two years later, Lacedelli would shed light on the radio silence:

> At Camp VIII, we couldn't make contact with Base Camp by radio, so we weren't able to tell them that we had reached 7,750 meters and established Camp VIII. That day, Desio was at "Sella dei Venti" [Windy Gap] on the left side of the mountain, looking down. Then, suddenly, we heard Desio on the radio. "I haven't got time for you," he said, "I need to get on with my studies." . . . He just got really annoyed. So I told him where he could go, and said, "From now on, if you want to know what's going on you can come up and find out for yourself!" End of radio contact.

Compagnoni, however, would insist that no radio communications were possible from Camp VIII and higher because the climbers no longer had line of sight to base camp.

According to Desio's orders, the first summit team was supposed to be Compagnoni and Ubaldo Rey, Compagnoni's regular tentmate, a thirty-one-year-old guide from Courmayeur. They were supposed to set out from Camp VIII, establish a camp high on the Shoulder, then go for the summit the next day. They would be supported by their other teammates, who would ferry loads up to Camp IX.

But after he started out on July 28, Rey gained only about 160 feet before dumping his load and turning back. According to Lacedelli, "Two of us actually had to help him back to the tent because he could hardly stand up." Stricken by some kind of altitude sickness, Rey gave up all hopes of the summit and headed down the mountain.

Thus, almost by accident, Lacedelli took Rey's place in the summit party. Lacedelli had never gotten along with Desio, who had relegated him to the "B team"—the "second group," which also included Bonatti and whose duty was mainly to carry loads in support of the five climbers in the "first group." A twenty-nine-year-old guide from Cortina d'Ampezzo in the Dolomites, Lacedelli was treated almost with contempt by Desio, as if he were a country bumpkin lucky to be invited on the expedition.

On July 26, at Camp VII, Bonatti had suffered from food poisoning—he thought he might have eaten spoiled sardines—and was so ill that he had had to stay in camp while his teammates pushed on to Camp VIII. Furious with himself and deeply depressed, Bonatti decided to force his way back into the action. He would recall in 1961, "I decided to eat at all costs, though the very thought made me feel sick; only in this way, I thought, would I be able to regain a little of my lost strength and resume my place up there." By July 29, he was almost back to his normal self. And, as it would turn out, Bonatti was fitter and stronger than anyone else on the mountain.

On July 30, Compagnoni and Lacedelli pushed up to the Shoulder, traversed it, and set up a Camp IX at 26,250 feet. Their choice of a camp-site was a curious one: instead of pitching their tent on the broad, almost level ridge of the Shoulder, they angled left and stopped at a narrow shelf hidden among the rocks at the base of the summit pyramid, very near where Fritz Wiessner had started climbing the final band on his first attempt, in 1939.

It was only after more than fifty years of silence that Lacedelli cast new light on the decision about where to pitch Camp IX. In 2006, he wrote,

> Compagnoni and I reached the place we had all agreed on for Camp IX. I said to Compagnoni, "Shall we pitch the tent?" but Compagnoni said, "No, here is no good, it's too dangerous." He then suggested we cross over to the left. I said, "Isn't it more dangerous that way?" But he wouldn't listen and so we carried on. . . . Eventually we reached a place that wasn't particularly good . . . it was precarious with a bit of a slope.

A camp at the base of the rock band would have made sense only if the two men planned to attack the cliffs above, as Wiessner had. But Lacedelli and Compagnoni intended to climb the Bottleneck couloir the next morning. On Wiessner's second attempt, he had had to lead the dangerous traverse across the lower edge of the rock band just to get to the foot of the Bottleneck.

The true reason for Compagnoni's insistence on the out-of-the-way location for Camp IX would not become clear until more than half a century after the expedition.

After pitching their tent on the "precarious" slope among the rocks, Lacedelli and Compagnoni were poised to make the summit attempt on July 31. But they were convinced they had no chance to get to the top without supplemental oxygen. Unable to carry heavy oxygen bottles to Camp IX along with their tent, stove, sleeping bags, and food, they counted on their teammates at Camp VIII to ferry up the critical cylinders.

Only there were two problems. The oxygen bottles that Lacedelli and Compagnoni needed were not at Camp VIII but down at Camp VII, at only 24,700 feet. And one by one, the other Italians up high who ought to have been able to ferry loads had succumbed to lethargy or altitude sickness. By July 30, only two men were capable of supporting the summit duo. They were Walter Bonatti and the Hunza Amir Mahdi.

In a heroic effort, on July 30 Bonatti recruited Mahdi to perform the ultimate load carry. That day the two men descended to Camp VII, picked up two racked sets of oxygen bottles (loads weighing almost forty pounds per man), carried them back up to Camp VIII, and then, with only a short rest, pushed up onto the Shoulder toward Camp IX.

It was dusk before an exhausted Bonatti and Mahdi reached the point on the Shoulder, at 26,000 feet, where the team had agreed to pitch Camp IX. But there was no tent in sight. Deeply alarmed, Bonatti cried out, "Lino! Achille! Where are you?" He scanned the frozen slope above him, as darkness began to engulf the mountain. The only answer was silence.

Bonatti guessed that his teammates must be less than 600 feet away, somewhere in the scattered rocks. The traverse to reach those rocks, however, would be perilous in the extreme, and it was now almost pitch-dark. Bonatti's headlamp had ceased to work, and Mahdi had no lamp of his own.

Abruptly, a light pierced the gloom, to the left and slightly above the climbers. At Camp IX, one of the summit duo must at last have heard Bonatti's cries and turned on his own headlamp to show the way. But now Bonatti heard Lacedelli call out, "Have you got the oxygen?"

"Yes!"

"Good! Leave it there and go straight down!"

What could Lacedelli mean? Was he simply unwilling to share his small tent with the two teammates who had worked so hard to support the summit bid? "I can't!" Bonatti protested. "Mahdi can't make it!"

The beam of light promised safety only a few hundred feet away. Crazed by exhaustion, Mahdi started scrabbling, out of control, across the dangerous slope toward Camp IX. Bonatti shouted at his partner to stop, but the language barrier now worked its sinister confusion. (Mahdi spoke only Urdu, Bonatti only Italian, with a mere handful of English words their common vocabulary.) "Mahdi! Turn back! No good!" yelled Bonatti, to no avail.

Abruptly the beam of light switched off. Once again, only silence came from above. A panicked Mahdi yelled in English, "No good, Compagnoni Sahib! No good, Lacedelli Sahib!"

At last Bonatti managed to coax the Hunza back to the precarious stance he had kicked in the slope. For another half hour, Bonatti screamed his own curses into the night. "No, I don't want to die!" he wailed. "Lino! Achille! Help us, damn you!" Not a word came from Camp IX.

Finally, in a fog of rage and despair, Bonatti turned to the slope before him and began to hack out a ledge with his ice ax. The two men had neither tent nor sleeping bag. Never before had anyone attempted, let alone survived, a bivouac in the open at such an altitude.

"I could have gone down in the dark by myself, even without a headlamp," Bonatti recalled in 2003. "But Mahdi was out of his mind. Several times I had to keep him from running away. Mahdi was like an unchained force of nature. Even in the night, he was yelling crazily. I had to find a way to calm him down just with the tone of my voice. I tried to invent my own English—convincing sounds, more than words. 'Good, Mahdi, good,' I said over and over. 'No! No!' he answered. That was his only word.

"It took a long time to dig a ledge out of the icy slope. We sat very close together. Mahdi was too tired to take his crampons off, so I did it for him. Otherwise his frostbite would have been even worse.

"I spent the whole night looking at my five fingers to see if they were still there. Making up problems in my head to see if I still think right. I kept banging my legs with my ice ax—that was before we knew it was a bad thing to do. It was as if one breath lasted the whole night."

In the wee hours, a sudden snow squall descended on the mountain. Bonatti and Mahdi were smothered in blowing snow. Three times Bonatti had to dig himself and Mahdi out.

As soon as first light arrived, Mahdi took off, almost running down the mountain toward Camp VIII. "In the morning," Bonatti remembered, "I was a piece of ice. I didn't have the strength to restrain him. All I could do was put on his crampons. My heart was beating fast as I watched him go. Then he reached a flat area, and I knew he was okay." Bonatti cached the oxygen gear in the snow, then gathered himself and slowly climbed down to Camp VIII.

It's a tribute to Bonatti's coolheadedness that both men survived that night. Other climbers, including Hornbein and Unsoeld on Everest, would later get through even higher bivouacs in one piece (though Unsoeld lost his toes to frostbite), but in 1954, most climbers would have said that to attempt to survive a night without shelter at 26,000 feet was to invite certain death. And just as I admire Wiessner for not abandoning Pasang Lama in 1939, I admire Bonatti, who could have saved his own skin by going down to Camp VIII in the dark, for not abandoning Mahdi.

At first light on July 31, Compagnoni and Lacedelli prepared for their summit push. In Desio's *Ascent of K2,* the short chapter covering the events of July 30 and 31 bears the footnote "As described by Achille

Compagnoni and Lino Lacedelli." The narrative veers awkwardly between the first and the third person. Sometimes it is "we" who act,
sometimes "Compagnoni" or "Lacedelli." But even though Desio must
have edited the chapter, it remains the principal source for Compagnoni
and Lacedelli's side of this unhappy story—or would remain so until
2006. In a small book he published that year, called *K2: The Price of
Conquest*, Lacedelli insisted that he had nothing to do with the contents
of the chapter in *Ascent* and that it was based entirely on Compagnoni's
diary.

In that chapter, on July 30 the two men installed at Camp IX see a pair
of tiny figures approaching from below, far too late in the afternoon. In
the first person, the narrative says, "As dusk was falling we heard shouts.
At once we came out of the tent. In the semi-darkness we could not see
Bonatti and Mahdi, but we recognized their voices. Unfortunately, the
high wind made conversation extremely difficult." At last Lacedelli
thought he understood Bonatti to be yelling that although he "could manage by himself," Mahdi wanted to return at once to Camp VIII.

> "Go back!" we shouted. "Go back! Leave the masks! Don't come
> any farther!" It did not occur to us that our colleague could be
> thinking of spending the night at such an altitude without a tent
> or even a sleeping-bag.
>
> Now Bonatti's voice was no longer audible. "Obviously," we
> thought, "he's taken our advice and gone down below."

The two men in the cramped tent spent a miserable, sleepless night.
At first light they emerged to see "an ominous carpet of mist" creeping
up from below.

> We searched the snow-covered slope below for the oxygen-masks
> which Bonatti and Mahdi were supposed to have left there the
> evening before. Suddenly, to our amazement, we caught sight of
> a figure receding into the distance. Who was it—Bonatti or

Mahdi? . . . We called out to the man at the top of our voices. He stopped and turned around, but he did not answer, and after a moment he resumed his halting progress down the precipitous slope.

We were simply flabbergasted. . . . How could we suspect the truth—namely that two men had survived the rigours of a whole night spent in the open at an altitude of more than 26,000 feet?

Is this account completely fictitious? It's true that high wind can make shouted conversations extremely difficult to understand. In 2005, when Veikka Gustafsson and I were camped at 22,000 feet on Annapurna, waiting for the wind to die down so we could go for the summit, our three Italian friends were in a tent only fifty feet away. Especially with the language barrier, shouting to each other over the wind made communication difficult at best. Eventually we resorted to hand signals, like thumbs-up or thumbs-down.

I suppose it's possible that Lacedelli and Compagnoni sincerely believed that the two men who had brought up the oxygen had descended in the dark, and only realized in the morning that they must have bivouacked. (Bonatti swears that no one called out to him in the morning.) But the obvious reason for Lacedelli and Compagnoni to have yelled out, "Go back!" was that they would have been extremely reluctant to share their cramped two-man tent with the refugees from the arduous load carry.

In Compagnoni's account, the two men left their tent at 5:00 A.M. They traversed across the slope, then headed straight down to the site of the cache Bonatti and Mahdi had left. He reported, "Having reached our objective, we hoisted the crates each containing three cylinders onto our backs." This is a key passage, for in it Compagnoni acknowledges that heavy oxygen bottles were the cargo Bonatti and Mahdi had hauled up to 26,000 feet. Yet in the dialogue quoted above, the men demand "Leave the masks!" Why masks, not bottles? A possible reason for this strange locution would not emerge until many years after the expedition.

By now, the mist had risen and the first snowflakes had started to fall. It sounds like a situation similar to ours on summit day in 1992. And the two men now uttered words very much like the ones Scott, Charley, and I exchanged. Their dialogue is captured in the summit chapter of Desio's *Ascent of K2*. "What do you say?" Lacedelli asked. Compagnoni answered, "I say we ought to have a try." (It's of course quite convenient that Compagnoni gives himself the credit for being the more committed climber.)

At the foot of the Bottleneck, the two men decided the couloir was too dangerous. Fifteen years earlier, insisted Compagnoni, Wiessner had found the ice "clear and firm," but now "it was covered with such a mass of snow that it would have been madness to climb it." Madness, one presumes, because it looked ready to avalanche, not because of the hanging ice cliff far above.

So the two men attacked the very edge of the rock band, several hundred feet left of the Bottleneck. Compagnoni took a short leader fall but was unhurt; Lacedelli led a hundred-foot cliff after taking off both his crampons and his gloves. "Here, in fact," Compagnoni writes, "we found that our resources were already taxed to the limit."

Hours passed by. The men slowly solved the edge of the rock band, then the ramp leading left to the summit snowfield. In one place, the snow was so deep, it took Compagnoni an hour to gain 50 vertical feet. Then: "Suddenly, at intervals of a few seconds, we both experienced a horrible sensation. We found ourselves gasping for breath." The two men had used up their bottled oxygen.

This event would prove to be a critical pivot point in the controversy that would, for half a century, hang over the first ascent. Strangely enough, rather than dump the useless bottles, the men kept the "crates" on their backs. Realizing that this would make little sense to other climbers, Compagnoni offers a four-point explanation. The key claims are two: that the pair wanted to leave something on the summit to prove their ascent, and that "in order to discard the crates we should have had to throw ourselves flat on the snow, which was very deep and unstable."

This sounds just plain weird. During the few expeditions on which

I've used supplemental oxygen—when I was guiding clients on Everest, for instance—I've always found that I can barely tolerate the weight even with the oxygen flowing. If I ran out of oxygen, I'd just chuck the thing, because you simply don't have the strength to carry useless bottles. In 1991 on Everest, when a faulty valve screwed up my oxygen rig, I simply shrugged off my pack and left the thing sitting in the snow. It's hard to imagine that Lacedelli and Compagnoni couldn't ditch those heavy bottles with a similar shrug of the shoulders.

The men plugged on. All the way up, Compagnoni insists, the men took not a single sip of water. He adds, "We had feared that the lack of oxygen would result in a loss of energy, but this was not so." That claim, too, doesn't quite ring true. When you're breathing gas for hours and suddenly run out, you crash with a vengeance. Jon Krakauer describes that happening to him on Everest in 1996, as he reached the Hillary Step on his way down from the summit: "My cognitive functions, which had been marginal before, instantly went into a nosedive. I felt like I'd been slipped an overdose of a powerful sedative."

At 6:00 P.M., Compagnoni and Lacedelli reached the summit. They embraced each other, tied flags to their ice axes for the summit photos, took a self-timed photo of themselves together—and finally threw off the dead weight of the oxygen crates.

The descent was a nightmare, as each man fell and slid several times, but fetched up in soft snow. Instead of downclimbing the edge of the rock band, they plunge-stepped straight down the Bottleneck, which did not avalanche. At one point in the night, the men thought they were lost. Their fingers were frostbitten (both would later undergo amputations). Finally they saw a light in the distance—a headlamp or a stove inside one of the tents at Camp VIII. The ordeal was over. According to their account in Desio's book: "Arms were flung around our waists, questions were fired at us, hands were clapped on our shoulders. Abram, Bonatti and Gallotti literally jumped for joy, and the two Hunzas, Mahdi and Isakhan, seemed hardly less delighted."

K2 had been climbed.

———————

Bonatti corroborates that joyous reunion. He wrote in 1961, in *Le Mie Montagne,* "At 11 P.M., five hearts were exulting over the same victory in the same tent. . . . At that moment, and only for that moment, I forced myself to forget all other reality."

Only for that moment. . . . Bonatti recalled in 2003, "I kept waiting for Lacedelli or Compagnoni to apologize. At Camp VIII, there was no 'Bravo, Walter.' Not a word of thanks, never. In base camp, I waited to hear excuses. I was conscious of what I had suffered, but I was young and ingenuous. The true of story of K2—the really bad story—begins after the expedition."

Amazingly, Bonatti had escaped from the bivouac unscathed. It was Mahdi who turned out to be the true martyr of K2, eventually suffering the amputation of nearly all his toes and fingers. The finest Hunza climber of his day, Mahdi had, just the year before, helped carry the badly frostbitten Hermann Buhl down Nanga Parbat. After K2, reduced to a virtual cripple, Mahdi would never again go into the high mountains.

In *Ascent of K2,* Desio makes no acknowledgment of Mahdi's sacrifice. The closest he comes to mentioning the man's terrible frostbite is in a single comment about the effort of the team to get down the mountain: "The Hunzas, however, postponed their departure from Camp V until they had administered first aid to Mahdi. As a result, the return of the climbing party was delayed for a whole day."

Back in Italy, the triumph on K2 made a titanic splash. Compagnoni and Lacedelli were instantly enshrined in the pantheon of their country's demigods of adventure. For decades, they remained Italy's most famous mountaineers. And in 2004, as the country engaged in a year-long celebration of the fiftieth anniversary of its greatest mountaineering achievement, Compagnoni and Lacedelli, then ninety and seventy-nine years old, were feted again as national heroes.

Bonatti, however, was lastingly embittered by the expedition. In 1961, he published *Le Mie Montagne,* a memoir of his finest climbs. There he revealed how Desio's expedition had changed his very character: "Until the conquest of K2 I had always felt a great affinity for and trust of other men, but after what happened in 1954 I came to mistrust people. I tended to rely only on myself."

The publication of Bonatti's version of what happened on July 30 and 31 caused quite a stir in Italy. Rather than the innocent miscommunication at dusk that Compagnoni's account had described, Bonatti made it clear that he thought his two teammates had hung him and Mahdi out to dry. "They didn't want to know if we were in the bivouac," he bitterly mused in 2003. "I was supposed to die. That would make the expedition even more glorious."

By the time I read *On the Heights,* the English translation of *Le Mie Montagne,* I was twenty-two years old. Bonatti was already a hero of mine, because his epic adventures—the terrible retreat from the Frêney Pillar on Mont Blanc, the amazing solo on the Petit Dru, and, of course, K2—were legendary. But after reading his own gripping accounts of these climbs, I saw him as even more of a supernatural character. He was obviously one of the most phenomenally gifted climbers of all time. Yet I never realized until recently just how bitter and prolonged the controversy in the aftermath of K2 had been.

In 1961, *Le Mie Montagne* had sent fireworks into the mountaineering sky above Italy. But the bombshell came in 1964, in the form of a pair of articles by a climbing journalist named Nino Giglio that appeared in the *Gazzetta del Popolo,* a widely read magazine. The first article was titled "After Ten Years, the Truth About K2."

Giglio claimed that Bonatti had tried to steal the summit from Lacedelli and Compagnoni. To enlist Mahdi in this ruse, he had promised the Hunza the glory of being the first Pakistani to stand atop K2. And the reason Lacedelli and Compagnoni had run out of oxygen short of the summit was that Bonatti had siphoned off at least an hour's worth of the precious gas as he huddled in his bivouac. In the morning, according to Giglio, Bonatti dashed down to Camp VIII, abandoning Mahdi.

At these accusations, Bonatti sprang furiously to his own defense. He instigated a libel suit against Giglio, which culminated in a 1966 trial in Turin. Not only the journalist but Compagnoni and two other teammates were called to testify. A deposition from Mahdi, in Pakistan, was conveyed to the court. Under oath, Giglio admitted that Compagnoni was the source of the incendiary charges.

Bonatti was quick to point out the impossibility of his having siphoned gas from the oxygen bottles, for he'd had no mask or regulator, without which there was no way to transfer the oxygen to his lungs. Lacedelli and Compagnoni had the masks and regulators at Camp IX.

Thus the curious cry at dusk—"Leave the masks!"—looks like a deliberate falsehood. It seemed to Bonatti that in misrepresenting the shouted conversation in the chapter of Desio's official book, Compagnoni was already planting the seeds of the claim that Nino Giglio would voice ten years later, that Bonatti had stolen the lead climbers' oxygen.

The outcome of the trial was total vindication for Bonatti. Yet the antagonisms indelibly tarnished Bonatti's reputation, especially in Italy. As he told an American writer in 2003, "It's stupid, but the whole world believed Desio and Compagnoni. Because it's a rhetorical formula that climbers always tell the truth."

If his K2 experience bred a lasting sense of mistrust of others, Bonatti was still determined to get some kind of revenge for his mistreatment by Lacedelli and Compagnoni. That revenge took the form of solo climbing, at a level of daring that was decades ahead of his time. In August 1955, Bonatti tackled the southwest face of the Petit Dru, above Chamonix.

Virtually no routes anywhere in the world that were, for their time, at the edge of the impossible had ever been attempted solo. Bonatti's six-day ascent of the pillar that would be named for him nearly cost him his life. But it was so visionary an achievement that the great British Himalayan climber Doug Scott later hailed it as "probably the most important single climbing feat ever to take place in mountaineering."

There followed, during the next decade, other visionary ascents:

Gasherbrum IV in 1958, by far the hardest climb yet done in the Himalaya or the Karakoram. The north face of the Grandes Jorasses in winter, in 1963. And then, in 1965, on the one hundredth anniversary of its first ascent, a new route *direttissima,* solo, in winter, on the north face of the Matterhorn.

The last achievement was Bonatti's swan song. At the age of thirty-five, he quit serious climbing overnight. (Virtually no other top mountaineer has ever ended his career in such a fashion.) He turned instead to other fields of adventure—deserts, rivers, jungles—as he reported for the magazine *Época,* often on daring solo expeditions.

The boldest of all Bonatti's projects, during his miraculous decade, was one that never happened. After the Dru, he recalled in 2003, "I was in a state of grace. I felt so strong that I thought I could do anything. And the name for 'anything' was K2."

For the summer of 1956, Bonatti plotted an attempt to climb K2 solo, without oxygen. "I planned it all very precisely," he said. "I would take four to six porters to base camp on the Baltoro Glacier. I had studied the route. Our fixed ropes were still there. I would carry only 25 kilos [55 pounds]. I could be self-sufficient for a week. And I knew that if I could survive a night in the open at 8,100 meters without oxygen, I could go to the summit without oxygen."

In the end, Bonatti failed to attract any sponsors who could have given him a shot at K2 solo, and he was far too poor to pay his own way. It is hard to appreciate today just how far ahead of its time Bonatti's scheme was. A comparable feat would not be performed for another twenty-four years, when Reinhold Messner climbed Everest solo, without oxygen, in 1980. I can relate to Bonatti's impulse: my own frustration with the lack of cohesion and teamwork on K2 in 1992 drove me to a solo attempt on Everest the next year.

Meanwhile, however, Bonatti could not put K2 behind him. In the end, he would write three books about his K2 experience, reprinting document after legal document as he sought vindication not only in the courts but in the eyes of the public.

Bonatti had always been convinced that Lacedelli and Compagnoni had placed their Camp IX out of sight—among the scattered rocks at the foot of the summit pyramid, above a dangerous traverse—in order to keep him and Mahdi from joining them in the cramped tent, and perhaps going to the summit with them the next day. After their heroic load carry on July 30, however, both men would have been too exhausted to try for the top the next day. But a shared tent could have saved their lives, and certainly would have prevented the frostbite that left Mahdi permanently maimed.

Vindication in this respect finally came in 2006, with Lacedelli's *K2: The Price of Conquest*. There the Cortina guide confessed to the very ruse Bonatti had long suspected. In Lacedelli's telling, the whole thing was Compagnoni's idea:

> I only understood later. . . . I believe he didn't want Bonatti to reach us. When I saw Bonatti come towards us I asked Compagnoni why he didn't want him to reach us and he said that it was just the two of us that had to make the final climb to the summit.

Lacedelli also confirmed that he and his partner had the crucial masks and regulators in their tent, and thus that the accusation that Bonatti had siphoned off oxygen was spurious.

Bonatti also never believed that Lacedelli and Compagnoni had used up their bottled oxygen and gone on to the summit without its aid. That was a myth, he believed, intended to make the summit push more dramatic. And after the 1964 accusations came out, Bonatti realized how the tale of running out of oxygen fed into the imputation that he had siphoned off gas during his bivouac, leaving less than enough for the summit duo.

In *K2: The Price of Conquest,* however, Lacedelli still insists that he and Compagnoni ran out of oxygen on the way up but carried the useless bottles all the way to the summit. By 2006, however, Bonatti had a new ally, in the curious form of an Australian surgeon and armchair climber named Robert Marshall, who had become fascinated by the controversy. Marshall taught himself Italian just so he could become a close student of the episode, met Bonatti, and eventually put together the definitive casebook of Bonatti's side of the story, published in the United States in 2001 in Bonatti's valedictory work, *The Mountains of My Life.*

Marshall contributed several key new insights to the muddled affair. Analyzing the rate of climb of the summit pair, and taking at face value their claim to have started upward on July 31 at 6:15 in the morning, he calculated that through nine and a half hours of climbing with gas, Lacedelli and Compagnoni would have averaged 168 vertical feet per hour. Then, from 26,700 feet to the summit, suddenly bereft of oxygen but carrying the weight of the useless bottles, they miraculously increased their pace to 320 feet per hour. This goes against everything other climbers have reported about progress at such altitudes with and without supplementary oxygen—just as it goes against my own experience. The higher you go, especially without supplemental oxygen, the slower you go. There's simply not enough oxygen to feed your muscles, so each step becomes more difficult than the previous one.

Even more damningly, Marshall stumbled upon a pair of summit photos published in 1955 in the Swiss anthology *The Mountain World,* although not in *Ascent of K2.* One shows Compagnoni with his oxygen mask still on his face. The other is of Lacedelli, maskless, but with exactly the sort of ring of congealed ice on his mustache and beard that would have formed around a mask he had just removed. This discovery demonstrated almost beyond a doubt that the story of running out of oxygen was a lie.

In 2003, an American writer questioned Lacedelli about these discrepancies. "We were using German-made Dräger bottles," the Cortina guide answered. "We didn't know how to regulate them properly. We had too much oxygen—it burned our throats, and we bled from the mouth. That's why we ran out." This did not speak to Marshall's point about the faster pace the two men would have had to manage after running out of oxygen.

Lacedelli also offered a new explanation for why they didn't chuck the apparatus to lighten their loads: "I couldn't take the bottles off because my fingers were frozen." I don't buy that reasoning, either. It's the simplest thing in the world to take off the oxygen crate.

Asked about the seemingly incriminating summit photos published in *The Mountain World,* Lacedelli answered, "Compagnoni put his mask on for just five minutes, to warm his breathing. I just put up my hand. I didn't want cold air in my throat." That, too, doesn't make sense. If you put a mask on your face when you're not getting oxygen through it, it's like breathing into a plastic bag. If you did it for five minutes, you'd probably pass out.

The American writer further probed Lacedelli about the strange cry at dusk, "Leave the masks!" In the original Italian edition of Desio's book, the key phrase is *"Lascia i respiratori!"* Strictly speaking, "respirator" refers to the whole apparatus, gas mask and regulator included. Had Lacedelli meant the bottles alone, he would have cried, *"Lascia le bombole!"*

"What did you say when you called out to Bonatti at dusk?" the writer asked.

"Lascia le bombole!" Lacedelli answered guilessly. "Leave the bottles! Go down to Camp VIII!"

"Lascia i respiratori!," then, must have been Compagnoni's deliberate lie in 1954, as he was already planting the charge he would make through Nino Giglio ten years later, accusing Bonatti of siphoning off the precious gas in his bivouac.

At his worst, Ardito Desio emerges from the story of K2 in 1954 as a pompous dictator, a self-important and somewhat mad scientist, even a semicomic figure. If there's a villain in the story, I'm afraid it would have to be Achille Compagnoni.

At the end of his interview with the American writer in 2003, Lacedelli sounded a wistful note. "For a long time after the expedition," he said, "I was friendly with Bonatti. Then we stopped writing and telephoning. I haven't seen him in 25 years."

Lacedelli sighed. "This was not war. Millions of people fight wars, and then shake hands afterwards. I hope one day to shake hands with Bonatti."

When all is said and done, what lingers about the first ascent of K2 is the feeling of just how sad a story it is. What should have been a great collective triumph ended up in backstabbing and endless controversy. The British team on Everest the year before had made its first ascent as a harmonious team. Decades later, the members of that expedition were still getting together in North Wales for reunions where they did a little climbing and a lot of nostalgic reminiscing.

Needless to say, the Italian K2 team never had a reunion. Instead, some of its members ended up suing each other. (Desio even went so far as to sue his own cinematographer, Marió Fantin, claiming that he'd withheld several reels of 16-millimeter film.) And in January 1955, all the team members except Compagnoni and one other climber signed a letter of protest against Desio's book, claiming it was full of distortions and outright lies. The first ascent of K2 may have been embraced by the Italian public as a great national triumph, but for the climbers, the victory was bittersweet at best.

Back in the States, Bob Bates and Charlie Houston learned of the Italian triumph on K2. Bates took the news philosophically. But for Houston, the ascent was deeply disturbing. He had already been granted a permit for a 1955 expedition, and, as he later recalled, "I thought that the third time we *must* succeed."

Within a day after learning of the Italian success, Houston (in the words of his biographer Bernadette McDonald) "wandered into the local hospital in Nashua, forty miles from [his home in] Exeter, with no idea of who or where he was and with absolutely no identification on him." Diagnosed with global amnesia, Houston was admitted to a hospital. A psychiatrist friend who visited him found him "weeping inconsolably," with his short-term memory gone. The shock of the news about K2's first ascent had apparently sent Houston over the edge.

He was soon restored to his wife and home, but it took him several weeks to recover. That autumn, Charlie Houston quit climbing for good.

7

THE DANGEROUS SUMMER

The second ascent of Mount Everest came in 1956, only three years after Hillary and Tenzing, when a Swiss party climbed the highest peak in the world and made the first ascent of neighboring Lhotse, the fourth-highest. The second ascent of K2 came only in 1977, twenty-three years after Lacedelli and Compagnoni. If anything, that second ascent represented logistical overkill far exceeding even Desio's 1954 extravaganza. The team of Japanese in 1977 had no fewer than fifty-three members and 1,500 porters! The climbers ascended via the Abruzzi Ridge and, like the Italians, used bottled oxygen up high. In early August, seven members reached the summit. One positive note was that for the first time a native Pakistani, the Hunza Ashraf Aman, also topped out.

The Japanese expedition, however, was viewed by mountaineers around the world as a throwback. Jim Curran writes in *K2: The Story of the Savage Mountain,*

This, then, was the long-awaited second ascent of K2: a total anticlimax.

If it proved anything it was that with enough money and man-power success was almost guaranteed. . . . Even in 1977, the expedition was seen as a dinosaur, totally out of step with the current thinking epitomised by Messner and Habeler two years earlier [on their landmark alpine-style ascent of Gasherbrum I by a new route].

The allure of Everest diminished almost not at all after its first ascent. Between 1954 and 1975, no fewer than seventeen expeditions attacked the mountain, their nationalities ranging from Indian to Argentine to Spanish to American to Japanese to Chinese. During that same twenty-two-year period, not a single major expedition ventured onto K2.

The main reason for that neglect was that, thanks to political turmoil, Pakistan closed the Karakoram to climbing from 1961 through 1974. But the intrinsic difficulty of the mountain also loomed as a prohibitive factor.

With the reopening of the Karakoram, Americans renewed their pursuit of K2, sending powerful parties in 1975 and 1978. The first attempt, which tackled the complex northwest ridge, was thwarted by route-finding problems and hideous internal dissension. It was this expedition that Galen Rowell chronicled in his tell-all book *In the Throne Room of the Mountain Gods*. The 1978 team was likewise torn with dissension, but finally placed four Americans on top. Jim Wickwire, John Roskelley, Lou Reichardt, and Rick Ridgeway—superb mountaineers, all four—made the third ascent of K2 via the long and intricate northeast ridge, which had been attempted before but never completed. (For the top 2,000 feet, the Americans' route coincided with the Abruzzi route.) Three of the four reached the summit without supplementary oxygen.

Though they're a bit older than I am, Wickwire and Roskelley became good friends of mine. Both of them were on the 1989 Kangchenjunga expedition with me, although they left the team early without reaching the summit—Jim because he developed a bad case of pneumonia, John essentially because he got fed up with the way the expedition was being run. Ridgeway's memoir about the 1978 expedition, *The Last Step*, also a tell-all inside account, was one of the books I devoured before I went to K2 in 1992. The sordid details of the team's interpersonal conflicts that Ridgeway captured are not the sort of thing I'd commit to print myself, but I found them fascinating all the same.

During the first years after the embargo ended, Pakistan limited the expeditions on K2 to one a year. The Ministry of Tourism, however, couldn't help noticing what the Nepalese were doing with Everest, granting permits to multiple expeditions within a single year. Since that's such an obvious moneymaker for the government, it's a wonder the Pakistanis didn't start the practice sooner.

By the early 1980s, K2 was "hot" in mountaineering circles. Four expeditions focused on the mountain in 1982, four again the following year, and four in 1985. In 1986, Pakistan at last opened the floodgates. That year, no fewer than eleven separate parties would congregate on the slopes of K2.

Meanwhile, in the years from 1978 through 1985, the mountain witnessed six more fatalities. There was Nick Estcourt from the British team in 1978, buried by an avalanche. The next year, two Pakistanis died, one of a heart attack, one by falling into a crevasse. In 1982, a Pole also died of a heart attack, and a Japanese climber fell on the descent after reaching the summit by a new route, the north ridge. And in 1985, a Frenchman died on the descent of the Abruzzi Ridge.

By the end of 1985, then, thirty-nine men (but no women) had reached the summit of K2, while twelve had died trying. With the summer of 1986, that ratio would become much worse.

There were two American teams on K2 that year. One of the ironies in my life that I'll never stop thinking about is that I was invited on one of those two expeditions, before I'd ever been anywhere in the Himalaya or the Karakoram. In 1986 I was twenty-six years old, in my fourth year of guiding during summers at Rainier Mountaineering, Inc. (RMI), but during the school year I was getting my doctorate in veterinary medicine at Washington State University. One of my RMI colleagues was a guy named John Smolich who'd been to Everest in 1984. John was a phenomenally strong climber, but he came across as soft-spoken and gentle. I really respected him.

John was the leader of an eight-man team from the Pacific Northwest. They were superambitious: instead of the classic Abruzzi Ridge, they were aiming at the beautiful, unclimbed route on the south face that Reinhold Messner had called the "Magic Line." Sometime that winter, John invited me to join the team. Andy Politz, another RMI guide, was also on board. He was an even closer buddy, the guy I'd bailed off Rainier with in a winter storm, when I survived the only unplanned bivouac of my life. Andy and I had also invented our "load wars"—an ongoing competition to see who could carry the most groceries to Camp Muir while guiding clients. And in 1983, Andy and I had served as junior guides under Phil Ershler on an RMI-led ascent of Denali—my first expedition ever.

I was deeply flattered to be invited to K2, and sorely tempted. There was no way, however, that I could skip out of my summer externship at Washington State. With great regret, I turned down the invitation.

The Americans had been at base camp for only three weeks when, on June 21, Smolich and teammate Alan Pennington started up the approach gully at the base of the Magic Line. Almost immediately, at 5:30 in the morning, they heard a loud roar. Morning sun striking the face had dislodged a huge boulder thousands of feet above. (That boulder had been considered so stable that on a previous foray up to Camp II, some of the team members had anchored a fixed rope to it.) The boulder started careening down the route. When it hit the top of the approach gully, it triggered a 15-foot fracture line that set loose a massive avalanche. Smolich and Pennington tried to run for it, but they didn't have a chance, and they were engulfed in tons of snow and ice debris.

Their teammates dug out Pennington, but it was too late to save his life. John's body was never found. After burying Pennington near the Gilkey-Puchoz memorial, the rest of the team abandoned the expedition and headed home.

John was the first guy I'd known personally who'd died in the Himalaya. (I didn't know Alan Pennington.) Later I dug out pictures of the route and tried to figure out if I could learn anything from the catastrophe. But in the end, I had to admit that the death of the two climbers was the result of sheer bad luck. If ever there was a pure case of what we climbers call "objective danger," it was that freak avalanche triggered by the boulder.

It's true that on big mountains, the very lowest slopes can be among the most dangerous. In 1999 on Shishapangma, Alex Lowe, considered by many to be the best climber in the world, was killed with his partner Dave Bridges in a very similar accident, as they strolled out to reconnoiter a route they eventually hoped not only to climb but to ski down. An avalanche broke off thousands of feet above them. Lowe and Bridges tried to run for it, but were smothered by the debris. Their bodies, like Smolich's, were never found.

But what can you learn from such grim accidents? If you want to climb an 8,000er, sooner or later you're going to be kicking steps up an approach gully that just might avalanche.

Smolich and Pennington happened to be in the wrong place at the wrong time. It *could* have happened to me.

None of the other ten teams on K2 in 1986 even considered giving up their attempts after the disaster on the Magic Line. But climbers who didn't know the two victims gathered from many different parties to attend the impromptu funeral service on the glacier for Smolich and Pennington, and they were moved by it. John Barry, one of the best climbers on a British team attempting the unclimbed northwest ridge, later described the service in *K2: Savage Mountain, Savage Summer*. After Pennington's body was lowered into a natural "sarcophagus," Barry wrote,

An American made a dignified little speech rounding off with a Mallory quotation to the effect that we eat and make money to live—not the other way around. It was a quotation equal to the occasion. A second American, Chelsea, their Base Camp Manager, said something plain, sensible and suitable too. Everyone was holding up well. Then their doctor spoke. He got three words into his bit and broke down, and brought a few others down with him too. But it was a fine funeral, if a funeral can be fine, and K2 is as good a headstone as any parish slate.

Among the scores of climbers on different teams trying K2 in 1986, you could have assembled an international all-star cast. The Pole Jerzy Kukuczka was locked in a battle with Reinhold Messner to become the first man to reach the summit of all fourteen 8,000ers. K2 would be his eleventh such success, putting him only one peak behind Messner. The great Tyrolean mountaineer, however, aced out Kukuczka by knocking off his last two, Makalu and Lhotse, in the autumn of 1986.

It was hardly a match waged on a level playing field. By 1986, Messner was the most famous climber in Europe, perhaps in the world. He had multiple sponsors, received large fees for speaking engagements, and earned royalties from a string of books he'd written. Messner is without question one of the greatest high-altitude climbers of all time, as he demonstrated with breakthrough ascents on Everest in 1978 with Peter Habeler, without supplemental oxygen, and again on Everest solo and oxygenless two years later. But in the highly competitive circles of Himalayan aficionados, many observers pointed out that Messner usually chose the standard routes on the 8,000ers.

Kukuczka, like most Polish climbers, could barely afford each expedition he went on. But what was most admirable about his campaign on the 8,000ers—in 1987, he became the second person to claim all fourteen—was that he almost never opted for the easiest route. Ten of his ascents of the highest peaks were by new routes, and four came in winter—including the first winter ascent of Annapurna, an achievement that still awes me, twenty-two years later. Sadly, Kukuczka died near the top of the unclimbed south face of Lhotse in 1989, when a rope broke. It's a dreary testament to this great mountaineer's continued poverty that the rope was a cheap six-millimeter cord he had picked up in a market in Kathmandu.

In 1986, Kukuczka was determined to climb a new route up the center of K2's south face. And he intended to pull off this deed alpine-style, with but a single fellow Pole as his partner.

Clear on the other side of K2, climbing out of China rather than Pakistan, a very strong American team was attempting the north ridge. Its members also included several superstars, among them Alex Lowe, George Lowe (no relation to Alex), Dave Cheesmond, and Catherine Freer, considered the best American woman alpinist of her day. Despite having such experts along, the team had to turn back a little above 26,500 feet, defeated by storms and terrible snow conditions. As mentioned above, Alex Lowe would die on Shishapangma thirteen years later. And Cheesmond and Freer vanished in 1987, on an incredibly bold two-person alpine-style attempt on the Hummingbird Ridge of Mount Logan, in Canada. Speculation had it that their tent, pitched on a narrow curl of the relentlessly steep and twisting ridge, broke loose with a cornice that collapsed, sending them hurtling to the glacier thousands of feet below. Their bodies, like Lowe's, were never found.

Another all-star on the mountain in 1986 was the Frenchman Benoît Chamoux. His project was to climb the Abruzzi faster than anyone ever had before. If you wonder just how dangerous trying to climb all the 8,000ers really is, you should contemplate the fates of Kukuczka and Chamoux. In 1995, the Frenchman would disappear near the summit of Kangchenjunga, which would have been his fourteenth and last 8,000er. The scuttlebutt had it that Chamoux wanted Kangchenjunga too badly, as he was running head-to-head with the Swiss mountaineer Erhard Loretan for the honor of being the third man to nail the whole list.

Yet another climbing celebrity was the Italian Renato Casarotto. His K2 plans were probably the most ambitious of anybody's that summer. The Magic Line on the south face had repulsed a number of previous attempts. Casarotto wanted to make its first ascent *solo*.

At age fifty-four, the Austrian Kurt Diemberger was well past his prime, but by 1986 he was a mountaineering legend. Way back in 1957, he had paired with Hermann Buhl (the man who had made the first ascent of Nanga Parbat solo four years earlier) and two other Austrians to become the first climbers to reach the top of Broad Peak, the twelfth-highest mountain in the world. Theirs was an admirably lightweight assault, accomplished virtually alpine-style, that set a new standard among the 8,000ers. Only eighteen days after summitting on Broad Peak, however, as Diemberger and Buhl retreated from nearby Chogolisa in a gathering storm, a cornice broke loose, taking Buhl to his death. (Like those of so many victims in the Himalaya and the Karakoram, Buhl's body has never been found.)

In 1960, Diemberger was a member of a combined Swiss-Austrian team that made the first ascent of Dhaulagiri, the world's seventh-highest peak. He and Buhl remain eternally the only two climbers to make the first ascents of two different 8,000ers. In 1986, Diemberger joined a large team on K2 to serve chiefly as a filmmaker, but he wanted very much to reach the summit with the woman who had become his regular climbing partner, Julie Tullis from Great Britain.

The strong British team attempting the northwest ridge was led by Alan Rouse, among the elite of his country's high-altitude mountaineers. That party had an additional incentive, for any members who got to the top would be the first Britishers to succeed on K2.

In 1975, the Japanese Junko Tabei had become the first woman to climb Mount Everest. By 1986, no woman had yet reached the top of K2. A number of women had tried, including the Americans Dianne Roberts, Cherie Bech, and Diana Jagersky in 1978. But no woman had yet even come close to summitting. (According to Rick Ridgeway's *The Last Step*, much of the dissension among the 1978 team sprang from the conviction among some of the climbers—notably the blunt, outspoken John Roskelley—that Roberts had no business on the mountain, but was along simply because she was the wife of expedition leader Jim Whittaker.)

Two women on K2 in 1986 seemed capable of making the first female ascent. One was Liliane Barrard from France, who had previously climbed Gasherbrum II and Nanga Parbat. The other was the Pole Wanda Rutkiewicz, widely regarded today as the finest high-altitude female climber of all time. Unable to afford an expedition of her own, Rutkiewicz joined Barrard's team, launching a friendly rivalry over which woman would get to the summit first.

By 1992, Rutkiewicz had summitted on eight of the fourteen 8,000ers. Many in the climbing world assumed that she would eventually join the ranks of the very few men who had bagged all fourteen. But that May—how often the paths of such ambitious climbers lead to the same dismal outcome!—she disappeared near the summit of Kangchenjunga, just as Chamoux would three years later.

Many of the climbers involved in the "dangerous summer" of 1986 would later write about it, but only one produced a comprehensive narrative of all the confusing events that took place between June and August. Jim Curran had joined Alan Rouse's northwest ridge expedition primarily as a cinematographer, but also to write a book, should the team succeed. Though not at the top level as a mountaineer, and with no ambitions to reach the summit, Curran was (and is) one of Britain's finest mountaineering writers. In the end, instead of writing only about his own expedition, Curran attempted to cover the stories of all eleven teams on the mountain, in his deft 1987 chronicle *K2: Triumph and Tragedy.*

By the time the avalanche snuffed out the lives of Smolich and Pennington, Liliane Barrard's team was high on the Abruzzi Ridge. The foursome was led by Maurice Barrard, Liliane's husband and inseparable climbing partner. Along with Wanda Rutkiewicz, the party was rounded out by another strong Frenchman, Michel Parmentier.

Afterward, Rutkiewicz wrote a short account in Polish of her team's adventure on the Abruzzi. (Translated into English, it is reprinted as an appendix in Curran's book.) Rutkiewicz's report is the only insider account of what happened to Barrard's team.

In the spring of 1986 in Paris, Maurice Barrard had met with Kurt Diemberger to discuss the Abruzzi route. In *The Endless Knot*, Diemberger's own account of K2, he quotes a statement by Barrard that, in view of what transpired on August 1, 2008, has an eerie prescience:

"I have serious misgivings about the serac wall on that hanging glacier," Maurice had confided . . . pointing to a photograph of the summit pyramid. "It is definitely worse now than it was in 1979. Look at this latest shot: the fracture zone along this great balcony bit looks to have more cracks than ever. Heaven knows how much will come off and funnel down through the Bottleneck."

From the start of their climb, Rutkiewicz got along so poorly with Parmentier that she refused to share a tent with him, camping instead in a small two-man tent she borrowed from the British. Trying to climb fast and light through deep, soft snow, the team managed successive gains of only 650 and 1,300 vertical feet on June 21 and 22. Their last camp was at the remarkable altitude of 27,200 feet. Rutkiewicz does not identify the site except to call it "a small rock platform"—my guess is that it was on the ramp after the climb of the Bottleneck and the delicate leftward traverse. Rutkiewicz wrote, "We spent the night there . . . without sleeping bags in a very bad condition, all four squeezed into one small tent."

The climbers had only just over 1,000 vertical feet to climb the next day to reach the summit, but on June 23 they gained ground at a snail's pace. It may be that they were simply too early in the season, for the snow on the summit cap stayed relentlessly deep and soft. Barrard's team was the first that year to reach the summit snowfield, so they had had no fixed ropes to rely on above about 24,000 feet, and no one had broken trail ahead of them.

The four climbers left their squalid camp at 7:30 A.M. on June 23. Halfway to the summit, however, Maurice Barrard made what seemed to Rutkiewicz a very strange announcement: "Now we will rest here for a couple of hours and cook something." Out of his pack he pulled a stove, a pot, and packets of instant soup.

That was indeed a bizarre decision. On summit day on an 8,000er, every minute counts. For liquid, you need to sip from a water bottle you've filled that morning or the night before, which you carry in a chest pocket to keep the fluid from freezing. I can't imagine sitting down at something like 27,800 feet on K2 to brew up soup!

Rutkiewicz felt the same way. "I didn't want to stay such a long time there drinking soup," she later wrote. "I was in a hurry. The summit was beckoning. So I left the others and started out on my own."

The Pole reached the top at 10:15 A.M., becoming the first woman to climb K2. She wrote a little note, signing it with both her and Liliane's names, and placed it in a plastic bag tucked into some rocks just below the summit. Given the frictions within the team, it's surprising that Rutkiewicz didn't immediately head down. Instead, she waited a long while for her teammates and then, after they arrived, shared an hour's celebration with them on top.

The upshot was that the foursome did not regain their 27,200-foot camp until late afternoon. Rutkiewicz was of a mind to keep heading down, but Maurice Barrard urged that they spend the night in the single tent pitched on the rock platform, and she acquiesced. She would later write, "I was tired, but not exhausted. The weather was still good and I was not worried. But I should have been. One should remain at that altitude as short a time as possible. I didn't know in the sunshine that death was following us down."

To try to sleep, Rutkiewicz took two and a half Mogadon tablets. As recently as 1986, climbers routinely popped sleeping pills at high camps, but it was later discovered to be a very dangerous practice. Pills such as Valium and Mogadon continue to depress one's pulse rate and other aspects of the cardiovascular system for twelve hours or more after waking, which isn't a good thing for any athlete, much less a mountaineer at 27,000 feet. I never took sleeping pills up high, mainly because I wanted to be fully alert in case a storm blew in during the night or something else went wrong.

In the morning, Rutkiewicz felt groggy and her balance was off, but she recognized the urgency of getting down the mountain. Parmentier set off first, but both Liliane and Maurice Barrard seemed completely lethargic and moved very slowly. The climb to the summit without supplemental oxygen, sandwiched between two nights spent with four people crammed into a small tent without sleeping bags at 27,200 feet, had taken its physical toll. Soon the gap between the Barrards and their two teammates widened. At Camp III, at 25,250 feet, Rutkiewicz caught up to Parmentier. Several Italians and the Frenchman Benoît Chamoux were there as well, heading up on an attempt they would abort the next day, in the face of a gathering storm. At Camp III, Rutkiewicz and Parmentier waited for the Barrards, but they never arrived. Their teammates were still not overly concerned, since the French couple were carrying the tent and could presumably have pitched it wherever they found themselves by nightfall.

In the morning, Rutkiewicz headed down, as did the Italians and Chamoux, but Parmentier insisted on waiting for the Barrards. It took the Polish woman three more days to reach advance base camp. By then, her hands were frostbitten and she was near collapse.

In a big dome tent at the Italian base camp, Jim Curran joined the vigil for the French climbers. Chamoux had tried to talk Parmentier into descending with him, but after the man had refused to abandon his teammates, Chamoux had given him a radio.

Eventually, Parmentier had started down in an all-out storm. At base camp, the listeners waited and waited beside the radio. Finally they heard a faint voice: *"Ici Michel, ici Michel"* ("Michel here"). Still above the top of the fixed ropes, Parmentier was lost in the storm. (One more example of how willow wands marking the route can make all the difference in the world.)

Chamoux got on the radio and did a remarkable thing: he tried to talk Parmentier down, giving him the "beta" of the route from memory. Curran captured some of the dialogue: "Keep right, keep right, don't veer to the left, then straight down for perhaps two, three hundred metres . . . over." Turning to the others in the dome tent, with the radio off, Chamoux said, "He has perhaps a fifty-fifty chance that he finds the ropes. If not . . . ." Curran fought back tears.

Hours passed. Parmentier's voice was weaker with each short burst of broadcast. But at dusk, after one more exchange, Chamoux turned to the others and said, "He has found piss stains in the snow."

The piss stains led the played-out climber to the top of the fixed ropes. Two days later, Parmentier staggered down to advance base, where Chamoux met him and helped him the rest of the way to base camp.

The Barrards never made it down the Abruzzi Ridge. A month later, an Austrian team discovered Liliane's body at the foot of the south face. Maurice's body was found two years later, in a crevasse on the Godwin Austen Glacier.

In the appendix to Curran's *K2: Triumph and Tragedy*, Rutkiewicz later coolly pondered the possibilities:

> How did the Barrards die? Possibly part of the summit serac broke off and hit them as they climbed down the Bottleneck. Perhaps the one behind [on the rope], Maurice, was exhausted and fell, taking Liliane with him. Perhaps they lost their way on the big snowslopes below the Bottleneck during the white-out and were avalanched down the South Face. I'm sure, too, we stayed too long at altitude. The cooking on the summit day, the slow descent from the bivouac at 8,300 metres [27,200 feet] both showed that the Barrards were more exhausted than Michel and I realised. That's how accidents happen.

At base camp, Parmentier was overcome with anguish about the loss of his partners and about the duty of getting in touch with their families. But Rutkiewicz, in Curran's opinion, was so blasé, she seemed in some kind of denial. He wrote in *K2: Triumph and Tragedy*,

> Wanda, whose frostbitten fingers were obviously very painful, seemed to be out of touch with reality, already planning to climb Broad Peak, which in her present condition she was not fit for. Even if she recovered physically, which at K2 Base Camp seemed unlikely, she would be risking much worse frostbite. She sounded vague, irrational, and quite obsessed with 8,000-meter peaks.

ABOVE: Chris Klinke's remarkable photo of the thirty-odd climbers going for the summit on August 1, 2008, shot just after the first fatality occurred.
© Chris Klinke

Detail from same Klinke photo, showing the "traffic jam" on the ramp above the Bottle-neck couloir. © Chris Kinke

K2 from near Broad Peak base camp. © Ed Viesturs Collection

K2 from high on Broad Peak. © Ed Viesturs Collection

Climbers ascending fixed ropes on the Abruzzi Ridge. © Charley Mace

ABOVE: Ed Viesturs (left) and Scott Fischer sharing a tent. © Ed Viesturs Collection

Camp IV at 26,000 feet.

© Ed Viesturs Collection

ABOVE: Ed Viesturs reaches the summit on August 16, 1992. © Charley Mace

Viesturs (left) and Fischer embrace on the summit. © Charley Mace

Left to right: Viesturs, Fischer, and Mace after climbing K2.

Paula and Ed, 2007. © Rick Burns

BELOW: Gil, Anabel, and Ella, 2008. © Rick Burns

Yet at the same time, he noted, "I remained in awe of the strength, skill and determination of the first woman to climb K2, and amazed that the experience had not left her, temporarily at least, satisfied."

Curran wrote that passage five years before Rutkiewicz would vanish on Kangchenjunga, but I think he hit the nail on the head. A disturbing fanaticism seizes many of the climbers who decide to go after all fourteen 8,000ers. That's a frame of mind I did my best to avoid during the eighteen years it took me to complete my Endeavor 8000, which is partly why, among my thirty expeditions, I returned from ten of them without a summit in my pocket. It's easy to see how a fixation with getting all fourteen peaks climbed becomes an ambitious climber's driving motivation. As soon as he or she knocks off one peak, plans for the next one go on the front burner. And in some cases, I believe, the climber's sense of haste is compounded by pressure from sponsors or the media.

The end of June 1986 had not yet come, and already K2 had taken four lives. The pattern of catastrophe during this "dangerous summer" would be utterly different from the tragedies of 1939 and 1953, which struck within the ranks of the only team on the mountain at the time. It would be different, for that matter, from the 2008 disaster on K2 or the 1996 debacle on Everest, each of which burst forth in a single dramatic two-day event—the freakish storm of May 10–11 on Everest, the serac collapse and benightment of August 1–2 on K2.

Instead, in 1986, one bad situation after another would develop through the summer, scarring the mountain with a series of isolated tragedies. Around each death, a collective grief would briefly bring members from the different expeditions together, as in the funeral service for Smolich and Pennington or the base camp vigil for the lost French climbers. But then the teams would go back to their separate missions.

Benoît Chamoux had been deeply concerned about the fate of his compatriots, and he may have saved Parmentier's life by talking him down to the top of the fixed ropes. But only a week after that hair-raising episode, Chamoux set off again up the Abruzzi in quest of his speed record. Climbing in loose association with the Italians, whose fixed ropes and blazed tracks he took advantage of, on July 4–5 Chamoux essentially soloed the mountain, climbing all the way from base camp to the summit in the astounding time of twenty-three hours. Instead of stopping to camp, he climbed straight through the night, taking short breaks to gulp down food and swallow drinks. He reached the top at 5:00 P.M. on July 5, spent half an hour there, then headed down into his second night. After a short sleep at 24,900 feet with the Italians, he bombed on down to base camp the next day.

Chamoux's performance was dazzling; in itself, it almost mocked the notion of climbing an 8,000er by going from camp to camp on successive days or retreating to base to gear up for another attempt, as we had to do in 1992. (" 'Gobsmacked' was the only word to describe our reactions," Curran wrote.) That summer, Chamoux was in fantastic shape. Only two weeks earlier, he had soloed Broad Peak in a comparable dash, an exploit that had honed the acclimatization he would need for K2.

Chamoux's twin killing was one of the first examples ever performed in the Himalaya or the Karakoram of what I would later call a "twofer" (as in "two for the price of one"). It turns out to be the most efficient way to go after 8,000ers, provided you can keep that edge of fitness and not get worn down by the sheer exertion of it all. In 1995, I would pull off my only "threefer," climbing Makalu, Gasherbrum I, and Gasherbrum II in a span of two months, though I had a two-week break back home between Makalu and the Gasherbrums. (I would actually have accomplished a "fourfer" had we not stopped less than 350 feet short of Everest's summit just before my Makalu expedition.) In 2003, J.-C. Lafaille notched his own threefer, climbing Dhaulagiri, Nanga Parbat, and Broad Peak in succession (the last two with me), although the pulmonary edema that felled him on the summit of Broad Peak might have been partly caused by the sheer intensity of his campaign.

One of the members of the Italian team who also reached the summit on July 5 was a Czech, Jozef Rakoncaj, who three years earlier had climbed K2 by the difficult north ridge. Rakoncaj thus became the first man to climb K2 twice. That's a remarkable achievement, too. Twenty-three years later, only two other men have climbed K2 twice. Yet I doubt that many K2 aficionados are aware of Rakoncaj's feat, or have even heard of the man.

Meanwhile, Jerzy Kukuczka was gearing up for his monumental alpine-style attempt on the south face—not by the Magic Line, but along an equally serious and committed route to the right, or east, of it. Kukuczka and his Polish teammate, Tadeusz Piotrowski, had bought their way onto a massive international team led by the notorious Dr. Karl Herrligkoffer—in the same way that Scott and I bought places on the Russian expedition in 1992. Herrligkoffer was the German martinet who had sued Hermann Buhl after the Austrian had disobeyed his orders and gone to the top of Nanga Parbat solo in 1953. Seventy years old in 1986, Herrligkoffer had led more than twenty expeditions to the Himalaya and the Karakoram.

In *K2: Triumph and Tragedy,* Curran pondered the enigma posed by the German expedition leader:

> An old man whose life had been dominated by mountains yet who had never been able to go above Base Camp; a man who despite his organisational experience, attracted feuds and con-troversy on almost every venture; and a man whose whole con-cept of leadership and power seemed to be profoundly at odds with the people who continually placed themselves under his command. Did he, I wondered, actually enjoy the mountains in the same way that I did? Did he enjoy the company of climbers?

Kukuczka apparently shared that disenchantment. About the rest of the motley international team, he later wrote, "Unfortunately, most of the members did not show enough sporting spirit to attempt even K2's normal route. I couldn't believe this since on Polish expeditions we al-ways try to attempt something different."

Kukuczka had a right to his national pride. Starting in the 1970s, if any country's climbers consistently tried really hard new routes and pushed them to the limit, it was Poles, despite their scrawny expedition budgets. They were and still are especially adept at winter ascents on the highest mountains.

In early June 1986, a team of six—Kukuczka, Piotrowski, three Swiss, and a German—started working their way up the south face. The climbing was so difficult and so scary that one by one all three Swiss and the German dropped out. Not until July 7 did the Poles launch their two-man alpine-style assault. To go as light as possible, they carried only four pitons and a 100-foot rope! Kukuczka led every pitch.

This was by far the hardest climbing that had been performed to that date on K2, and it took its toll on those tough men. Kukuczka spent a whole day mastering a single desperate pitch. The men had accidently dropped a gas canister, so their stove was useless. The first night, all they had to drink was a small cup of water from snow melted over a candle.

On the second day, economizing further, they left behind their tent, sleeping bags, sleeping pads, and even food. All they carried was a pair of bivouac sacks and their cameras. In doing so, they made a commitment to go up and over the top, then descend the Abruzzi Ridge, instead of downclimbing the difficult line they had ascended. That was a bold yet somewhat desperate move. By late afternoon, Kukuczka and Piotrowski reached the summit snowfield, where they actually came upon the empty packets of powdered soup left by Maurice Barrard. Kukuczka reached the summit of his twelfth 8,000er at 6:25 P.M., Piotrowski a bit later.

Descending with a single headlamp, the men had to halt when the bulb abruptly burned out. They dug a hole in the snow at around 27,000 feet and settled in for a second bivouac, "shaking with cold," Kukuczka later wrote, "until the morning."

Growing weaker, desperately thirsty, the men were able to descend only 1,300 feet of the Abruzzi Ridge on July 9. They worried about losing their way on a route they had never ascended, since they had no good knowledge of its landmarks. They endured another bivouac, a night of "absolute torture."

By July 10, the two men had gone almost three days without food or water, and their bivouac sacks were full of holes. But that day they spotted the tents of a Korean party far below, and so knew they were on route. Below the Shoulder, at about 24,500 feet, very near the slope from which Art Gilkey had been swept to his death in 1953, in Kukuczka's telling, "When I asked Tadeusz for the rope, I discovered that he had forgotten to bring it with him from the bivouac."

Rappelling was no longer an option, and the men had not yet reached the top of the fixed ropes. In their exhausted state, they would have to downclimb every foot of the way, each man on his own. Kukuczka wrote in *The American Alpine Journal,*

> I started down with Tadeusz behind me. The ice was harder than usual. Just after I warned Tadeusz to go a little to my left, I saw one of his crampons slip off. When he tried to bang his other foot into the ice, the crampon shot off his other boot. I was directly below him. He fell full force onto me. I braced and could barely keep my footing, but I was totally unable to catch him. He hurtled down over the edge.

In shock, Kukuczka continued the descent alone. He was so addled that, as he approached the Korean tents, he later related, "I was under the strange illusion that somehow I might see Tadeusz there alive."

The tents were unoccupied. Kukuczka found a radio, but its batteries were dead. "There was a little gas cookstove and I drank and ate," he would recall. "Then I fell into a deep sleep and woke up the following afternoon. I had slept for 20 hours."

Two days later, Kukuczka reached the Godwin Austen Glacier and stumbled back to base camp. He had survived only because, at the time, he was probably the strongest high-altitude climber in the world.

As a feat of sheer gutsy climbing and endurance, I can admire Jerzy

Kukuczka's ascent of the south face and his skin-of-the-teeth descent. But what he did on K2 went so far beyond the boundaries of what I would ever attempt on an 8,000er that I can't even imagine participating in such a climb. My guess is that the reason Piotrowski's crampons came off is that he was too tired, or his fingers were too numb, to tighten the straps properly. We know that he was not wearing the newfangled clip-on crampons but an old-fashioned strap-on pair. If the straps are cinched tight, those are actually less likely to twist off than clip-ons.

Like so many other Poles in the high mountains, Kukuczka had stuck his neck way, way out there—and gotten away with it. And sadly, like so many great climbers who take risk to the ultimate, he would cut his margin too thin only three years later, on the south face of Lhotse.

The joy Kukuczka had felt on the summit ("We were both ecstatic," he recalled) was canceled by the loss of his partner. "My experiences on that mountain were too tragic," he later noted, ending his account, "and the price we paid for victory was too high."

At base camp Kukuczka embraced Wanda Rutkiewicz. Stunned by the death of Piotrowski, one of her dearest friends, she at last abandoned her own plan—despite her frostbitten fingers—to try Broad Peak that summer.

Meanwhile, Renato Casarotto was attempting the Magic Line solo. His wife, Goretta, who had climbed Gasherbrum II with him the year before, served on K2 in effect as his base camp manager. The two were in radio contact several times each day.

Casarotto was motivated by a personal vendetta as well as by the aesthetic appeal of the Magic Line. He had been a member of Reinhold Messner's 1979 K2 expedition, on which he had not performed well. What should have been a private disappointment became a public humiliation when Messner disparaged Casarotto in his book about K2: "I invited Renato Casarotto because I believed him at the time to be one of the ablest European climbers. . . . [But] I felt let down . . . by Renato as a climber." And according to Jim Curran, at a meeting of high-altitude climbers in the Tyrol in 1985, when someone told him about Casarotto's ambitions for the next summer, Messner spat, "He'll never make it!"

In 1986, Casarotto went after his monumental goal with admirable cautiousness. On two attempts, he reached 26,900 feet before turning back because of weather and dangerous conditions. In mid-July, he made his third attempt. This time he got above 27,000 feet, but ferocious winds once again defeated him. Kurt Diemberger, who was close friends with the Casarottos, overheard a radio conversation from that third attempt, which he quoted in *The Endless Knot*:

> GORETTA: How are you feeling, Renato?
> RENATO: I'm OK . . . fine, really. So far. But I'm tired now. and so fed up with this whole business that I'd like to pack it in, come down, get away from here.

On July 16, Casarotto headed down once more. He had been on K2 for two months and had come within only about 1,000 feet of the summit, but he had promised Goretta that the third attempt would be his last. Once he got back to base camp, the pair would pack up and head for home.

Slowly and carefully, Casarotto descended the dangerous route. At last he reached the foot of the face and started to trudge across the glacier toward base camp.

Standing beside his own tent, Diemberger saw "a small dot . . . actually more of a comma" approaching from a little more than a mile away. He continued to watch: "Now the comma was moving forward almost horizontally across the plateau—there! Then, suddenly, it vanished. Wiped out. I rubbed my eyes in amazement and peered again. Nothing. Nothing at all. Yet I hadn't dreamt it, had I?"

With his decades of mountaineering experience, Diemberger feared the worst—that Casarotto had fallen into a crevasse. Hesitantly, he approached Goretta, who had been waiting for the scheduled evening radio call from her husband. "Ciao, Kurt, what's the matter?" she greeted him.

"Renato—where is he now?" Diemberger asked.

> "Still on the ridge."
>
> For a moment, I felt relief. Then fear clutched at my heart again: *somebody* was on the glacier . . . if not Renato, then who? . . .
>
> "It's just that I saw someone, something, further down." I didn't want to say more than that.

Diemberger persuaded Goretta to try the radio. "The next moments will stay with me forever," Diemberger later wrote.

"Goretta, I have fallen . . . ," said the weak voice. "I am dying . . . please send help quickly."

Diemberger and several Italians grabbed ropes and gear and dashed toward the invisible crevasse. Along the way, one of the Italians managed to keep up radio contact with Casarotto. Then the rescuers saw the telltale hole in the glacier. The crevasse was only a couple of feet wide, and the snow bridge that had broken beneath the soloist lay right on a well-beaten path that many others had blithely hiked during the previous weeks.

An Italian rappelled into the crevasse. Narrow it might have been at the top, but it swelled beneath the surface into a monstrous cavern. One hundred and thirty feet down, the Italian found Casarotto "leaning against his rucksack in total darkness, with water running everywhere." The two men embraced, and the rescuer put a waist harness on his stricken comrade.

Even with several men hauling on different ropes, it is a very difficult task to pull an inert victim out of a crevasse. Because the ropes tend to cut into the snow on the lips of the fissure, they must be run over ice axes laid flat near the edge. It took several attempts before the men could hoist Casarotto almost to the surface. By then, he was unconscious.

Once they got him onto the level glacier, the rescuers wrapped Casarotto in sleeping bags. An Italian shined a headlamp on the victim's face. His eyes flickered briefly. He was still alive.

But moments later, he was dead. Internal injuries from the fall had doomed him from the moment he'd landed on the snow ledge in the darkness, 130 feet down.

Word of her husband's death was carried down to Goretta. She started up the glacier to say good-bye to Renato, but changed her mind halfway there and returned to base camp. Before leaving the scene of the accident, the men who had tried to rescue Casarotto dropped his body back into the crevasse. To nonclimbers, that may seem like a brutal act, but it's the most common grave for mountaineers in the great ranges. On an 8,000er, it's almost logistically impossible to carry a dead climber back to base camp, somehow summon a helicopter to lift the body back to the nearest village, and then arrange to ship it home. (It's been done in a few rare cases, among them that of Chantal Mauduit, my friend from K2, after she died on Dhaulagiri in 1998.)

There are worse places to be buried than in a crevasse at the foot of a great mountain. If I had died on some 8,000er, I wouldn't have minded too much if my friends had consigned me to the nearest crevasse. It would have been much easier for everyone involved to leave me on the mountain. It wouldn't have made sense for them to go to all the trouble and expense (not to mention paperwork!) of bringing me home just so I could be buried on U.S. soil.

The British team had gathered at base camp upon learning of Casarotto's demise. Jim Curran wrote, "I mumbled my condolences to Goretta, lost for words." With dignified control, she answered in English, "Please thank your friends for trying to help to save my husband."

Is there anything to be learned from Casarotto's death? Perhaps, after the ordeal of safely descending thousands of feet on the Magic Line, once he reached the glacier, he let down his guard. One of my favorite mountaineering mottos is "Crevasses don't care if you're a pro or not." The crevasse into which Casarotto fell was so narrow on the surface that he could easily have jumped across it. But snow bridges are fiendishly deceptive: they often look exactly like any other harmless patch of glacial surface. If you're going to try to solo an 8,000er, you almost have to cross crevasses on snow bridges that could collapse under your weight. A number of great mountaineers have died falling into crevasses—including Louis Lachenal, the conqueror of Annapurna, who perished in 1955 on a routine ski descent of the Vallée Blanche above his home town of Chamonix. And ever since my close partner J.-C. Lafaille disappeared high on Makalu on a solo winter attempt in 2006, I've thought that his death was most likely caused by his falling into a crevasse. Even a lifetime of climbing experience is no safeguard against a hidden crack in a glacier.

I've always been supercautious about crevasses, roping up where other climbers blithely travel solo, as I did on every trip through the funky icefall just below the foot of the Abruzzi Ridge. On my only solo expedition, to the north side of Everest in 1993, I dealt with the crevasses by wearing snowshoes or skis whenever I could, thereby spreading my body weight over a larger surface. I also made sure to climb the glacier only in the predawn cold, when its surface was as hard as it gets. Even so, traveling alone on the glacier was probably the scariest part of the climb, since I had so little control over what might happen.

Some of my climbing friends are astonished to learn that despite all the expeditions I've been on, I've never fallen into a crevasse. I've plunged into holes up to my waist several times, but always caught myself with my arms and managed to extricate myself without breaking loose more of the snow bridge and taking a nasty plunge. (And believe me, the insides of crevasses are nasty places!) The absence of crevasse falls on my mountaineering résumé is partly just sheer luck, but I like to think it's mainly the result of my healthy respect for those hidden death traps.

The latest tragedy sent shock waves reverberating all over the mountain. As Jim Curran would write:

For many of us the death of Renato Casarotto was the last straw. . . . The circumstances were so harrowing that I felt it was surprising that anyone had the willpower to stay on, yet even after six deaths some of us felt that there couldn't possibly be any more and that going home wouldn't change anything. And so, as July dragged on and the warm, wet monsoon-like weather kept everyone at Base Camp, the remnants of nine expeditions re-formed and regrouped for one last big effort.

On August 3 and 4, however, two more deaths occurred. One was the result of an almost absurd fluke: Mohammed Ali, the sirdar of the Pakistani high-altitude porters for a Korean team trying the Abruzzi Ridge, was making a routine shuttle between advance base camp and Camp I, on the lowest slopes of the spur, when a falling stone struck him in the head, killing him instantly.

The other accident occurred at the end of yet another epic ascent. After the deaths of Smolich and Pennington on the Magic Line, and of Casarotto on the glacier just below it, another team, made up mostly of Poles, went to work on that route, which was already being called K2's "last great problem." At the end of an epic struggle, three members completed the route, arriving nearly exhausted on the summit at 6:00 P.M. on August 3. The trio decided to descend the Abruzzi Ridge rather than the Magic Line. Just before midnight, the men were rappelling fixed ropes that had been recently strung up the Bottleneck couloir by the Korean team. Coming last was Wojciech Wróż, an experienced Himalayan veteran making his third attempt on K2.

In the dark, his teammates noticed a "one-meter gap" between the bottom of one fixed rope and the top anchor of the rope below it. They warned each other about the gap, and the first two men reached the bottom end of the last rope without mishap. Only a relatively easy snow slope lay between them and Camp IV, on the Shoulder.

The two men waited for Wróż to join them. The expedition leader later reported, "Suddenly they heard the noise of a fall. They feared the worst, but, exhausted, could do nothing more than to wait." Wróż never appeared. His partners could not be sure what had happened, but they guessed that Wróż must have rappelled off the end of the rope above the one-meter gap. There was nothing the two men could do but head on down themselves.

At base camp, a bitter argument broke out between the Polish and the Korean team leaders about the placing of the ropes and the one-meter gap. Curran's view was more philosophical: "The Poles should not have been relying on the Koreans' fixed ropes in the first place. But when the ropes were there and others were using them, it would be ridiculous to expect them to ignore them, either on purist or practical grounds."

I think all this blame casting misses a more basic point. What happened to Wróż is what happens to climbers when they're pushed to the very limit. If you have to call on your last reserves just to get down a mountain, it's the easiest thing in the world to make a simple mistake, like rappelling off the end of a rope in the dark. In forging the first ascents of the south face and the Magic Line, the Poles proved they were the toughest climbers on the mountain in 1986. But both Wróż and Piotrowski paid for their brilliant conquests with their lives.

Like Kukuczka and Piotrowski, the trio on the Magic Line had climbed a route so difficult, and had so deeply drawn on their reserves of strength, that their only hope for survival was to come down an easier route that had been fixed by others. Some observers see that as cutting-edge alpinism, but for me, it's leaving too much up to luck. Sometimes you get away with it; sometimes you don't.

Another eternal verity about the 8,000ers cannot be emphasized too much. In general, more climbers die on the descent of a great mountain than on the ascent. The Poles solved all the extreme technical problems as they fought their way up their breakthrough routes. It was only on the way down the relatively easy Abruzzi Ridge, with almost no gas left in their tanks, that they came to grief. Thus by the second week in August, eight climbers had lost their lives on K2 in a single summer, by far the deadliest toll in the mountain's history. And yet the worst was still to come.

The British team on the northwest ridge was coming apart at the seams. Besides the leader, Alan Rouse, the team was made up of some of the crème de la crème of British mountaineering: John Barry, John Porter, Brian Hall, and the infamous Burgess twins, Alan and Adrian—hippie iconoclasts who were nonetheless top-notch, quite conservative mountaineers.

As they attacked an unclimbed route on K2, with the prospect of becoming the first Brits to climb the mountain, the team was buoyed by promises of book and film contracts. In the middle of the expedition, the climbers got a letter from the wife of one of their Himalayan cronies back home, informing them that the word was out that the climbers would be knighted by the queen if they got to the top. This was apparently a spoof, but such an honor would not have been inconceivable. After all, John Hunt and Edmund Hillary had been knighted after the first ascent of Everest.

But the team never jelled on the mountain. Rouse divided his climbers into two foursomes, infelicitously calling them the "A Team" and the "B Team." (He put the Burgess brothers on separate teams, even though they were used to climbing together.) And no one seemed happy with Rouse's leadership, which was constantly vacillating and indecisive. In *K2: Triumph and Tragedy,* Jim Curran painted a basically sympathetic portrait of Rouse, to whom he was loyal to the end. But John Barry wrote his own book, called *K2: Savage Mountain, Savage Summer,* culled mainly from his own diary entries, which are scathing about Rouse:

> As a leader, his is an inept performance. He admits that he wants the commercial benefits of being a leader but is unwilling to take the responsibilities that go with it—mainly the reduction of his chances of making the summit. Overheard him say that he'd prefer to go alpine style and abandon the expedition.

Barry is as gleeful a tell-all narrator as Galen Rowell and Rick Ridgeway were in their K2 books. The diary entries paint a dreary picture of constant bickering: "Big row. I tell Al-R [Rouse, to distinguish him from Al Burgess] that I think he's a fool. Al goes off to tent in tears. Jim-C[urran] follows to comfort him. But still there is no apology or commitment to Wilkie. Wilkie pulls out."

The biggest problem for the British expedition, however, was that despite repeated efforts, the climbers made little headway on the northwest ridge. The intricacies of the route, the misery of the snow conditions, and the danger posed by avalanche slopes and precarious seracs defeated these crack alpinists. The team reached an altitude of only 24,300 feet before giving up. The northwest ridge would finally be climbed in 1991 by a pair of dedicated French mountaineers, Pierre Béghin and Christophe Profit, but even their ascent line deviated onto the north face high on the mountain.

As early as July 7, Rouse's party threw in the towel on the northwest ridge. In his diary, Barry laconically recorded:

> We are quitting the NW Ridge. I'm disappointed. We have
> 3 weeks left at least.
> Reasons: team too small . . . route too long.
> Abruzzi a clear run.

By this early date, a number of Rouse's teammates had suddenly remembered that they had job obligations back home. By ones and twos over the following weeks, they abandoned the expedition and started the long hike out. John Barry himself defected on July 28. As a result, his book is hugely anticlimactic, the long last chapter devoted to his humdrum hike back to civilization rather than to the drama that would soon unfold on the mountain.

In changing routes from the northwest ridge to the Abruzzi, Rouse was breaking all the rules, for his permit covered only the former route. As Barry wrote, "There's great secrecy surrounding our switch to the Abruzzi. Al-R doesn't wish to be banned from Pakistan for ten years; which he says is what the punishment would be. Phil [Burke] says that it would be a reward. I'm beyond caring."

The Brits had sardonically nicknamed the mass base camp at the foot of the Abruzzi "the Strip." Now, to get on the route themselves, the climbers still committed to the mountain transferred all their gear to a new base camp, as they sneaked past the Strip, hoping that the various liaison officers from other teams would not discover their transgression. The two narratives of the British expedition start to take on a comic tone at this point. The whole expedition, in fact, could have been treated as a comedy (this seems to have been John Barry's intention from the start), had it not ended in the disaster of early August.

By the beginning of that month, among the Brits only Al Rouse was still fully committed to an attempt on K2. Jim Curran would linger on, but strictly in the role of chronicler, scarcely climbing above Camp I. And now Rouse completed his defection from his own team, as he announced that he was pairing up with a woman from the Polish team to climb the Abruzzi. Whether Rouse and Dobroslawa Wolf (known as Mrufka, Polish for "ant") had started having an affair is pretty much irrelevant. What matters is that all semblance of teamwork—except the dogged loyalty of Curran at base camp—had vanished from the British expedition.

Kurt Diemberger and Julie Tullis had spent most of their time so far on K2 filmmaking for the Italian team to which they were attached. Calling themselves Quota 8000, those climbers had started work on the Magic Line, but after the deaths of Pennington and Smolich, they had bailed and switched over to the Abruzzi. Unlike the British, the Italians claimed they had obtained permits beforehand for both routes, though climbers from other teams were skeptical.

Diemberger and Tullis's not-so-secret agenda was to climb K2, rather than simply make a film about their teammates. They were an odd pair, the subject of gossip all over the mountain. Tullis, at forty-seven, and Diemberger, at fifty-four, were both married—apparently happily—and Diemberger's *The Endless Knot* unabashedly credits the help and goodwill of Terry Tullis and Teresa Diemberger. But when he writes about the bond between himself and Julie, passage after passage reverberates with an intimate passion. For example:

Each step is a step into boundless possibility.

Julie says it more simply: wherever I go, anything is possible.

I say: where anything is possible, there I go.

That's why we are together.

Or:

If just one of us, as a conclusion of our first years together, reached the summit of K2—wouldn't that be fulfillment for both? Even if only one trod the dream summit? Only one made the dream come true?

Granted, Diemberger has always been a writer inclined toward the mystical and the emotional. What matters is not whether Diemberger and Tullis were lovers (with or without the knowledge of their spouses) but whether the very emotionality of their relationship, like that newly formed between Rouse and Mrufka, interfered with good judgment on this dangerous mountain.

At first, Jim Curran took a slightly jaundiced view of the Tullis-Diemberger pairing. He had known Tullis for years, though not well, through encounters at climbing meets and festivals in Britain. She struck him as, on the one hand, "a bright, attractive, and apparently conventional housewife" and, on the other, as "a rather bossy 'head girl.' " He was not at all sure Tullis was ready for K2, for "her actual mountaineering experience was rather limited and certainly had not got the foundation of Scottish winter and extreme alpine climbing," which the best British alpinists considered mandatory before one tackled the most serious mountains.

Diemberger, whom Curran had also known casually over the years, "radiated a massive self-confidence, amounting at times to self-importance." But at K2 base camp one day, as Diemberger reminisced about Broad Peak with Hermann Buhl in 1957, Curran was won over by the legend: "I was suddenly conscious that here was a major part of Himalayan climbing history in the flesh."

The crux of Curran's analysis of the bond between the British woman and the Austrian man was that Julie, "through her devotion, almost amounting to hero-worship, of Kurt, had come to see herself as a world-class mountaineer in her own right." And that spelled trouble.

On K2 in 1992, despite my undeniable attraction to Chantal Mauduit, and even as I wondered whether she was flirting with me, I had no intention of getting involved with her during the expedition. My own concentration and commitment, I absolutely believed, depended on having no relationship with another climber that might undercut my motivation or cloud my judgment. All of my energy and focus needed to be on trying to climb K2. Anything less could spell failure or even disaster.

On August 2, Tullis and Diemberger, along with Rouse and Mrufka and three Koreans, all reached the Shoulder, at 26,000 feet. They had been preceded by three Austrians—Willi Bauer, Alfred Imitzer, and Hannes Wieser—who that day were attempting to go for the summit but had to turn back at 27,500 feet. This created a serious space problem at Camp IV, where only three tents stood, normally capable of housing seven climbers. When the Austrians returned late that afternoon, they pleaded to be allowed to jam in with the others, so that they could make one more try for the top. At last the Koreans generously accepted two of the Austrians, so that night five men slept piled together in a three-man tent. Rouse and Mrufka invited the third Austrian into their tent. But Diemberger refused to share his and Tullis's tent, despite (or because of) the fact that the Austrians were his compatriots. (Afterward, there would be hard feelings between Diemberger and Bauer.)

On August 3, the Koreans set out for the summit. They reached it late in the afternoon and were overtaken by night on the descent. Two of the Koreans regained Camp IV, while the third survived a bivouac above the Bottleneck, having tied himself off to a piton. (That same night the three Poles who had made the first ascent of the Magic Line came down the Abruzzi, only to lose Wojciech Wróż in the darkness.)

Later, many would wonder why the "Europeans" (Brits are not, strictly speaking, Europeans)—Tullis and Diemberger, Rouse and Mrufka, and the three Austrians—didn't go for the summit with the Koreans on August 3, while the weather was still fine. The vague explanation offered by the survivors was that they needed a day of rest and wanted to avoid a traffic jam in the Bottleneck. Another factor may have been that, of all the teams on the mountain that summer, the Koreans were felt to be climbing in the poorest style. Using old-fashioned heavy logistics, their nineteen-man team had strung the route with fixed ropes up the Bottleneck and across the leftward traverse above it. On August 3, the three summiteers used bottled oxygen all the way, the only climbers that season to rely on gas. Yet the Koreans survived where others did not.

With the addition of the two Poles from the Magic Line, the tent situation at Camp IV on the night of August 3 became drastic. Showing remarkable magnanimity, Rouse let the Poles move in with him and Mrufka, even though that meant that he spent the night halfway out of the tent, his upper body nestled in a snow hole. The third Austrian moved into the Korean tent. Once again, Diemberger and Tullis refused to accommodate any of the refugees.

In *The Endless Knot,* though he acknowledges the overcrowding problem, Diemberger never explains why he and Tullis were unwilling to share their tent—in fact, he dances so cleverly around the truth that if you had only his account of the expedition to go by, you'd never uncover that selfishness.

It seems clear that the later debilitation of many of the climbers at Camp IV was partly a result of the miserable nights they spent in crowded tents on August 2 and 3. At 26,000 feet, it's hard enough to sleep in "normal" quarters, let alone with too many climbers crammed into too small a tent.

On August 4, the seven "Europeans" set out for the top. Rouse and Mrufka were the first out of camp, but they departed only at dawn, not in the middle of the night, as Charley, Scott, and I would do six years later. Despite two nearly sleepless nights, Rouse was the strongest climber among the seven, and in fact he broke trail nearly all the way. Mrufka quickly fell behind. One of the Austrians, Hannes Wieser, turned back a short way above Camp IV. Willi Bauer and Alfred Imitzer caught up with Rouse not far below the summit and took over the trail-breaking. They reached the top at 3:15 P.M., Rouse not long afterward. After two and a half months on the mountain, he had finally claimed the first British ascent of K2.

Tullis and Diemberger had actually set out from Camp IV before the Austrians, but they'd quickly been overtaken by Bauer and Imitzer. The weather was holding perfect. Diemberger's account of the summit climb in *The Endless Knot* is so rich in mystical transport that you have to read between the lines to figure out what was going on with Tullis and himself. They climbed roped together, as no one else did, and they were very slow. Sensibly, they vowed not to reach the summit later than 4:00 P.M., but by 3:00 P.M. they were still 650 vertical feet below the top.

Suddenly they came upon Mrufka, leaning immobile against the slope. To their shock, they saw that the Polish woman was asleep. Diemberger woke her up and offered her a candy. "She reacts with alarm, looking up full of surprise," he later wrote. " 'No . . . Up . . . I have to go up!" As Diemberger and Tullis continued on, Mrufka put on a burst of speed and tried to pass them. Tullis suggested that she follow in their tracks, for she was clearly half out of her mind, but Mrufka blurted out, "I don't want to climb behind an old man."

For long moments, Mrufka flailed away clumsily on the steep slope above Diemberger and Tullis, who were terrified that she would fall and knock them off their feet, or snag their rope and pull them off. Eventually Mrufka passed out of sight to the right.

At 4:00 P.M., Bauer and Imitzer suddenly appeared, heading down. Diemberger recounted their conversation.

"Are you sure you still want to go up?" Bauer asked him.

"It shouldn't take us more than an hour at most," he replied.

"You're wrong. It took us four hours!"

Diemberger could not believe what he was hearing. Finally he deduced that Bauer meant four hours from the top of the traverse out of the Bottleneck, not from their present position. (It sounds as though no one was thinking very clearly that day high on K2.) Reassured by this rationalization, Diemberger and Tullis pushed on, violating their own turn-around deadline. But first Diemberger asked Bauer, "Are there any crevasses where you can bivouac?"

Diemberger was indisputably a world-class mountaineer, but he was also fifty-four years old. I suspect that he and Tullis wanted the summit too badly, and that the "endless knot" of their interwoven partnership, combined with hypoxia, goaded them into making the foolish decision to push on. In their situation, no matter how much I might have craved the summit, if it was after 4:00 P.M. I would have given it up and descended.

My own turnaround time is an inflexible 2:00 P.M. I've never violated that deadline. And I've never had to stop and turn back because it got too late. It's all about planning beforehand and starting early enough in the day. Too many times I've seen climbers invite trouble just by leaving for the top too late in the morning.

Diemberger and Tullis reached the summit at 5:30 P.M. In *The Endless Knot,* he recalls that triumph:

> The joy! The happiness! We cling to one another. For this one moment of eternity, K2—beautiful K2—is ours.
>
> "Julie—the peak we most desired!" I feel my voice trembling as I look into the big, dark eyes under the hood. . . .
>
> "Our very special mountain," she whispers. It is, it is—our own and very special mountain.

This sounds like the perfect recipe for an unfolding disaster. But the most extraordinary thing about the summit push on August 4, 1986, is that all seven climbers made it back to Camp IV in one piece. On his way down from the top, Rouse found Mrufka still inching her way painfully upward. After a heated argument, he persuaded her to turn around and descend. At Camp IV, Willi Bauer said later, "She cried in her tent because she hadn't made it to the top. . . . I told her, 'Mrufka, be happy that we're alive.'"

Diemberger and Tullis did not leave the summit until after 6:00 P.M. By then, the weather was deteriorating. All the way down, Tullis was near collapse. Diemberger went first on the rope to find the route. Suddenly he heard her call out his name: she had fallen and was cartwheeling down the steep slope. Diemberger plunged his ax in, put his weight on the head, and almost stopped her fall before he was wrenched from his stance by the rope. The two fell several hundred feet, out of control, before miraculously sliding to a stop.

The only headlamp the pair carried had failed to work. In the dark, with a belay from his partner, feeling more than seeing his way, Diemberger climbed into a crevasse to scout it for a bivouac site, only to discover that he was standing on a fast-crumbling snow bridge. He screamed at Tullis to pull him out, but, much lighter than the heavyset Austrian, she could barely hold him in place. With a desperate effort, Diemberger clawed his way back to the surface with his ice ax.

The pair finally bivouacked in a hollow snow niche they excavated out of the slope, at 27,500 feet. Since they had left their rucksack anchored to a piton at the top of the traverse out of the Bottleneck, they did not even have the space blanket Diemberger had stuck in his pack as an emergency shelter. It was a blessing that the storm held off until morning, but in the night both climbers suffered serious frostbite. At first light on August 5, in a whiteout, the two started down again, but they were effectively lost. Zigzagging back and forth, they finally struck the Korean fixed ropes and managed to get down the Bottleneck; in the mist, however, they could not locate Camp IV. Diemberger began shouting, and at last Bauer heard his cries and shouted back, guiding the two stricken climbers into camp.

Bauer later reported that he had dragged Tullis on her back the last stretch into camp, that "her nose and cheeks [were] quite black showing definite signs of first degree frostbite," and that her gloveless "right hand

[was] swollen and bits of flesh [were] hanging down." In *The Endless Knot,* Diemberger vehemently disputed these assertions, insisting that Tullis had made it into camp under her own power.

In any case, Bauer and Imitzer took Tullis into their tent, the largest of the three at Camp IV, fed her hot drinks, and tried to warm her with a spare down jacket. Eventually she returned to the tent she and Diemberger had pitched on the Shoulder on August 2.

Five of the seven climbers ensconced in Camp IV had reached the summit. To avert catastrophe, all they needed to do now was head down the mountain, following a route that was hung with fixed ropes most of the way. But the looming storm had finally arrived. The climbers stayed in their tents all through August 5. They would not try to descend, in fact, for another five days.

At base camp, Jim Curran and the other watchers could only guess what was happening high on the mountain, for there was no radio in Camp IV. In the storm, it would not be possible to climb up the Abruzzi Ridge to attempt a rescue, and as day succeeded day, the thoughts of those below turned dark. On August 5 and 7, there were lulls in the storm. On the latter day, Curran could see all the way up to the Shoulder. He said to the others in base camp, "If anyone is up, they will be, I imagine, hot-footing it down." But no one arrived that day, or the next, or the next.

What happened at Camp IV from August 5 to 10 is still something of a mystery. Al Rouse, who had been the strongest of all seven climbers on summit day, had repeatedly vowed that one must spend as few days as possible at 26,000 feet. It seems that a kind of apathy took hold, the inevitable concomitant of the hypoxic states that perhaps all seven had entered on August 4; and that apathy most likely was reinforced by the complete exhaustion of Tullis and Diemberger.

On the night of August 5, winds that Diemberger estimated at sixty miles an hour piled heavy drifts of snow against the walls of the tent he shared with Tullis, threatening to break the poles. The Austrian was incapable of punching his way loose from inside, and by now Tullis was snowblind as well as shivering with cold. In the morning, the two called out for help. First Rouse, then Bauer tried to dig the tent loose from outside, before giving up in the blizzard. Their furious ice ax blows tore holes in the tent fabric, however, forcing Tullis and Diemberger to abandon their shelter.

Dashing through the storm, Tullis tumbled into the Austrian tent, while Diemberger crawled inside Rouse's. The man who had refused to share his tent with the refugees on August 2 and 3 now had to beg, "Please, let me in!" Without hesitation, Rouse and Bauer granted the same mercy Diemberger had denied others. But now the misery of overcrowded quarters once again sapped the willpower of the seven. They spent another night without leaving their tents.

During the night, the storm eased up, and the climbers prepared to make their getaway in the morning. At first light, however, as Diemberger later wrote, "there was no visibility. . . . With only the one line of escape, the risk of getting lost in thick fog or cloud on the Shoulder was great." So the climbers stayed put.

In my view, this is a crucial passage. It's startling that in all the subsequent discussion of the 1986 disaster, no one brought up the question of willow wands. That was the first thing that leapt to my attention when I read *The Endless Knot* and *K2: Triumph and Tragedy* before my 1992 expedition. Had the climbers wanded the route between the top of the fixed ropes and Camp IV, they could have managed to get down on August 7, whiteout or no. But neither Curran nor Diemberger even mentions this oversight as contributing to the tragedy.

There's a curious passage much earlier in Diemberger's book, however, that illuminates the thinking of the "Europeans." On the way up to the Shoulder on August 2, he remarks, "I notice that only one of the bamboo sticks the high-altitude porters have brought up bears a red pennant; the other marker flags have either been lost during the transport along the ridge or have not yet been fixed. No time to sort that out now."

The porters, of course, were Pakistanis working for the Korean expedition. Why didn't it occur to Diemberger and Tullis, or Rouse and

Mrufka, or the three Austrians to bring and plant their own willow wands? That's porters' work, Diemberger seems to imply. Even more curiously, on that crucial slope below the Shoulder, the Austrian comes across a cached bundle of wands but declines to pick them up. He recalls, "I look at the bundle thoughtfully: they're no protection against avalanches, that's for sure. To put them in now, so near to the end of our time here, seems pedantic, an over-scrupulous precaution."

Of course willow wands are no protection against avalanches! That's not what they're for. When I first read that passage, I wondered how such an experienced mountaineer as Diemberger could have been so blasé about willow wands. Now I realize, as I said earlier, that's it's just not chic for Europeans to climb with those garden stakes sticking out of their packs. And the same goes for Brits: unlike Americans, they have little or no tradition of wanding routes in the great ranges to safeguard a descent in a storm.

Thus on August 7, the climbers at Camp IV decided against going down in the whiteout for fear of getting lost. It makes you want to weep with frustration: a string of willow wands below Camp IV could have saved lives.

On the morning of August 8, Diemberger awoke to hear Bauer's voice over the wind. At first he could not make out the words. He called back for clarification.

"Kurt!" Bauer shouted. "Julie died last night."

"It was like a hammer blow," Diemberger later wrote. "Alan, at my side, tried to comfort me. I heard his words without grasping their meaning."

Bauer carried Tullis's body to the abandoned tent, cut a hole in the roof with his ax, and deposited the corpse inside it. As heartless as that may seem, it was obviously preferable to keeping a dead body in the cramped Austrian tent.

That same day, August 8, the stranded climbers ran out of stove fuel. They could no longer turn snow into pots of life-saving water. They tried to scoop handfuls of snow and melt them in their mouths. Many a person dying of thirst in the cold has tried to do the same, but it's a desperate remedy that doesn't really work, because the loss of precious energy in melting the snow outweighs the minimal gain of liquid.

Meanwhile, Al Rouse, who had been the strongest of the seven, began to fade. Diemberger recalled,

> Last night was bad, he was thrashing about, agitated, like a chained animal. He would lunge suddenly, delirious, quarreling with destiny. I tried in vain to calm him. . . . He begs continuously for water, which we no longer have. I put a piece of slush to his lips, which he sucks greedily.

The survivors knew better than to hope for rescue from below. But all through the day on August 9, they stayed in their tents, certain that they could not get down in the ongoing storm. Only the next morning, when they woke to blue sky (though the wind was still raging), did they rouse themselves to action.

Willi Bauer was the motivating force. "*Aussa! Aussa!*" he yelled at Wieser and Imitzer—colloquial German for "Out! Out!" In the other tent, Diemberger and Mrufka slowly put on their boots. They knew that Rouse was now beyond help, but, as Diemberger put it, "The prospect of leaving him here is a ghastly one." Tottering around outside the tents, he noted, was "like having to learn to walk again."

Diemberger paid a last visit to Tullis. He later wrote, "I cannot see her face. The tent is half caved-in, but has not collapsed. I move the sleeping bag sealing the opening, and put the down jacket over her feet. . . . For the last time, I touch her—then I leave her alone."

By this point, the other four survivors had already started down, but almost at once, the catastrophe deepened. Wieser and Imitzer were able to walk only a little more than 300 feet before they fell down in the snow. Mrufka and Bauer desperately tried to get them back on their feet, but had to give up.

Only minutes later, Diemberger came upon the doomed men.

I reach Hannes. He is sitting in the snow, with his back to me. A few metres further on Alfred is lying face down on the furrowed surface, completely still. He must be dead. Hannes moves his arms weakly, rowing the air in slow motion. . . . Then I see his face. His eyes, blank, stare into space. He does not see me. I shout his name, but he does not even move his head.

To save himself, Diemberger, too, had to leave Imitzer and Wieser behind.

Throughout the early stages of the descent, Mrufka was stronger and faster than Diemberger, and the equal of Bauer. But all three were in a hallucinatory trance. When Diemberger finally caught up to the other two, Bauer suddenly asked, "Do you have anything to eat? Have you brought a stove?"

"No, of course not," Diemberger answered in astonishment.

It is a testimony to the sheer will to live that the three survivors were able to keep descending over tricky ground, on a route unsecured by fixed ropes. Their thoughts were fixated on Camp III at 24,100 feet, where they expected to find tents still standing, perhaps with food and stoves and fuel still in them. Late that afternoon they reached the camp, only to find to their horror that ice avalanches had destroyed everything.

The only blessing was that fixed ropes had been strung continuously from camp to the lower slopes of the Abruzzi. But here a trivial technical detail worked its cruel mischief. Neither Bauer nor Diemberger had a descending device, so each man simply clipped in to the fixed ropes with a carabiner and went down hand over hand. Mrufka, however, had a Sticht plate, which she insisted on affixing to each rope. A Sticht plate is a good belay tool, but for rappelling, it's far less easy to use than a figure-eight device. At each anchor, Mrufka had to fiddle arduously with her plate to disengage it from the upper rope and attach it to the lower one. Diemberger tried to persuade her to use a carabiner instead, but Mrufka either refused or didn't understand.

As they forged on down into the darkness, the two Austrians lost track of Mrufka. They assumed she was just behind them, but they would never see her again.

Trailing behind Bauer, Diemberger could barely hold on to the fixed ropes. He half-fell, half-slid down the cords strung along the nearly vertical fissure of House's Chimney. But at Camp II, he found Bauer in a tent, melting snow over a stove. The two men drank as much as they could, then fell asleep.

It was not until evening of August 11 that the two refugees completed their descent. The first person to greet Diemberger was Jim Curran, who of course hoped it would be Al Rouse emerging from the high death trap. According to Diemberger, Curran said, "You're safe at last!"

"I've lost Julie," he answered.

Later Curran wrote,

> If you had lined up every member of each expedition and asked yourself who would survive an ordeal like this, Willi and Kurt would come at the bottom of most people's lists. But in the end their slow, plodding, energy-conserving approach must have paid off.

Of the seven climbers who had headed for the summit on August 4, five had perished. The toll for the "dangerous summer" had reached thirteen.

To this day, in the long annals of mountaineering in the Himalaya and the Karakoram, only one season on any peak has ever been more deadly than K2 in 1986. In 1937 on Nanga Parbat, seven German climbers and nine high-altitude porters were crushed to death by a monstrous avalanche as they slept in their tents at Camp IV. That calamity, however, occurred in a single instant, as a result of a collapse of a hanging glacier far above—an act of God, as it were. In terms of a season punctuated by one unrelated disaster after another, snuffing out the lives of some of the world's best mountaineers, K2 in 1986 remains unmatched.

The terrible summer had its impact in mountaineering circles in the United States, though it did not really reverberate among the general public. For one thing, "only" two of the thirteen victims were Americans. The hue and cry in this country about the Everest tragedy of 1996 had everything to do with how many of the principals involved, from Scott Fischer to Beck Weathers to Doug Hansen to Jon Krakauer, were Americans. And though K2 had an able chronicler in Jim Curran, the British writer did not play a pivotal role in the drama, as Krakauer did on Everest. Finally, on K2 there was no simple morality play to which the public could reduce the complicated chain of accidents—nothing like the perversely satisfying "they got what they deserved" formula so many readers took away from *Into Thin Air.*

A lead article in the *American Alpine Journal* by Charlie Houston, titled "Death in High Places," tried to wring a moral lesson from the 1986 season. Among other criticisms, Houston wrote,

> Too many of the deaths were avoidable. . . .
>
> Also commonplace were outrageous behavior, intense rivalry, and disregard of mountain ethics—which caused several deaths. Not many years ago some of the things that were done would have led to excommunication by the climbing fraternity.

Houston's strictures were among the first in a vein that has now become commonplace, especially in response to the "circuses" on Everest every spring, as selfishness, competition, and dehumanization overwhelm compassion and brotherhood.

The most balanced and comprehensive coverage of the K2 tragedies in the American media came in an article in *Outside* magazine titled "The Dangerous Summer," cowritten by Greg Child (four years before he would climb K2) and Jon Krakauer (ten years before he would climb

Everest). For the most part, Child and Krakauer avoided finger-pointing, but they ended the piece with a quote they had elicited from Jim Curran:

> "If anything was common to most of the deaths, it was that a lot of people were very ambitious and had a lot to gain by climbing K2—and a lot to lose as well. Casarotto, the Austrians, Al Rouse, the Barrards were all—the word that comes to mind is overambitious. If you're going to try alpine-style ascents of 8,000-meter peaks, you've got to leave yourself room to fail."
>
> Too many people on K2 last summer, it would appear, did not.

Twenty-two years later, commenting on the 2008 K2 catastrophe for *National Geographic Adventure,* Child would strike a more sardonic note: "What the hell—climbing is dangerous."

In Great Britain and Europe, however, the K2 season caused a huge furor. The British press, including some of the climbing journals, raked the Austrians over the coals for "abandoning" Al Rouse. This charge was, of course, ridiculous: by August 10, Rouse was too feeble even to stand, and it was all Diemberger and Bauer could do to get themselves down the mountain. Likewise, British journals and newspapers castigated Diemberger for making a martyr of the supposedly reluctant Julie Tullis—despite all the evidence that their "endless knot" was very much a mutual passion.

Some of the French press went so far as to blame Michel Parmentier for abandoning Maurice and Liliane Barrard, even though he almost lost his own life by waiting for them as long as he did at Camp III. In the German-language press, Bauer and Diemberger, both of whom lost frostbitten digits to amputation, feuded bitterly, with the public taking one side or another. Even the Koreans were scapegoated for climbing too slowly, in too old-fashioned a style.

On the last page of *K2: Triumph and Tragedy,* Curran stepped back from all the accusations to editorialize:

> Exploring and pushing the limits has always been the name of
> the game, whether in rock climbing, alpinism, or Himalayan
> mountaineering. But the disastrous summer of K2 must remain
> a salutary reminder that the limits are still there: pushing them
> is one thing, ignoring them another. Mountaineering will never
> be a safe activity and would not be worth doing if it were.

That last line is a credo by which all climbers live. When I look back on the summer of 1986 on K2, I can see all kinds of small mistakes that led to fatal outcomes. But the scenario that most haunts me is the picture of those seven climbers stranded at Camp IV waiting, day after day, when they must have known that their only hope of getting off K2 alive was to head down at once. It reminds me of a very wise saying about mountaineering that my wife, Paula, repeats often: "Just when you think you've got it figured out, you don't." No wonder the mantra that kept running through my head on K2 in 1992 was "Remember '86!"

In the summer of 1987, not one climber reached the top of K2. But a Japanese-Pakistani expedition pushing up the Abruzzi Ridge came upon Mrufka's body between Camps II and III. She was frozen in place on a steep slope, her Sticht plate still clipped to a fixed rope, which was also wrapped around her wrist. In a remarkable operation, the team carried her body down to the foot of the Abruzzi Ridge and buried her there.

That summer, several Japanese and several Spaniards reached the Shoulder and climbed into the Bottleneck couloir before being turned back by bad weather. They found no trace of Alfred Imitzer, Hannes Wieser, Julie Tullis, or Alan Rouse. The two Austrians may have been avalanched off the ridge between August 1986 and July 1987. Tullis and Rouse were most likely entombed by the winter snows. As is true for so many victims of K2, the bodies of those four climbers have never been found.

Epilogue: The Holy Grail

Despite the title of Jim Curran's book about the 1986 season, in the story of K2, there's more tragedy than triumph. The first ascents of other 8,000ers unfurled as glorious sagas of perseverance and daring—the French dashing up Annapurna in 1950 after wasting a month simply trying to find the mountain, Hermann Buhl going solo in 1953 to the top of Nanga Parbat, Hillary and Tenzing blithely solving the last obstacles on Everest the same year, Joe Brown and George Band stopping twenty feet short of the top of Kangchenjunga in 1955 out of respect for the beliefs of the people of Sikkim, for whom the mountain was a god and a protector. (Our team did the same on Kangchenjunga in 1989.)

But the first ascent of K2, in 1954, will forever be clouded by the bitter and interminable controversy it spawned. If you believe Walter Bonatti's version of the events of July 30 and 31—and by now, most people in the climbing world do accept that version—the dominant character in the summit duo, Achille Compagnoni, must go down in history as one of the indelible bad guys of mountaineering. For fear of sharing the triumph with the younger, better climber, Compagnoni was apparently willing to let Bonatti and Amir Mahdi freeze to death in an open bivouac. And the premeditated ruse Compagnoni devised to prevent that sharing—hiding

Camp IX behind rocks above a dangerous traverse—turned the bravest Hunza climber of his day into a frostbite victim who would never be able to go back to the high mountains.

The heroes of K2—for me, the list is headed by Bonatti, Fritz Wiessner, and the whole 1953 American team—remain men lastingly scarred by defeat and, in the cases of Bonatti and Wiessner, by betrayal. Toward the end of Curran's book, he tries to enumerate the triumphs of the 1986 season: Wanda Rutkiewicz becoming the first woman to climb K2, Benoît Chamoux's dazzling twenty-three-hour ascent, the Poles claiming the Magic Line after it had turned back others—but those deeds are so far overshadowed by the thirteen deaths that 1986 will forever figure as a black season in the annals of mountaineering in the Karakoram.

Ever since Bob Bates and Charlie Houston wrote their classic narrative of the 1953 campaign, "the savage mountain" has become the sobriquet that has stuck to K2. John Barry and Jim Curran (in his historical survey) incorporated that label in the titles of their own K2 books. Last summer, the nickname recurrently appeared in the media accounts of the 2008 disaster.

It doesn't work for me, though. K2 is not some malevolent being, lurking there above the Baltoro, waiting to get us. It's just there. It's indifferent. It's an inanimate mountain made of rock, ice, and snow. The "savageness" is what we project onto it, as if we blame the peak for our own misadventures on it.

There's no denying how dangerous a mountain K2 is, however. According to the website EverestNews.com, in 2008 alone at least 290 climbers reached the top of Mount Everest, while only 1 person died on the mountain. No fewer than 77 men and women topped out on a single day in late May. On K2 that summer, 18 climbers reached the summit, while 11 died trying. According to the most accurate count, by May 2009, 299 people have stood on top of K2, while 77 have died on its flanks. That's a pretty daunting ratio—it means that for every 4 climbers who reach the summit, at least 1 dies. (The ratio for Everest is roughly 19 to 1.)

Those cold statistics mask a discrepancy that only further underscores the danger of K2. Every spring and fall, Everest now swarms with relative novices, the clients on guided expeditions who make up the bulk of the traffic. It's not surprising that some of them should come to grief. K2, however, is still almost exclusively the province of experienced mountaineers, men and women who are used to extricating themselves from the most perilous predicaments.

It's also true, though, that on Everest experienced "professional" climbers make mistakes and get in trouble. In the public eye, all clients get scapegoated as dilettantes who have no business being on the mountain. But many clients, including ones I've guided, have been training as amateur climbers for years before they sign up for Everest. In 1996, the clients got most of the blame for the tragedy. Shouldn't the leaders have absorbed much of the criticism for mistakes that led to the disaster?

In 2004, the French climbing writer Charlie Buffet wrote a deft little book called *La Folie du K2* (K2 Madness). In it, he listed the ten French mountaineers who had reached the top of K2 to that date: Éric Escoffier, Daniel Lacroix, Benoît Chamoux, Maurice and Liliane Barrard, Michel Parmentier, Pierre Béghin, Christophe Profit, Chantal Mauduit, and Jean-Christophe Lafaille. That list reads like a Who's Who of French mountaineering. Laconically, Buffet commented, "At this time, only two of them are still alive, Profit and Lafaille. All the rest died in the mountains."

Since my great friend J.-C. Lafaille disappeared on Makalu in 2006, that reduces Buffet's list of the living to one: Christophe Profit, who with Béghin made the first ascent of K2's northwest ridge in 1991. And with the death of the Frenchman Hugues d'Aubarède in August 2008, Buffet's roster becomes even more doleful.

Buffet closes his book with a powerful quotation from Lafaille. Since I don't read French, I'd been unaware of J.-C.'s comments until this year, when a friend translated the passage for me. (In the book, it's not clear whether J.-C., who got to the top of K2 in 2001, wrote the passage for a climbing magazine or simply spoke it during an interview with Buffet.)

It's a superb, immense mountain that crushes you. Here the risks are palpable, you can see them. Not far from base camp, there's this memorial [the Gilkey-Puchoz memorial]. You feel as though you're in a cemetery. To reach the foot of the [Abruzzi] face, you walk along the Godwin Austen Glacier, where a Spanish friend of mine found the body of Maurice Barrard two years ago. It's only a fifteen-minute walk from the tents where we lived for two months. And every time that I took that path, I found human debris there—clothes, shoes, a pelvis. The whole history of this mountain lies heavy on your shoulders.

K2 was the greatest adventure of my climbing life. It was the ultimate test of my mountaineering skills. It had everything: close calls, interminable waits during storms, retreats to base camp, desperate rescues of other climbers. I not only needed all my ability to get up the mountain, I needed all my patience. (Sometimes I call K2 the "full meal deal" of mountaineering—everything you could ask for in a climb, and more.) In all of my expeditions to 8,000ers, I've never spent so long on a peak before getting to the top. K2 was a lifetime of expeditions packed into one summer.

It was also one of the two or three most important turning points in my life. As I hiked out the Baltoro that August, I could finally say to myself, *I really do have the skills to get up the 8,000ers. I've climbed the three highest. What about the others?* Ultimately, K2 gave me the push and the confidence to conceive of my Endeavor 8000.

By 2008, I'd been on ten expeditions to Mount Everest. I'd reached its summit six times. Ever since 2005, when I finished the cycle of the fourteen 8,000ers by climbing Annapurna, I'd always entertained the thought that, given the right circumstances, I might give Everest another go.

Then, just last spring, the right circumstances fell into place. On

March 25, 2009, I set out once more for the world's highest mountain, trekking up the Khumbu Valley for the seventh time on the way to base camp on the south side. Three months shy of my fiftieth birthday, I still felt as physically fit as I ever had.

The expedition was organized by the Eddie Bauer company. By now, I'm part of a team helping design a new line of technical gear, called First Ascent. Showcasing the products on Everest was to be the final stage of the company's official launch of that line of products.

It was an honor for me to be part of the Eddie Bauer campaign. The primary draw for me in returning to Everest, however, was the challenge of trying to climb to 29,035 feet again. People often ask when I'm going to quit climbing. My response is "I'll quit when I no longer enjoy it, or can't do it anymore."

Everest was as crowded as ever last spring. My biggest problem on the mountain, besides the usual spells of bad weather, was the traffic congestion up high on the South Col route. But I bided my time through late April and early May, and finally the weather forecast seemed favorable for a summit push. It's always a bit of a gamble to leave base camp, with high camp still three days away, and to time it just right for a summit attempt. We had originally hoped to go for the top on May 17, thereby beating the crowds. But May 17 was a bust, with extremely high winds and near-zero visibility. So we waited in our tents on the South Col all day and night. And as we waited, many other climbers arrived. We knew the traffic would be heavy the next day.

Finally, at 11:00 P.M. on May 18, four teammates and I left the South Col. It was not only pretty crowded on the route, but it was quite cold—somebody said minus 30 degrees Fahrenheit. Even so, we made good time, reaching the Balcony at 3:00 A.M., the summit at 8:00 A.M.

By the time the sun rose, it was a nice day, slightly breezy but warm enough and gloriously clear. The descent was uneventful, and we got back to the South Col at 1:00 P.M. As I wrote on my website, "So, 14-hour round trip. My seventh ascent of the mountain and more than likely my last ascent of the mountain. It was a great place to revisit, to come back to Everest, but I don't have the desire anymore to come back and climb the mountain for the eighth time."

On Everest in spring 2009, I made a choice I'd never resorted to before, which was to use supplemental oxygen even though I had no client to guide. I explained the decision on my website: "Knowing that the next day would be rather cold and windy, as a safety issue I felt it would be better to stay with the team and use supplemental oxygen. So it was more based on safety, and sticking with my group. So I kind of compromised my ascent but it still worked out well." It was gratifying later to learn that the people following our expedition online uniformly praised my decision, rather than needling me about compromising my purist style.

Climbing Everest again seemed reasonable. But there's no way I'd ever try K2 again. Objectively, it's not that severe a climb, at least on the Abruzzi Ridge. It's gnarly, and it's not easy to descend in bad conditions. It's colder than Everest, because it's situated a full eight degrees of latitude farther north, the equivalent of the distance between Charleston, South Carolina, and New York City. On Everest, every spring you can usually count on a stable window of clear weather, when the high jetstream winds start to get pushed away by the approaching monsoon. But the monsoon doesn't reach the Karakoram. Instead, you have to throw the dice with the weather. There's no guarantee that you'll get a single prolonged spell of good days all summer.

During the climbing campaigns of 1987, 1988, and 1989, no fewer than fifty-three climbers reached the summit of Mount Everest. In that same three-year period, although fifteen different expeditions, including some of the best mountaineers in the world, attacked K2, not a single person got to the summit. I'm not surprised.

Many climbers have made repeat ascents of Everest, including me with my seven. The record holder, Apa Sherpa, upped his own total of

Everest summits to nineteen in 2009. But as of May 2009, only three climbers have gotten to the top of K2 more than once, each of them making only a second ascent.

The ultimate barrier on K2, I think, is psychological. If you've been fortunate enough to hold the holy grail of mountaineering briefly in your hands, you don't want to get greedy and try to take it home with you. If you do, as with Sir Gawain and Sir Lancelot in the Arthurian legend, only bad things will happen.

In recent years, there's been gloomy talk about whether K2 will soon be "trivialized" the way Everest has been. The South Col route on Everest is now usually strung every spring with fixed ropes, in a continuous chain from advance base camp to the summit. That hasn't happened yet on the Abruzzi Ridge on K2, but there's no saying it couldn't sometime soon. The expectations of last year's climbers that the Bottleneck and the traverse at the top of it had to be strung with fixed ropes indicates a huge mental shift from the 1990s.

A few paying clients have gone on K2 expeditions in recent years. As far as I know, none has gotten to the summit. But the gloomy observers predict a future in which guide services will charge affluent wannabes big bucks to be hauled up the Abruzzi. If those outfits hire Sherpa or Hunzas to fix the ropes and pitch the camps, and if they routinely use supplemental oxygen, then K2 will move toward the situation Everest is now in. Fixed ropes are the linchpin for commercial guiding, for if a client only has to slide his jumar up one rope after another, rather than actually climb the rock and ice, a formidable challenge is reduced to a treadmill test of stamina. It's inevitable, I think, that companies will try to commercialize K2, especially now that it's becoming a "sexier" prize than Everest. And that will be a sad day for mountaineering.

Another recent trend on Everest is the bagging of "firsts" that range from the monumental to the absurd. For the critics, this is one more measure of the mountain's trivialization. The first winter ascent, the first descent by ski and by snowboard, even the first descent by parapente represented truly skillful and extreme deeds. But within the last ten years, Everest has been climbed by a blind man, by a double amputee, by a seventy-one-year-old man, and by a fifteen-year-old Sherpa. The speed record for Everest keeps getting ratcheted downward.

It frightens me when I hear from people who say they want to be the first this or the first that on Everest; often they ask for my endorsement. Those are not good reasons to climb the mountain, so I always decline. These folks obviously hope to garner attention, rather than just to be on the mountain for the joy of the experience. Climbing the mountain for its own sake should be reason enough to go there.

Still, the firsts continue to proliferate. It's gotten so that Everest expeditions in search of sponsors will cook up "firsts" so arcane that any experienced climber would laugh at them—except that they seem to be effective fund-raising gimmicks. Such developments may be in the cards for K2, but I wonder. Skiing down the mountain, for instance, strikes me as extremely difficult and scary but conceivable. Who knows what the next generation will pull off? Indeed, in 2001, the great Tyrolean climber Hans Kammerlander planned to ski down the Abruzzi after a solo ascent. But after teaming up with J.-C. Lafaille to struggle up the route in hideous conditions, he changed his mind about strapping on his skis for the descent.

In 1980, a Polish expedition accomplished the first winter ascent of Everest, as Krzysztof Wielicki and Leszek Cichy reached the top by the South Col route on February 17. This was a genuine landmark, one of the great feats in Everest history. So far, there have been two attempts on K2 in winter, both by Polish teams, in 1987 and 2003. The second effort, led by Wielicki, fought to an altitude of 25,000 feet on the Abruzzi Ridge before throwing in the towel. I suspect that this tantalizing "first" will be accomplished by someone in the next five to ten years.

I climbed Gasherbrum I with Wielicki in 1995, after my partner Rob Hall had gone home. It was simply by chance that Wielicki and I met on the mountain, but as a partner he was a man you could trust and rely on. He loved being in the mountains, and he was like a tiger on the hill. I can only imagine how strong he was in the 1980s, when he was at the top of his game. I would gladly go on another expedition with Krzysztof if the opportunity arose.

I believe it will be the Poles, with their legendary stamina, tolerance for pain, and tenacity, who will be the first to get up K2 in winter. They seem willing to go back time and time again until they succeed. But even so, a future triumph will depend on phenomenally good conditions during the winter the climbers mount their attack.

On Everest, every plausible route—except the Fantasy Ridge, a line on the east face to the right of the two routes that have already been climbed—has been knocked off. On K2, there are still a number of high-quality routes awaiting their first ascents, including the east face and the complete northwest ridge. And the passion to put up first solo ascents of difficult routes is alive and well on the world's second-highest mountain.

In recent years, helicopter rescue has—thanks to some astonishingly gutsy aerial feats by Nepalese and Pakistani pilots—begun to transform the game all over the Himalaya. There is already evidence that some self-styled hero-alpinists are willing to stick their necks out on 8,000ers farther than they otherwise would, as they count on choppers to get them out of trouble. This is, on the whole, a deplorable trend, for the pilots, who routinely go nameless in the media, risk their own lives to save showboating climbers who are only after personal glory.

If you doubt whether aerial rescue can transform an exploratory "game," just look at the north and south poles. For centuries, the poles were the most remote places on earth, and such genuine heroes as Amundsen, Scott, and Peary gave everything they had to reach them by the best means available—sleds, dogs, and skis. Nowadays you can book a trip to skydive over the north pole or be flown there to compete in a marathon. Ninety degrees north can be "bagged" in merely a long weekend away from your home in suburban America. There are still daring explorers pushing new "firsts" in the Arctic and the Antarctic, although when they get in trouble, they are routinely spirited to safety by helicopters.

Will choppers transform climbing on K2, or is altitude an impenetrable barrier for aircraft? It remains to be seen. No climber has yet been lifted by helicopter from the summit of Everest, but a few years ago a nervy French pilot touched down there; with his rotors still going and only one skid balanced on the summit, he stayed for several minutes before peeling off into the empyrean. No one could have safely jumped aboard and been whisked to safety, as the helicopter was already at its limit. But who knows what the next few years may bring.

For me, it would be a sad turn of events if helicopters could pluck stranded climbers off the highest summits. In the last decade, cell phones have transformed the rescue of backcountry hikers and climbers in the United States. A lot of folks go out now believing that if they get into trouble, all they have to do is dial 911. God forbid if the same thing came to pass on the 8,000ers. I've always liked the sense of disconnection from the rest of the world that I get on high peaks, and the self-reliance that imposes, as I realize that my safety depends entirely on my own careful decision making. There aren't many places left on earth where a rescue by outsiders is still literally impossible.

It's clear that in recent times, climbers on 8,000ers, like some of the ones stranded in August 2008 above the Bottleneck, have simply sat down to await a rescue from other climbers. Such a thing was always inconceivable to me. On all my expeditions, I said to myself, *If I get in trouble here, it's my problem to get myself out.* In a way, I kind of liked that mandate. It made me test myself. It taught me self-confidence. And in the end, it made me a more conservative climber.

I'll never forget peering over the ridge crest on the summit slope on Dhaulagiri in 1999, and suddenly seeing a dead man sprawled in the snow. That was another wake-up call. As I fought down the shiver that crawled up my spine, I vowed, "Ed, if you fuck up, that'll be you lying there."

For several years after 1998, there was a macabre mystique about women and K2. By that date, only five women had reached the summit: Wanda Rutkiewicz, Liliane Barrard, Julie Tullis, Chantal Mauduit, and Alison Hargreaves. And by 1998, all five were dead. Barrard and Tullis died descending the Abruzzi in 1986, as did Hargreaves in 1995, when she was apparently blown off the mountain by a tremendous gust of wind. (Hargreaves's death caused a huge and to my mind ridiculous furor in her native Great Britain, where she was posthumously censured—by the popular press, not the climbing community—for leaving two small children motherless. Any number of male climbers over the decades, including Mallory, have done the same, without being tarred and feathered as irresponsible fathers.) Then Rutkiewicz died on Kangchenjunga in 1992, and Mauduit on Dhaulagiri in 1998.

The fact that no woman alive had climbed K2 sparked a competition among a small sorority of ambitious female alpinists. Jennifer Jordan wrote a popular book called (here we go again!) *Savage Summit,* chronicling the life stories of the five who had climbed K2 and died. And in 2002, her husband, Jeff Rhoads, organized an expedition to the mountain, while Jordan made a film, called *Women of K2,* that pivoted around Araceli Segarra's attempt to become the sixth woman to get up the mountain, thereby breaking what was already being called "the curse of the women of K2."

Araceli was one of the on-camera stars of David Breashears's IMAX film about Everest in 1996. She's a strong climber and a great teammate, and she also happens to be beautiful enough to make a living as a model in her native Spain. Her effort on the Cesen route, however, was turned back by weather and snow conditions at only 23,300 feet. It was on this expedition that Jordan and Rhoads discovered the remains of Dudley Wolfe on the Godwin Austen Glacier.

Despite Araceli's failure to climb K2, the film won several awards. It also provoked an odd backlash among feminists, who thought that what Jordan was saying was that women simply aren't good enough to climb K2 safely. She was dumbfounded, since her real point was to dramatize just how dangerous a mountain K2 is, for men as well as for women.

The so-called curse produced a far more opportunistic response than Jordan's film, when a publicity-hungry American climber named Heidi Howkins published a book called *K2: One Woman's Quest for the Summit,* about how she *planned* to climb K2. Give me a break! Do the climb first, then write the book! Howkins never did get very high on the mountain, but that didn't prevent *National Geographic Explorer* from making a film about her self-styled "quest." It was titled (wouldn't you know it?) *Savage Summits.*

As of May 2009, no American woman has yet climbed K2. This is a first that will undoubtedly keep a heated rivalry alive until some female mountaineer from this country pulls off the feat.

Meanwhile, in 2004, a Spanish woman, Edurne Pasabán, quietly ended the curse, as she reached the summit by the Abruzzi Ridge as part of an Italian-Spanish team. At the moment, she stands tied with the Austrian climber Gerlinde Kaltenbrunner, both of whom have climbed twelve of the fourteen 8,000ers. Back in the 1980s, a lot of people thought that Wanda Rutkiewicz would be the first woman to join the elite company of men who had completed all fourteen. She was way ahead of any other woman in the world, in terms of 8,000ers on her résumé. But seventeen years after Rutkiewicz's death, no woman has yet completed the list.

Because they are Europeans, and because they don't have the kinds of publicity machines up and running that Heidi Howkins (or for that matter, Reinhold Messner) deployed, this friendly competition—and both women insist it *is* friendly—has flown under the radar in the United States. But I think it's an interesting and admirable challenge, and I'm following it pretty closely. I'd be the first to congratulate Pasabán or Kaltenbrunner the minute either woman joins our little club, of which at last count there are still only sixteen members.

In a postscript I wrote for the paperback edition of *No Shortcuts to the Top,* I admitted that after my eighteen-year-long campaign to climb all fourteen 8,000ers had come to a close, there were times when I felt at loose ends. Appearances on shows such as *The Colbert Report* and *The Daily Show with Jon Stewart* were fun and gratifying, as were the numerous letters and e-mails I got from readers, and the enthusiastic receptions that often greeted my slide shows and "inspirational" talks. But I didn't really envision my future as that of an after-dinner speaker, living off an endless recounting of the climbs I'd done in my prime. I enjoy those speaking events, but I still need to push myself physically and mentally in the outdoors. The future would seem empty to me if I had no more mountains to climb.

Since May 2005, when I returned from Annapurna, I've also found other kinds of adventures to keep my juices flowing. One was running the New York City Marathon with Paula in November 2006. As much fun as the run itself (notwithstanding all the sore muscles we strained on that twenty-six-mile course) were the weeks of training together near our home on Bainbridge Island. Paula and I were able to share a workout regimen with a common goal in a more satisfying way than we could ever share 8,000-meter expeditions.

My dogsled trip with Will Steger on Baffin Island in the spring of 2007 was another novel form of adventure for me. I had to learn a whole new art of traveling, and I was fascinated by the culture of the Inuit villages we visited, so different from the cultures of Skardu and Askole or Dingboche and Namche Bazar. Yet as grueling as that overland journey was at its toughest, it didn't test me to the limits as the 8,000ers—especialy Annapurna and K2—had.

A year later, I returned to Baffin Island with my dog-mushing friend John Stetson. This time, rather than using dogs to haul our gear, we pulled our own sleds, which weighed 220 pounds each, almost 150 miles over the barren, frozen landscape in a long loop out of the small town of Pond Inlet. This was a physically more demanding trip than the one with Steger, and for me a more rewarding one.

In January 2009, I climbed Aconcagua, at 22,841 feet the highest peak in South America, as part of a gear-testing expedition organized by the Eddie Bauer company—a trial run, in effect, for the launching of the First Ascent line that we would undertake on Everest in the spring. Aconcagua's not as hard a mountain as an 8,000er, but it can be deceptively lethal: many climbers die on its slopes from altitude sickness, pulmonary or cerebral edema, hypothermia, or getting lost in a storm. Several folks died, in fact, while we were on the mountain.

I'd first climbed Aconcagua twenty years earlier, when I was twenty-nine and in prime shape. I expected to find it a little harder at the age of forty-nine, but I surprised myself. On the summit, I thought, *Hell, I feel great, I want to go farther.* And also: *Hey, this is still what excites me!*

The pleasure I had on Aconcagua was what motivated me to go to Everest with the Eddie Bauer First Ascent team last spring. I'm sure that skeptics may have said, "What's in it for Viesturs to go back to Everest for the eleventh time? A lucrative deal with his sponsors, more publicity via online dispatches?" But the number one reason for me to go to Everest in 2009 was the simple fact that I still find high mountains intriguing. I'll always love the mountain environment. And as I learned on Aconcagua, climbing is still fun.

Skeptics might also say, "Hey, he's scared of turning fifty. He still thinks he's got something to prove." But the fact is, I'm not afraid of the big five-oh. I still feel really active, strong, and intelligent. If I didn't know my own birth date, I'd guess that I'm only thirty-five. Maybe forty, tops. Calendar age had nothing to do with that eleventh attempt on Everest.

When I was closing in on the end of Endeavor 8000, some of Paula's friends would say to her, "How can you stand it that Ed's away so much? Don't you worry about him? And don't the kids miss him?" It's true, I was gone for long stretches, and mountaineering is inevitably dangerous. But I liked to point out that when I was home, I was really there for Paula and the kids. I even told the kids that I probably spent more time with them each year than a dad who went off to his dreary nine-to-five job every day.

Ever since Paula and I got married, in February 1996, and especially after Gil, Ella, and Anabel were born, family has been the most important thing in my life, even more important than big mountains and climbing friendships. And since the summer of 2005, when I got home from

Annapurna, I've been a true full-time dad. In the last year, we've divided our time between Bainbridge Island and Sun Valley, Idaho, where we've owned a condo since 2006. During the winter of 2008–09, the kids went to public school in Sun Valley, but we returned to Bainbridge for the summer. Time will tell how we'll manage our dual residences in future years, but it's nice to have options.

This year, the kids really missed their friends back home, but they love the recreational possibilities of Sun Valley. Gil and Ella have become demon skiers. I'm a pretty good skier myself, but when those two bomb straight down the slope, it's all I can do to keep up with them.

At age eleven, Gil is the extrovert of the family. He loves conversation, and he just talks and talks. Paula and I tell him he has a future as a talk-show host. Both friends his age and adults think he's hilarious. And he's still madly into Seattle Seahawks football, even though, after the team went to the Super Bowl in 2006, their last three seasons have been pretty disappointing.

If Gil's the extrovert, Ella, who just turned nine this June, is our introvert. She's strong and stoic, never complains about a minor accident or some chore she has to do. Like me, she's quiet in company, tending to recede when others dominate the conversation. She's a great athlete, able to keep up with Gil on the ski slopes. She's also taken up indoor sport climbing whenever she gets the chance. If one of our three kids becomes a mountaineer, it'll probably be Ella.

Anabel, at four, is the little lover in the family. Without any particular pretext, she'll come over to Paula or me and give us a kiss. Or she'll crawl into my lap and say, "I love you, Dad." But she's not clingy—she's a solid, independent gal in her own right.

As for Paula, she's turned out to be a wonderful companion and the great mom I always knew she would be. She has a God-given talent for motherhood. And she doesn't do it by spoiling the kids, or by using baby talk with them. I'm pleased to say that I've never heard any scuttlebutt from friends in Seattle or Sun Valley about our children being pampered or overindulged. Paula is, quite simply, the cornerstone of our family.

Before I decided to go to Everest again, Paula and I had some good long talks about it. We deliberated, in fact, longer than we had before any other expedition I've ever considered. Of course she worries about me every time I try an 8,000er. But Paula has always fully supported me, and the mental strength she sends my way while I'm climbing is, I'm convinced, part of why I've been successful. Without her support, I would never go on another expedition.

Paula has always insisted, "Don't call me from the summit. Call me when you get back to camp." She knows from experience that standing on the summit doesn't mean that you've climbed the mountain.

In the spring of 2009, she knew I'd be gone for eight or nine weeks. She knew firsthand that Everest is dangerous—particularly the Khumbu Icefall, which you have to climb through several times on every ascent of the South Col route. But by now she trusts me on the mountain. She knows that I know how to be safe. Since I wasn't going to be bound to anyone else's schedule, I could go through the icefall as fast as I needed to. That's one place where speed equals safety.

It was, I have to admit, a bit hard telling the kids that I'd be gone for all of April and May. But they're troupers. When I told Gil, he got a slightly stricken look on his face; then he said, "Oh, yeah, Dad, I'll be okay." But I knew already that I was going to miss the three of them as I never had before.

It's been seventeen years since I climbed K2, but in a sense, that great mountain has never been far from my thoughts. And writing this book has plunged me back into the fascination with K2 that had me in its grips when I read everything I could as homework for our 1992 expedition.

No mountain in the world has a more interesting history. And even though the cynics feel that the second-highest mountain is about to be tarnished by the kinds of commercialization that have tainted Everest, I'm optimistic about the future of K2. In 2009, the mountain remains an ultimate test of the ambitions of the best climbers in the world. The gold that gilds the holy grail is still intact.

One way I know this to be true comes from having sat in on the chat of high-altitude climbers all around the world. In their company, if you mention climbing Everest, the remark may elicit nothing more than a shrug. But if you let on that you've reached the top of K2, a hush comes over the room. And then, invariably, someone will say, "Tell us about it."

Acknowledgments

In 1992, when I went to Pakistan to attempt K2, I traveled there with friend and partner Scott Fischer. Young, ambitious, filled with energy and enthusiasm, we committed ourselves to giving all we had to climbing this test piece among mountains. We had nothing to lose, everything to gain, and no limit of time. In the throes of our campaign to climb the second highest peak in the world we teamed up with climbers who also aspired to do what we were doing. The climbers I connected with, related to, and enjoyed climbing with became lifelong friends, who still bring back the fondest memories of that difficult yet successful season. The friends and partners whom I wish to thank specifically are Charley Mace, Neal Bei-dleman, the late Scott Fischer, Rob Hall, and Gary Ball. I enjoyed their companionship immensely and had the pleasure of climbing as partners with them on K2 and elsewhere. There were others on the mountain that season, and they all contributed in some way. I acknowledge them as well.

I would also like to thank those who forged the way on K2, specifically the 1953 American Expedition. Those men displayed to me the indelible example of team work, camaraderie, trust, and commitment in expedition climbing. When someone mentions "the brotherhood of the rope," that band of mountaineers instantly comes to mind.

One member of that expedition I wish to thank specially and with my utmost gratitude and respect is Dee Molenaar. After my ascent of K2, Dee presented me with a bound and illustrated copy of his private expedition journal. For this book, he allowed me to quote passages from the journal that I thought were important in highlighting details of the 1953 expedition.

K2 in 1992 came quite early in my career, when I still had very little in the way of support or sponsors. But to everyone who supported our K2 climb, I say thank you.

Thanks also to family and friends who gave me emotional support and waited for word to trickle out from the Baltoro about our expedition. Those were the "good old days" when we often got home before anyone received word as to how things had gone on an expedition. We literally walked off the map and then a few months later, walked back on.

There are certain events in one's life that are cornerstones. My climb of K2 was one such event. I believe that one becomes a better, more rounded climber, and also a more thoughtful and patient human being, after having successfully climbed and descended K2. There is no comparison. K2 is the ultimate test of climbing ability, judgment, and patience at extreme altitudes. The bonds that form during the hardships we undergo on such climbs stand the test of time, even while they are difficult, if not impossible, to explain.

—Ed Viesturs

My strongest link to the fascinating history of K2 lies in long-term friendships with some of its principal characters—especially Charlie Houston, Bob Bates, Bob Craig, and Fritz Wiessner. The privilege of listening to them tell their stories has been one of the joys of my life as a mountaineer. In addition, I was delighted by more sporadic friendships with K2 veterans Dee Molenaar, Paul Petzoldt, and Jim Curran, and as a journalist, I had the rare experience of meeting and getting to know Walter Bonatti and his teammate Lino Lacedelli.

Many people helped Ed Viesturs and me gain access to important photographs, for the use of which they gave unstinting permission. They include Polly Wiessner, Charlie Houston, Greg Glade, Ed Webster, Charley Mace, and Chris Klinke. Ed and I hired freelance researcher Alice Gifford to hunt down the availability of and rights to the historical photos. She accomplished this difficult task superbly.

Dee Molenaar not only let us quote from his K2 diary, but also he helped us adapt his own incomparable maps and diagrams for this book. Many thanks to Dee for his involvement and aid.

Our editor at Broadway Books, Stacy Creamer, not only got this project off the ground, but also championed it through a series of frantic deadlines and logistical mine fields. Upon her abrupt departure last spring to another publishing house, Charlie Conrad stepped in and smoothly guided the book toward its finish line. Throughout the whole process, assistant editor Laura Swerdloff performed many valuable tasks.

Once again, Ed and I are deeply indebted to our masterly agent, Stuart Krichevsky, who not only "closed the deal" but offered his constant advice about matters as minor yet consequential as finding a subtitle and getting the cover photo right. Stuart's colleague Shana Cohen and his assistant Kathryne Wick came through (as usual) with all kinds of important chores and details.

The American Alpine Club library in Golden, Colorado, proved an invaluable research resource. And I am grateful to my longtime climbing buddy Ed Ward, and to my wife, Sharon Roberts, for reading the book in manuscript and offering pithy comments and vivid reactions.

—David Roberts

Bibliography

Barry, John. *K2: Savage Mountain, Savage Summer*. Sparkford, U.K., 1987.

Bonatti, Walter. *Le Mie Montagne*. Bologna, 1961.

———. *The Mountains of My Life*. New York, 2001.

———. *On the Heights*. London, 1964.

Bowley, Graham, and Andrea Kannapell. "Chaos on the 'Mountain That Invites Death.'" *New York Times,* August 6, 2008.

Buffet, Charlie. *La Folie du K2*. Chamonix, France, 2004.

Carter, H. Adams. "The August Catastrophe on K2." *American Alpine Journal: 1987*. New York, 1987.

Child, Greg. "A Margin of Luck." *Mixed Emotions*. Seattle, 1993.

———. "Another Tragedy on K2." *Postcards from the Edge*. Seattle, 1998.

———. "The Dangerous Summer." *Mixed Emotions*. Seattle, 1993.

———. "Death and Faxes." *Postcards from the Edge*. Seattle, 1998.

Cranmer, Chappel, and Fritz Wiessner. "The Second American Expedition to K2." *The American Alpine Journal: 1940*. New York, 1940.

Crowley, Aleister. *The Confessions of Aleister Crowley.* 1929. Reprint. New York, 1969.

Curran, Jim. *K2: The Story of the Savage Mountain*. London, 1995.

———. *K2: Triumph and Tragedy*. London, 1987.

Desio, Ardito. *Ascent of K2: Second Highest Peak in the World*. London, 1955.

———. "The Italian 1954 Expedition to the Karakoram," *The Mountain World: 1955*. New York, 1955.

Diemberger, Kurt. *The Endless Knot*. Seattle, 1990.

Filippi, Fillipo de. *Karakoram and the Western Himalaya*. London, 1912.

Hornbein, Thomas F. *Everest: The West Ridge*. San Francisco, 1966.

Houston, Charles S. "Death in High Places." *The American Alpine Journal: 1987*. New York, 1987.

Houston, Charles S., and Robert H. Bates. *K2: The Savage Mountain*. New York, 1954.

Houston, Charles S., Robert H. Bates, et al. *Five Miles High*. New York, 1939.

Jordan, Jennifer. *Savage Summit: The True Stories of the First Five Women Who Climbed K2*. New York, 2005.

Kauffman, Andrew J., and William L. Putnam. *K2: The 1939 Tragedy*. Seattle, 1992.

Kodas, Michael. "A Few False Moves," *Outside*, November 2008.

Kukuczka, Jerzy. "K2's South Face," *The American Alpine Journal: 1987*. New York, 1987.

Lacedelli, Lino, and Giovanni Cenacchi. *K2: The Price of Conquest*. Hildersley, U.K., 2006.

Maraini, Fosco. *Karakoram: The Ascent of Gasherbrum IV*. New York, 1959.

McDonald, Bernadette. *Brotherhood of the Rope: The Biography of Charles Houston*. Seattle, 2007.

Messner, Reinhold, and A. Gogna. *K2: Mountain of Mountains*. London, 1981.

Molenaar, Dee. "K2 Diary 1953." (Unpublished.)

Petzoldt, Patricia. *On Top of the World: My Adventures with My Mountain-Climbing Husband*. New York, 1953.

Power, Matthew. "The Killing Peak." *Men's Journal*, November 2008.

Ridgeway, Rick. *The Last Step: The American Ascent of K2*. Seattle, 1980.

Ringholz, Raye. *On Belay! The Life of Legendary Mountaineer Paul Petzoldt*. Seattle, 1997.

Roberts, David. "Five Who Made It to the Top." *Moments of Doubt*. Seattle, 1986.

———. "Is K2 the New Everest?" *National Geographic Adventure*, October 2008.

———. "K2 at 50: The Bitter Legacy." *National Geographic Adventure*, September 2004.

———. "The K2 Mystery." *Moments of Doubt*. Seattle, 1986.

Rose, David, and Ed Douglas. *Regions of the Heart: The Triumph and Tragedy of Alison Hargreaves*. Washington, D. C., 2000.

Rowell, Galen. *In the Throne Room of the Mountain Gods*. San Francisco, 1977.

Rutkiewicz, Wanda. "The First Woman's Ascent of K2." In *K2: Triumph and Tragedy*, by Jim Curran. London, 1995.

Schoening, Pete. *K2 1953*. (Privately published, 2004.)

Tenderini, Mirella, and Michael Shandrick. *The Duke of the Abruzzi: An Explorer's Life*. Seattle, 1997.

Viesturs, Ed. "Russian-American K2 Expedition." *The American Alpine Journal: 1993*. Golden, Colo., 1993.

Viesturs, Ed, with David Roberts. *No Shortcuts to the Top: Climbing the World's 14 Highest Peaks*. New York, 2006.

Wiessner, Fritz H. "The K2 Expedition of 1939." *Appalachia,* June 1956.

Wilkinson, Freddie. "Perfect Chaos." *Rock and Ice,* December 2008.

Index

76° 15'

Chiring *Glacier*

Nera
▲ 20800

Changtok
23260

Moni
Brangsa

SINKIANG

SARPO   *LAGGO*   *GLACIER*

16600

20480
▲

20310
▲

19880
▲

Moni

Glacier

Mustagh La
17800

Pyramid
22100

Sarpo Laggo
Pass
18520

35°
50'

KASHMIR   PAKISTAN

▲ 22080

Lobsang
20420

Mustagh

Biale   *Glacier*

Chagaran   *Glacier*

Surgus Glacier

Glacier

Dunge

18720
▲

Borum Glacier

Trango

Trango

Nameless
Tower
20530

18870

Glacier

Choricho Glacier

22160 ▲

19260
▲

BALTORO

Uli Biaho

Uli Biaho
▲ Tower
19957

Urdukas
● 13000

Paiyu ▲
21658

Liliwa
● 12000

11000

Urdukas
20890
▲

Mundi   *Glacier*

35°
40'

Paiyu
●

Biaho   *River*

Liliwa   *Glacier*

Yermanendu

Bardomal
●

Masherbrum
25660

Liliwa
20510

76° 15'